Personal Pleasures

Also published by Handheld Press

Personal Pleasures

by Rose Macaulay

Handheld
Press

Handheld Classic 21

This edition published in 2021 by Handheld Press
72 Warminster Road, Bath BA2 6RU, United Kingdom.
www.handheldpress.co.uk

ISBN 978-1-912766-50-5

1 2 3 4 5 6 7 8 9 0

Series design by Nadja Guggi and typeset in Adobe Caslon Pro
and Open Sans.

Printed and bound in Great Britain by Short Run Press, Exeter.

Contents

Kate Macdonald is a publisher and a literary historian. She has published a number of books, chapters and articles on twentieth-century publishing history and the book business, and assembled *Rose Macaulay, Gender and Modernity*, the first edited collection of essays on Macaulay (Routledge 2018). Some paragraphs of the Introduction in the present volume are revised and updated from her essays 'Introduction' and 'Constructing a public persona: Rose Macaulay's non-fiction' (from *Rose Macaulay, Gender and Modernity*), and 'Home is where the Art is: Rose Macaulay's resistance to domesticity' (*Women. A Cultural Review*, 31:4, 416–32, 2020).

Introduction

BY KATE MACDONALD

Rose Macaulay was born in Rugby in 1881, and was the second daughter of a family of seven children. She lived in Italy with her family for seven years during her childhood, and returning to Britain as an adolescent, she went to school in Oxford. Later she attended Somerville College, where she was awarded the equivalent of a degree in history in 1903. In 1901 the family moved from Oxford to live in Aberystwyth, on the mid-west Welsh coast, at whose university her father was Professor of English Language and Literature. When Macaulay left Oxford to move to rural Wales, she began to publish poetry. In 1906, two months before her first novel was published, the family moved again, to Great Shelford, a village south of Cambridge, where Professor Macaulay now taught English literature at Trinity College.

In 1912 Macaulay's sixth novel, *The Lee Shore*, won a Hodder & Stoughton literary prize of £600 (equivalent to over £50,000 now), finally giving her financial independence. She moved to London in 1913. When the First World War broke out Macaulay volunteered as a VAD in a hospital for a few months but was much happier when she began working on the land. After nearly a year in the Women's Land Army Macaulay succeeded in her application for an office job. From January 1917 she worked in the War Office on cases of exemption from military service and conscientious objectors.

When the war ended Macaulay was already a professional woman of letters. Her second volume of poetry came out in 1919. She published twenty-two books between 1919 and 1939: only half of these were novels, but at least one, *Potterism* (1920) was a best-seller. Her two most well-known novels would appear after the Second World War, during which, at the age of sixty, she had been a volunteer ambulance driver. *The World My Wilderness* (1950) and

The Towers of Trebizond (1956) would bring her widespread fame at a level that her earlier novels had not achieved.

Although she is best known now as a novelist, in her day Macaulay published far more essays and newspaper columns than books. These shorter pieces took much less time to write, and as newspaper and magazines paid well, writing for them in the 1920s earned Macaulay a living while she worked on her books. She was also energetic in creating a public perception of herself as a pundit, by giving talks, and writing her own opinions into public discourse, on paper and on the air by radio, until the end of her life. In 1958 she would be made a Dame for services to literature, a few months before her death.

Reading Macaulay's essays is to read the progression of a career through her changing preoccupations. In the 1930s these included sixteenth- and seventeenth-century culture, ruins, travel around the Mediterranean shores, and the arcane lore of the early Church Fathers and their liturgical disagreements. Her sprightly article-writing in the early 1920s for *Good Housekeeping* and *Nash's and Pall Mall Magazine* would develop into weightier and intellectually lively 'middles' in *The Spectator*, then into full-length scholarly commentary, with her essay on linguistics in *Catchwords and Claptrap* (1926), and on pacifism as a philosophy in *An Open Letter to a Non-Pacifist* (1937). In parallel, she wrote books of formal scholarly criticism: *Some Religious Elements in English Literature*, 1931; *Milton*, 1934, and *The Writings of E M Forster*, 1938. As her status as a critic and a literary authority rose, she became a regular contributor to BBC radio programmes, to weightier periodicals, and then to books of informed commentary on public topics. In 1935 her essay 'Linguistic changes' was published in a volume for the English Association by the Clarendon Press, as serious and scholarly a publisher as a non-academic public intellectual could desire. She was elected a Fellow of the Royal Society of Literature in July 1945. Her contributions to miscellanies and other collections of essays were printed alongside those by prominent British thinkers of her day. The contents list for the 1945 volume of the heavyweight literary periodical *Orion*, to which she contributed an essay on the poet Southey's visit to Portugal, is a good example. This essay was the second in an issue containing contributions by (in publication order) Walter de la Mare, Cecil Day Lewis, Ivy Compton Burnett and Margaret Jourdain, Edith Sitwell, Stephen Spender, Edwin Muir, John Piper, Maurice Bowra, Mary MacRae, William Plomer, Frank O'Connor, Andrew Young, Walter Allen, Margiad Evans, Leonard Woolf, John Lehmann, John Russell, Henry Reed and Willa Muir. In this assemblage of British cultural authority, Macaulay was firmly established as a serious literary figure.

Macaulay's essay anthology *Personal Pleasures* is a collection of joys. On its first publication in 1935 a publisher's advert for the book repeated phrases in bold type from the previous month's reviews: 'Delicious', 'Most amusing', 'Delightful', 'How brilliantly ...', 'The perfect book', 'A delightful bedside book', 'The literary gem' and 'The ideal gift' (Gollancz 1935). Its early reviewers seem most struck by the sense of pleasure taken as well as given by Macaulay, and the uncommon quantity of unusual words that she used.

The modern reader of *Personal Pleasures* is most likely to notice a palimpsest of dense allusions and quotations, mostly presented without attribution. At surface level, where the authors' names or the titles of their poems, pamphlets or books are unfamiliar to the reader, these names work as decorative flourishes, merely suggesting but not explaining a historical period or a tone. Reading an essay more closely is to delve into a bran-tub of references dating from the third century CE or even earlier, although – aside from Plato – Macaulay rarely quoted from pre-Christian philosophies. These continue up to the nineteenth century, but twentieth-century quotations are rare. The sixteenth and seventeenth centuries are well represented, and some favourite texts appear again and again, such as Sylvester's translation of

Du Bartas his divine weekes and works (1608) and Bishop Wilkins' *Mathematical Magick* (1708). As the reviewer for *The Times* noted in 1935, Macaulay's delight in quoting from much-loved volumes and authors (John Milton was well in the lead) is infectious, encouraging the reader to relish her enthusiasms and to enjoy the eccentric juxtapositions which Macaulay took on excursions into the ridiculous and back again. The *Times* reviewer put this more baldly: 'Miss Macaulay has obviously enjoyed writing this book so much that it is impossible to read it without receiving some reflection, however faint, of her own pleasure' (Anon 1935, 22).

Locating the identity and contexts of these allusions is now made possible, thankfully, by digitised facsimiles and easy availability online. While researching the Notes for this edition it was a repeated marvel to me that I could type a phrase or name into an internet browser and almost always find my way to the answer and to corroborating evidence through secondary routes. Serendipitous quotations in long-dead magazine articles that had been archived online would lead me to the right Book, Homily or Address and locate the exact words that Macaulay had quoted. I found myself making repeated visits to a digitised copy of a fifteenth-century translation of a fourteenth-century travelogue, the Early English Books project website, the hymnary of Isaac Watts, the works of Cicero, the essays of Montaigne, the *Biographical Dictionary*, an encyclopaedia of Greek mythology, and the complete works of William Cowper.

This enflourishment of sources was compounded by Macaulay's enthusiasm for inventing new words to suit the meaning and sounds she desired. She used her father's edition of the *Oxford English Dictionary* with gusto, hunting down word history and derivations for her own pleasure. When her flat was bombed in 1941 she would be distraught at the loss of all the *Dictionary*'s volumes along with her other books (Smith 1964, 120, 157). Eight years later she was still regretting the loss of all her books: 'I can still smell those acrid drifts of smouldering ashes that once were live books' (Macaulay and Third Programme 1949, 65). But not all her research was lost. She had a passion for spotting usages that the *Dictionary* did not contain, and in 1936 she would send 'her notes to the OED's editor, which was fortunate. When she tentatively wrote again in 1941 after the destruction of her flat to enquire if the Press still had them, they returned her list, having first made copies that were to be used in the 1990s when the revision of the first edition of the Dictionary was finally undertaken' (Florio 2018, 163).

The *Times* reviewer had noted, uneasily, that the essays 'are written in rather a pedantic style, with out-of-the-way words and unusual turns of phrase, but luckily Miss Macaulay is one of the few writers who have enough real wit not to let their ever-present humour be weighed down by their deliberate pedantry' (Anon 1935, 22). Miss Macaulay had so much enjoyed herself that she created brand new out-of-the-way words for her own and her readers' enjoyment. In the first thirty essays of *Personal Pleasures* we can discover unentomologous, cantiferous, sedilian, philoclinic, empatining, lectisternia, hagiary, agoral, miniations and cuculan. None of these are in the *Oxford English Dictionary*, which is odd because they seem quite suitable words, derived from logical sources and already seeming familiar because of their close relationship with existing words. For example, hagiary must be something to do with saints, and agoral, in its context, is clearly about speaking in wide public spaces.

✕

In August 1928 Macaulay had written an article for *The Daily Herald* entitled 'The witchery of words and the charm of elsewhere'. As 'the famous novelist' she answered the question 'What most interests you, and why?', with 'language' as her choice for 'the most interesting study in the world', and praising the *Oxford English Dictionary* as the most readable book in English (Macaulay 13 August 1928). Earlier in 1928 Macaulay had written articles on 'Bad names' and 'Travelese' for *The Saturday Review*, in which she expanded on her remarks on language usage and its changes in her earlier anthology *A Casual Commentary* (1925). In 'Bad names' she asked why 'suburban' should apply to all people living just outside London, and what were the characteristics of such boroughs are that were so universally despised. She objected to snobbery, the 'language of opprobrium' and 'popular fallacies', giving precise discussions of the derivations of 'Philistine', 'magazine fiction', 'provincial' and 'circulating library'. A few months later her essay 'Travelese' excoriated the 'genteel and ponderous style' in language (Macaulay 5 May 1928, 14 July 1928). By her challenge to 'the language of opprobrium' in the mouths of the intelligentsia, in how they criticised those tastes they snobbishly disapproved of, Macaulay was a natural champion of 1920s middlebrow culture.

Yet she was a trenchant critic of the incorrect use of words. 'Into human speech' from *A Casual Commentary* is on the misuse of common words, for example 'suggestive', 'literally', 'problem novel', 'spinster', 'decimated', 'annihilated' and 'nominal'. She discussed common speech patterns, repetitions, locutions and the idea of half-educated speech (Macaulay 'Into human speech, 1925). There is an unmistakeable sense in these remarks of Macaulay judging unknown strangers by their use of language in comparison with her own practice, and by what she held to be right. This is repeated in 'Lonely souls', also in *A Casual Commentary*, in which Macaulay discusses a lonely hearts advertisement magazine, and the language used to indicate the class and education of advertisers: she is not entirely kindly (Macaulay 'Lonely souls, 1925).

In 1931 she wrote a bravura demonstration of her knowledge of endangered words in *The Spectator*, beginning by explaining her fondness for older forms of English, and blasting common and hackneyed phrases into oblivion with a spectacular display of uncommon, archaic and dictionary words 'to tale the high rodomontical banners of our speech' ('tale' in the archaic sense of enumerating). She asked for leadership from writers and public citizens to use the older, more poetic words as a good example so that 'the unclergied, cowish, docible common kind might ape the trick' (Macaulay 'Autumn Meditation', 1931). This exuberance can also be seen in this volume in 'Logomachy', in which Macaulay shows that the art of arguing about words can be an immersive and loudly enjoyable spectacle, especially on a summer afternoon out of doors where everyone with open windows can hear you and your friends discuss the meaning of 'pornography' (154).

Macaulay's continuing interest in language and word pronunciation was connected to her work for the BBC Advisory Committee on Spoken English, of which she was a member from 1934 to its dissolution in 1939 (BBC Written Archives; Schwyter 2016). She may have been selected for membership of this committee after her article 'How to Speak English' appeared in *The Spectator* in January 1934. This discussed how variation in pronunciation had been exacerbated by the popularity of radio, and the effect of this exposure on different pronunciations among the listening nation (Macaulay 'How to speak English', 1934). She would reinvigorate her crusade against what she regarded as mispronunciations when she became the *Time and Tide* monthly reviewer of the BBC's radio broadcasts after the Second World War. In March 1945 she would note that 'BBC English' was only now being heard for the first time by people who did not speak it, and described being nonplussed at BBC English being considered unusual, when she thought of it as 'standard' (Macaulay 'February on the Air', 1945). (This provoked correspondence on the subject in subsequent issues of the magazine.) Macaulay would continue to niggle at what she considered to be incorrect pronunciation, in early 1946 laying into modern 'Board School' pronunciation (Macaulay 'February on the Air', 1946), and writing about the (to her) repellent voices and opinions of 'young people' on air (Macaulay 'January on the Air', 1946). This refrain of grumbles about the speech of the nation continued for a further year, until Macaulay's retirement as the *Time and Tide*'s radio talks reviewer.

She then was over sixty. Her standards for language had been fixed many decades earlier, and had been shown to be outdated by 1939 when the BBC committee was disbanded, as no longer the right forum to determine pronunciation for national use. Macaulay's concern for the maintenance of high standards and a rich and varied vocabulary for the nation's English came from her own passionate enthusiasm for words as tools and embellishments, but she resisted debasement and restriction in English. Innovations, if they could be proved to be necessary and legitimate, she would accept willingly. Her 1935 essay 'Linguistic changes' was written in this spirit. In it she translated letters from a current issue of *The Times* into past and future speech patterns, and repeated the experiment on the new Highway Code alterations (Macaulay 'Linguistic changes, 1935'. This imaginative flight of fancy demonstrates clearly that, for her, language should be employed to enrich life.

✕

In *Personal Pleasures* Macaulay explained that the charm of writing comes from 'arranging words in patterns ... to hunt language, to swim lazily in those enchanted seas' (207). Creating her own words was a step beyond what she had described in *Catchwords and Claptrap* in 1926, when she had described 'her formulation of "nimbuses of association"' and of "words and their haloes" made of associated meanings (Macaulay 1926, 7, 21). By making up her own words Macaulay could satisfy her readerly requirement for the right word to fill a particular gap in the lexicon. And she could tease her readers by persuading them to join in the game, or fool her reviewers with new words so perfectly tuned that it would have needed some solid work with the dictionary to discover that they had not, hitherto, existed.

This teasing extended to making up entire texts that ought to have existed. In *The Minor Pleasures of Life*, Macaulay's 1934 anthology of favourite extracts and quotations from plays, prose and poetry of the past, there are some texts that are so obscure as to – suspiciously – have no known provenance. Macaulay's most recent biographer Sarah LeFanu has identified at least one, possibly two, faux-seventeenth-century poems written by Macaulay herself (LeFanu 2003, 208). Macaulay also wrote an elaborate faux obituary for herself, first tried out in 'Album' (14), and later published in full in the *Listener* in 1936 (Macaulay 'Full Fathom Five', 1936). More teasing is evident in Macaulay's essay on 'Heresies'. After a brief trot through some standard heresies from the early Christian church, she skips forwards to the seventeenth century to quote Jeremy Taylor's phrase 'rustick impudence'. The *Oxford Dictionary of National Biography* and Wikipedia both offered extensive entries on the seventeenth-century Anglican divine Jeremy Taylor, latterly the Bishop of Down and Connor. As an alternative, Google Books presented the digitised copy of a pamphlet from 1701 purportedly by two Ladies discussing Lawful and Unlawful Additaments to Natural Beauty, in which the phrase 'of rustick or *Adamitick* impudence' was helpfully highlighted (see 240).

The literary detective is now alert: Macaulay had mentioned the Adamites earlier in her essay, and one of the authors of this lively pamphlet was a Jeremy Taylor. But before the literary detective can crow with delight at this apparent revelation of a frivolous side in the sober Bishop's writings, a more cautious reader will note the Bishop's death date of 1667, which makes it unlikely that the pamphlet of 1701 is the Bishop's child. It must have been written by another Jeremy Taylor entirely. It would be in character for Macaulay to have identified and laid this scholarly trap, hoping that her readers would spot it, swerve gracefully, and continue to follow her through the outer reaches of early Christian belief tangents, feeling all the better in themselves for not having been fooled by simple dating.

※

The first reviewers of *Personal Pleasures* acknowledged the intelligence of these essays almost despite themselves. Ifor Evans in the *Guardian* remarked that *Personal Pleasures* fell 'into no known category; it is compact of originality both in conception and detail. Much of it is humorous with that individual humour which Miss Macaulay gains by a pretty pretence at shyness and stupidity when actually she is piercing to the depths of our oddities' (Evans 'Books of the Day', 1935). Three weeks later in the *Observer* he had decided that *Personal Pleasures* 'looks like a gift book and is a gift book, but an unusual quality in the writing – wit made subtle with learning, and learning dissipated with wit – will give it a reputation more than seasonal' (Evans 'Letters and Criticism', 1935).

Basil de Selincourt in the *Observer* preferred the more lyrical essays to the ironical ones, and gently objected to Miss Macaulay being too literary (de Selincourt 1935). Harold Nicolson noted in the *Telegraph* that 'in these essays the memories of a fastidious scholar are combined with the shameless curiosity of a debutante; the humour of a sceptic with the delightful credulity of an adolescent' (Nicolson 1935).

Macaulay was then aged 55. The narrative voice of the 'implied author' that is such a constant feature in Macaulay's novels is also delightfully present in *Personal Pleasures*, giving the impression that we are eavesdropping on Macaulay's own conversations (Bensen 1964, 33). This narrative voice may have been based on Macaulay's own personality, but it was maintained consistently across the decades as a definite and probably separate persona in her essays.

'Abroad' is a witty account of travelling in this separate Macaulay's company, but did any of it really happen, even in part? Reading the essay 'Album' is to be the admiring and acquiescent foil to Macaulay's sardonic commentary on a family photograph album and the lives of the people it depicts, including a version of herself. 'Astronomy' is a recollection of her Italian childhood, an aspect of her private life rewritten for the public, as are 'Bathing', and 'Bed', particularly the intimate complaint of 'companions lapped and chrysalised in robbed blankets and close-gripped sheets': she was, let us not forget, one of seven children (37). Reading 'Cinema' is to be there with her, watching a film and listening to her murmured sparkling remarks. These essays, which acknowledged the interest of readers in Macaulay's own life, seem to actively encourage contact, yet Macaulay the 'famous lady novelist' had had trouble in 1926 with a 'mawkish female admirer', who would only accept rejection when it was clear that Macaulay would not meet her alone (Smith 1964, 33). Controlling the contact when it became unwelcome, in impact if not in quantity, was important.

The essays in *Personal Pleasures* are relentlessly witty, closely argued, conversational and erudite, written in a tone one can imagine being used at a literary cocktail party, in a senior common room or in a cathedral vestry. 'Heresies', for example, is a comic skit on the different beliefs of heretics, only comprehensible without a glossary to a High Church scholar. Yet it was also quite characteristic for Macaulay to write about something utterly recognisable from everyday life, for instance on royal jubilees, or 'Talking about a new car'. She was self-deprecating and did not pontificate, nor was she ever pompous. The reader needed to be amused, and so (for example, in 'Hot bath' and 'Listening in') Macaulay would often ground her perorations with a sly, puncturing joke.

A more light-hearted depiction of her professional life as a writer is given in 'Finishing a book'. She described the torment and labour of writing a book, and the relief, on finishing it, of having an empty and peaceful life once more. Her enjoyment in entertaining others by her writing is revealed in the layers of reflection in 'Flattery'. Macaulay wrote about receiving flattery in the letters that an author is sent by admirers, and laughed at the author's natural egotistical instinct by noting how intelligent and kind the writers of such letters must be. A second thought brought the stern reminder that all pleasures must be paid for: how tedious these letters really were because they required answers, and effort to be invested in the replies. By interrogating her practice as a writer over more than twenty years in *Personal Pleasures* Macaulay was making plain for the careful reader her beliefs about how she wrote and for whom. These essays also make it clear what writing meant to her as an educated woman, with a sound grounding in the mechanics, varieties and modes of the English language.

Macaulay exposed her prejudices when she wrote about language, and matters of daily or national import: this was an unavoidable side-effect of being a public commentator. Writing about her own life could also be fashioned into a version for the public to see. Apparently reliable fragments of autobiography could be made public, at long intervals, in the absence of a full autobiography. She published the four-page memoir of her childhood, 'Villa Macioli', in 1932 in a collection of similar reminiscences, in which she aligned her freedom and happiness as a child in Italy with overwhelming feelings of displacement and mundanity on the family's return to England (Macaulay 1932). 'Candlemas' is a brief autobiographical fragment on keeping the Candlemas feast as a child in Italy, and 'Canoeing' is a recollection of paddling the family canoe solo out into the Gulf of Genoa, out of sight of land, and imagining an epic struggle with a shark. 'Chasing fireflies' is a description of catching fireflies as a child, and 'Christmas morning' describes the clangour of Christmas Day bells in late nineteenth-century Italy, waiting for daybreak when the Christmas stockings could be examined properly. These are safe and distant memories, not closely relatable to the adult Macaulay, famous woman novelist and wit. They add lustre to her personality, and burnish her reputation for unconventionality and free thinking.

'Fraternal' repeats this process, by narrating how the (surviving) Macaulay siblings meet as adults, and recollect reckless stories from their childhood, while behaving in a respectable and adult way. A similarly sanitised picture of unconventionality is revealed in 'Departure of visitors', in which Macaulay gives heartfelt thanks for the glorious solitude after guests have departed, for the comfort of the empty room and the freedom to put books on any surface she wanted. 'Getting rid' presents Macaulay's decidedly eccentric routine of living among accumulating litter, in a cycle of first getting rid of letters, newspapers, circulars, rags and clothes she will never wear again, to create space and emptiness, to be filled again by incessant, creeping accumulation. These are tailored anecdotes for public amusement, designed to bolster a public persona that was known for being learned, witty, feminist, and opinionated.

The pleasure these essays convey came from external circumstances as well. Sarah LeFanu noted that in 1935 Macaulay had had at least 'a decade of happiness with her lover' Gerald O'Donovan and was 'full of joy' (LeFanu 2003, 220, 207). Macaulay was fizzing with intellectual energy, and was a respected, money-earning popular author with her own flat and agreeable friends, and moved in fascinating literary circles. She dined out on her own, a lot, and at 'a Sunday evening dinner from the mid-1930s' that she attended at the house of novelist Sylvia Lynd and her newspaper editor husband Robert, the guests included the comic geniuses Max Beerbohm and A P Herbert, the recently famous Margaret Kennedy, author of *The Constant Nymph* (1924), publisher Victor Gollancz and his wife Ruth, and Bryan Guinness, a poet, erstwhile Bright Young Thing and a former Mitford husband (LeFanu 2003, 185). The conversation ranged widely, and the party seemed to have continued well into the small hours.

In 1935 Rose Macaulay was living life to the full, in all the ways she could. Writing about personal pleasures now was good timing. In the next ten years she would watch her lover die painfully slowly from cancer, and be unable to grieve openly as to the world he was merely a family friend. The war would come, as would the Blitz and the loss of all her possessions. But in the post-war years, in her seventies, life would look worth living again.

References

Anon, 'Miss Macaulay enjoys herself', *The Times* (22 October 1935), 22.

BBC Written Archives, Caversham: R6/196/5, Advisory Committee of Spoken English, File 5, 1934 January–June.

Alice Bensen, *Rose Macaulay* (New York: Twayne Publishers, 1969), 26.

B Ifor Evans, 'Books of the day. Early Travellers', *Manchester Guardian* (5 December 1935), 5.

—, 'Letters and Criticism, *The Observer* (29 December 1935), 4.

Maria Stella Florio, 'The Towers of Trebizond. Language and the joys and paradoxes of the modern world', in *Rose Macaulay, Gender, and Modernity*, Kate Macdonald (ed.) London; Routledge, 2018), 161–173.

Gollancz advert, *The Sunday Times*, 3 November 1935, 9.

Sarah LeFanu, *Rose Macaulay* (London: Virago, 2003).

Rose Macaulay, 'Into human speech', *A Casual Commentary* (London: Methuen, 1925), 101–106.

—, *Catchwords and Claptrap* (London: Hogarth Press, 1926).

—, 'Lonely souls', *A Casual Commentary* (London: Methuen, 1925), 233–236.

—, 'Bad names', *Saturday Review of Politics, Literature, Science and Art*, 145:3784 (5 May 1928), 553–54.

—, 'Bad names', *Saturday Review of Politics, Literature, Science and Art*, 145:3794 (14 July 1928), 42–43.

—, 'The witchery of words and the charm of elsewhere', *Daily Herald* (13 August 1928), 10.

—, 'Autumn Meditation', *The Spectator* (21 November 1931), 42.

—, 'Villa Macolai', *Little Innocents. Childhood Reminiscences* ed. Alan

Pryce-Jones (London: Cobden-Sanderson, 1932), 46–49.

—, 'How to Speak English', *The Spectator* (12 January 1934), 43.

—, 'Linguistic changes', in *Essays and Studies*, By Members of the English Association, vol XX, collected by George Cookson (Oxford: Clarendon Press, 1935), 108–22.

—, 'Full Fathom Five: Auto-obituary VIII', *The Listener* (2 September 1936), 434.

—, 'February on the Air', *Time and Tide* 26:9 (3 March 1945), 184.

—, 'January on the Air', *Time and Tide* 27:5 (2 February 1946), 103–04.

—, 'February on the Air', *Time and Tide* 27:9 (2 March 1946), 200.

Rose Macaulay and Third Programme, 'Books destroyed – and indispensable', *The Listener* 42:1068 (14 July 1949), 63–65.

Harold Nicolson, 'Travellers, painters, writers and scientists', *Daily Telegraph* (25 October 1935), 6.

Jürg Schwyter, *Dictating to the Mob: The History of the BBC Advisory Committee on Spoken English* (Oxford: Oxford University Press, 2016).

Basil de Selincourt, 'Genius in enjoyment', *The Observer* (20 October 1935), 5.

Constance Babington Smith (ed.), *Letters to a Sister from Rose Macaulay* (London: Collins, 1964).

Note on the text

The text for this edition was scanned non-destructively from the 1935 first edition, and then proofread. The very few typographic errors have been silently corrected.

Personal Pleasures

Pleasure …
That reeling goddess with the zoneless waist
And wand'ring eyes.

—W Cowper, *The Task*

But every pleasure hath a payne, they say.

—George Chapman, *The Blind Beggar of Alexandria*

FRATRIBUS SORORIBUSQUE

Foreword

Compiling, as I recently did, a selection from the records of the pleasures enjoyed by other people has forced on me the conclusion that other people, though they have doubtless (between them) enjoyed all the pleasures accessible to our mortal state, have left very many of them unrecorded in print. Be that as it may, everyone has his own pleasures, enjoyed after his own manner, and much perusal of those of others has moved me to record a few of my own. Necessarily only a few. Had I but world enough and time, I might have continued this agreeable pastime for ever, leaving no joy unspelt, unwrit, no mirthful hour unsung. When I look through my collection and note its gaps, I feel, like Clive, amazed at my own moderation. There are here, for instance, no games; that is, no set games, with rules. There are all too few picnics, no riding, no separate heading for conversation, no presents, no money, no friends, no maps. There are a thousand pleasures, even of my own, left unrecorded in this brief choice. But a choice it had to be, owing, as I say, to this perhaps fortunate limitation of world and time which sets so brief a term to all our undertakings. So I have set down a few pleasures randomly, as they came to mind. They are pleasures of different, sometimes of contrary, moods; they include parties, and not going to parties, believing and disbelieving, solitude and showing off, and other seemingly opposed diversions.

But how true it is that every pleasure has also its reverse side, in brief, its pain. Or, if not wholly true, how nearly so. Therefore I have added to most of my pleasures the little flavour of bitterness, the flaw in their perfection, the canker in the damask, the worm at the root, the fear of loss, or of satiety, the fearful risks involved in their very existence, which tang their sweetness, and mind us of their mortality and of our own, and that nothing in this world is perfect.

Abroad

The great and recurrent question about Abroad is, is it worth the trouble of getting there? Delicious as is the prospect we see beyond this travail, shall we be enabled to conquer sloth's enticements, and emerge from what Mr Thomas Coryat, that enterprising Jacobean tourist, contemptuously termed our domestical lurking corners? Is there any peace, the voice of indolence protests, in ever climbing up the climbing wave?

Let us hearken rather to the stirring exhortations of Mr Coryat, who must have been minded much like Mr Thomas Cook, and spoke with his very accents. 'Let us,' cried Mr Coryat, 'propose before our eyes that most beautiful theatre of the universe, let us behold whatever is abroad in the world, let us look into provinces, see cities, run over kingdoms and empires. Surely we shall find,' said he, hopefully, 'those people which have used no journeys to be rude, slothful, uncivil, rough, outrageous, foolish, barbarous, void of all humanity, civility, and courteous entertainment, proud, arrogant, puffed up with self love and admiration of themselves, also effeminate, wanton, given to sleep, banquetings, dice, and idleness, corrupted with the allurements of all pleasures and the enticements of all concupiscence.'

But this is getting to sound agreeable; if home offers all that, one might do worse than stay there. Our tourist perceives this, and hurries on in different vein: 'Such is the sweetness of travelling and seeing the world, such the pleasure, such the delight, that I think that man void of all sense and of a stony hardness, which cannot be moved with so great a pleasure … O sluggish, abject, servile, and most dejected mind, which includeth itself within the narrow bounds of his own house.'

Perhaps it is the expense you dread? 'As though the dice and dicing box, domestical idleness, domestical luxury, and the gulf of domestical gourmandizing, doth not far exceed the necessary charges of travel.'

That is as may be. Perhaps one would do well not to balance the nicely calculated less and more, but to remember the spring cleaning, or the house painting, and consider how many by their travels have procured themselves evasion from domestical calamities and miseries.

Arise, then, from abject and home-keeping sloth. Cease to regard with effeminate distaste those hurdles which stand between you and Abroad, looming high, barred, enthorned, only by the strong to be o'er-leapt. Do tickets, passports, money, travellers' cheques, packing, reservations, boat trains, inns, crouch and snarl before you like those surly dragons that guard enchanted lands? A little firmness, a nice mingling of industry, negligence, and guile, and the hurdles will be leaped, the dragons passed; snapping your fingers at what you have left undone, you launch yourself into space.

Yes, you are on the boat train; you make once more the Grand Tour; you are full steam ahead for Dover, for Boulogne, for the silver seas whereon trumpet and pipe these enticing sirens against whose penetrating call even Ulysses would have cered his ears in vain. Hola, Captain! where is the packet for France? Here, Sir, here, and a fair wind in our sails. Honest gentlemen who will for Calais, let them make haste. To Calais ho! Aboard ho! The wind is at North, North, and North-West. Is the ship well armed, Captain? Fear nothing, Sir, for the ship is very well equipped with artillery and munition. Go into the prow. The wind blows, the tide swells, see the waves mount. The sea begins to rise and rage from the very bottom. See how those huge waves beat against the sides of our ship. Hear you these terrible whirlwinds, how they sing over our sailyards? We shall have by and by a storm. The tempest makes a great noise. The heaven begins to thunder from above. It thunders, it lightens, it rains, it hails; it is best to strike sail, and to veer the cables. This wave will carry us to all the Devils … O my friends on shore! O thrice and four times happy are those who are on firm land setting of beans! O St James, St Peter, and St Christopher! O St Michael, St Nicholas! O God we are now at the bottom of the sea. I give eighteen hundred thousand crowns to him who will set me a land. Let's land, let's go a shore. Captain, I will give you all that I have in the world to set me ashore. Will you go a shore in the midst of the ocean sea, Sir? What a horrible tempest! By St Grison what means this? Shall we take our sepulture here among these waves? I pardon all the world. I die, my friends. Fare you all well.

The tempest is now ended. Oh, it is fine weather again. A fig for the waves. We are in the haven of Calais. We are saved. Cannoneer, shoot off a piece of artillery. Les passeports, s'il vous plait. Oh, yes, indeed, anything. Par ici pour la douane. By all means yes, even that. How delighted I am to be arrived! Here is all my luggage, and all its keys.

Yes, you may look at everything, tumble everything about. No, nothing to declare, nothing at all; still, by all means rummage. This one too? Of course. And now you will chalk them; that is nice. Now for the train; allons, allons, facteur! Second-class, n'est-ce-pas. No, nothing else about it matters, and I have no reserved seat. Put me anywhere. What? All reserved? Then I must wait for another train, n'est-ce-pas. No, I never reserve seats in advance, it is quite too much trouble. What I say is, why make a business of what is meant for a pleasure? If a railway ticket does not get me on to a French train, then France is not the land of liberty, equality, of fraternity. But then, one never supposed that it was. There will be another train presently, free to all? That is excellent news. I will settle down; I will wait. Attention, there is a train. Allons, allons, facteur; deuxième classe, s'il vous plait. Ah, Ah, I am on the train, n'est-ce-pas. Mettez mes bagages on the rack, on the seat, on the floor, all about me. Je suis bien entourée, n'est-ce-pas. But see, there lacks one bagage; where can it be? Oh, Oh, you have left it on the platform over there. Vite, vite, facteur! The train departs. You have not been vite enough; the train is departed. I shall not see my bag again. Je me plaindrai au consul anglais.

Eh bien. Life is like that. Abroad, in particular, is like that. And now I am abroad; I am entrained; I am launched on my enchanting error across Europe. Where shall I go? France, Spain, Italy, everywhere; perhaps even Portugal. How fast and how loud foreigners talk! It is a gift; the British cannot talk so loud or so fast. They have too many centuries of fog in their throats. Besides, they are nervous; they dare not talk loud; they mumble and murmur, afraid lest some one will hear. Never mind them; forget them; too many of them are, indeed, on this train, on all trains, since the English cannot keep still or stay at home, but still we will ignore and forget them, we will feign that we are alone abroad among the foreigners. Allons, allons, mes braves compagnons! To Paris ho! But only to make a change of train; we will not linger in Paris, it is drab and cold. Across it quickly to the Gare de Lyons, the Gare d'Orléans, and off to the South. East or west, Marseilles or Bordeaux, Mediterranean or Atlantic, Italy or Spain, it matters not, it is all south, Palms, pines, pepper, eucalyptus, oranges, lemons, juniper, myrtle; Alps, Apennines, Pyrenees; Basque, Catalan, Castilian, Mallorquin, Ligurian, Tuscan, Sicilian, Venetian, Greek, Portuguese – any language you like, I have the phrase-books of some of them, and can do the rest by signs. To Greece with little English ladies and schoolmasters, questing after ancient Hellenes. Ἀθήναςε! Ὀλυμπίαςε! To Athens! To Olympia! Ἀθῆναι εἰσι καλαί, Athens are beautiful. Oh, how beautiful

Athens are! That is to say, they are vulgar and modern and dirty, but never mind, we rummage among them, we find the Acropolis. Schoolmasters, dons, little eager ladies, we swarm about the Acropolis, among the modern Hellenes, who do not comprehend their own ancient tongue when we speak it to them, who desire only that we should give them money. Over the hills to Corinth; Greece is terra-cotta coloured, and silver with olives; tortoises and lizards scuttle over it. The Vale of Tempe is dark and deep, and Peneius shines in it like an agate. All the plains of Thessaly; Olympus, Ossa, and Pelion; Thermopylæ, Parnassus, Thebes, Cithæron; the schoolmasters, the dons, the little ladies, are overwhelmed. Greece is really excessive. One cannot idle in it, or be stupid or inert, no, not for a moment, or one will miss something, one wastes one's time, since it is possible that one will not be this way again. One cannot, in Greece, be happy merely in being Abroad. For Abroad, Italy and France and Spain and Czecho-Slovakia and Scandinavia and the Americas and the South Seas are better. Back, then, to Italy; Sicily and Calabria and Naples; look how Vesuvius smokes! Stroll about Pompeii, so gay, so coloured, so still; if you are encouraging, one of the custodians will show you a house freshly dug, and perhaps embrace you in it. Rome, Florence, Siena, Umbria, Venice, the lakes; having seen all these, settle down on the Ligurian sea shore and bathe. Nothing to see here but sea and shore and fishermen and nets and mountains and some small town. No buildings, no pictures, no churches, nothing but Abroad. Buon giorno, signorina, sta bene oggi? Benissimo, grazie, signore; mi bagnerò nel mare, dopo di prendere il caffé. Caffè latte! how it froths into the thick white cup! Sugar tablets wrapped in paper, coarse white crusty roll, church bells clanging, fishermen shouting, small waves lisping on the sand. You can stay in the sea all day if you wish, coming out to dry and toast, and slipping in again. It is deep sky-blue, and there is a rock far out on which you can sit. Great Britain can give you buildings, picture galleries, cities, (though of no great moment and of inconsiderable antiquity), and scenery, but only Abroad can give you real bathing.

For that matter, only Abroad can provide a great deal else. Meals, for example, in the streets. Trams that blow horns; indeed, traffic horns in general play a sweeter, liltier music than ever they play in Britain. How their gay tune, on two notes, like a cuckoo's song reversed, lifts the heart! Mountains of a height, a jaggedness, a grandeur, that surpasses those of Caledonia, Westmorland and Wales. Terraces climbing up their lower slopes, set with olives, chestnuts, figs, and vines. Large white oxen drawing loads of marble. Mules drawing sand. Nets being hauled in from the sea heavy with bianchetti, and perhaps a tunny or two. Processions round the town, led by nasally chanting acolytes and magnificently dressed wax saints, and followed by the citizens. Rose petals scattered and flung from every window on to the Corpus Christi procession: Little St John, the Baptist, his hair just released from a week's curling-papers, leading his unruly lamb in the procession on his day. Brown and beautiful Basques dancing the fandango in the squares after a pelota match on Sunday evening. Redwood forests, giant cactuses in a pale Arizona desert, palms and orange trees and futbal in the plaza, the great blue sweep of Mexican mountains, the brown adobe of Mexican villages, the yucca standing high like blossoming swords, the wild roads not mended since the last revolution, the tiny burros carrying Mexicans, the estancias, haciendas, chile con carne, tortillas, the comida con vino incluso, the mandolins twanging in the plaza while you sit on the pavement and eat. The hot dog stalls, the camping cabins, San Francisco on her hills above the Golden Gate, Santa Barbara in white adobe, set with lit fir-trees on a warm Christmas night, San Diego, Tia Juana, and the Old Spanish Trail. The Florida seas and their leaning palmettos, the Keys and their twisted mangroves, Cuba across the straits. A small Provençal estaminet on the foothills, a mountain road twisting above it. Sunshine and warmth, sunshine and warmth, and the scent of lemons on the air. And, naturally, foreigners. I do not prefer foreigners to the English, except that they speak another language. Otherwise they are, I find, essentially much the same, though the Italians and Spanish are handsomer and browner, and the Americans more cordial. But they all belong to Abroad, that great, that delightful English picnic. So, like Walt Whitman, I make a salute to all foreigners. As he so exuberantly exclaimed, 'You Sardinian, you Bavarian, Swabian, Saxon, Wallachian, Bulgarian! You Roman, Neapolitan, you Greek! You little Matador in the arena at Seville! You mountaineer living lawlessly on the Taurus or Caucasus! You thoughtful Armenian! You Japanese! All you continentals of Asia, Africa, Europe, Australia, indifferent of place! You benighted roamer of Amazonia! You Patagonian, you Feejeeman! ... I do not say one word against you! Salut au monde!'

He was right. It is all Abroad, all that vast camping-ground, pleasure garden or paradise in which we may wander at large; or might until recently, when passports, bureaucracy and suspicion are attempting to hamper and limit our tranquil and happy errors over our errant celestial ball. Les Passeports s'il vous plait! Par ici pour la douane! Apra la sua valigia! Sin duda quejaré al consul ingles. I guess we'll have to put you on Ellis Island, if that's all the dollars you have.

Yes; we are hampered, invigilated, kept in on every side, very likely flung into gaol, directly we step into our pleasure-ground. But, when governments and their watch-dogs have done their worst, it is still Abroad.

Album

How enchanting your relations are! Mine, too, look much the same. I suppose people do; I mean, so much depends on the clothes, does it not? I like your aunts; how they ripple from the waist down, bending in the middle like swans; their hair piled high in chignons; see, how much of it they have – or was some, perhaps, attached, or rolled over cushions? Your Aunt Amy, did you say? What long ear-rings! She is very elegant, *mondaine*, refined, yet *capable*, do you not think, *de tout*? Or was she not? Married a curate, do you say? One wonders what life in the curate-house was like, after your Aunt Amy entered it. Nine children? So that was what it was like. Yes, I see, here they all are. The little boys in sailor suits or jerseys, holding bats; the little girls in sashes, their hair cut across their foreheads. Du Maurier children. Oh, yes, I see, that is Phyllis, and there are Olive and Ruth. I should know them anywhere; by the way, I hear Ruth's grandchildren are at that fashionable school in Dorset, and can already change wheels, top batteries, and milk cows. They are going to learn to read next year, you say? At ten and twelve? Isn't that a little soon? One is so afraid of over-exciting their brains. Still, if they *want* to learn, anything is better than repressing them ...

A clergyman: of course, Aunt Amy's husband. A Tractarian, was he? Well, he was a little late for that; but I see what you mean, he was whatever High Church clergymen were in the eighties. Wrote tracts about the Eastward Position? I think he was so right. And, of course, they all face that way now, so that shows.

Who is that old military man? He looks like a splendid walrus, with his long whiskers. Your paternal grandfather?

Of course; the General. Didn't he fight in the Crimea? Charged with the Light Brigade? How exciting! And how fortunate that he was one of those who rode back. He looks the kind of military man who might have been very much annoyed with whoever it was who had blundered. I should not care to face your grandfather if I had blundered. The lady in the crinoline is your grandmother, of course. She looks full of spirit; I dare say she needed it all. A crinoline gives such dignity, such deportment. No one could look *dowdy* in a crinoline. How her chatelaine hangs over it, full of the store-room keys. What a bore, to have to unlock the store-room whenever anyone wanted stores. I suppose stores are used by the cook daily, and always at the most inconvenient moment.

Look at those lovely girls, all in crinolines, ready to swim along like balloons in a breeze. Your great aunts? They are very sweet. No doubt they had a delightful time, waltzing, shooting with bows and arrows, riding, skating with gentlemen (for there was real ice in those days, was there not?). See, there is one of them on a horse, in a long habit, her hair in a net under a dear little feathered hat. Great-aunt Helen? Famous all over the county for her riding and jumping? Broke her back at a water-jump, and lay crippled for forty years ... Oh, dear, let us turn the page.

Here we have bustles. Your mother? Now, that is *really* the swan period. What a bend! The Grecian bend, was it not? The Greeks were first with everything, of course; but I do not recall this bend in any of their statues. Perhaps they could not hold it long enough to be sculptured. Of course, it is not *altogether* genuine; the bustle helped. But how adorable! How sorry your mother must have been when she had to go into those horrible clothes of the nineties, puff-sleeved jackets (by the way, I see they are in again; strange how even the worst things always come round) and stiff collars and sailor hats – yes, there she is in them.

And your Aunt Elizabeth, in a college group wearing large cricket pads – Newnham, is it? What year? 1890. Well, of course Newnham had been going for about twenty years then ... It was quite the thing to go to college, I suppose; now it seems to be less thought of, to be considered no use for getting jobs. I dare say your Aunt Elizabeth didn't have to think about jobs. Became a doctor, did she? I never knew Mrs Robinson had been a doctor; why did she give it up? She left six forceps in? But that's nothing, surely ... Oh, all in the same wound; yes, I suppose that *would* be rather many ... *And* three swabs? Well, I dare say her mind was on cricket. It may happen to anyone, they say. Most people who have ever had an operation are simply full of forceps and swabs, I believe; they think it is rheumatism or neuritis ... It is wonderful, I often think, what additions, as well as subtractions, the human frame can stand. I suppose really we are put together *quite* at random, and a few objects more or less make very little difference; though I must say, when you see a picture of our insides, you wonder where extra forceps and swabs would go. But of course, they take the place of whatever the surgeon has just taken away, I forgot that ... Well, perhaps your Aunt Elizabeth was right; she goes in for chickens now, doesn't she?

You as a child; how pretty. How people change; still, I would know you anywhere. Quite in the nude. That has the advantage that you can't be dated by your clothes. Your school lacrosse team ... and your first dance dress. Empire style. Clothes were pretty that year; nice high waists and simple lines.

But let us turn back to the Victorians. They fascinate me. There is a *je ne sais quoi* about them, a subtlety; they might have strange experiences, commit strange deeds, and say nothing. They are proud, reserved, self-contained. Your Aunt Geraldine looks like a mermaid, your Uncle Frank, behind his moustaches, seems to brood on strange lands. Had to leave the country suddenly? That would account for it, I suppose. Poor Uncle Frank. Did he have to be long away? It was hushed up? That always takes a little time, of course. And then Uncle Frank came home, and married a Miss Jones. Had to leave the country *again*? What bad luck he had! Now-a-days, they seem to manage better, without so much travelling. Was he long abroad the second time? Always? Dear me. Yes, I see, this is his *hacienda* in the Argentine, with himself and Miss Jones, grown nice and plump, in the porch … Oh, not Miss Jones? She Stayed in England, with the children? Then this would be some other lady, more of the Argentine type … I expect your uncle Frank was wise to settle there, among cattle; as your Aunt Elizabeth was wise to settle among chickens. Animals are a great resource. And so much nicer to rear them than to go and shoot them.

Photographs of ancestors are really much more interesting than the paintings of them they had before, because the camera cannot lie, so we know that they really did look like that. Now-a-days they touch them up more; the camera has learnt to lie. Besides, do we look as interesting? I am sure we do not. I could look at our ancestors for ever. Thank you so much for showing me yours. It has been a charming evening. You must come and see mine.

A charming evening. But as I drive home, the small cold wind of mortality hums round me with sighing breath. The way to dusty death seems to stretch before me, lit by those fading yellow oblongs wherefrom someone's ancestors gaze, pale pasteboard prisoners, to be wondered about, recalled, lightly summed and dismissed by us as we turn a page. So too shall we gaze out some autumn evening, prisoned and defenceless, to stir in posterity a passing idle speculation, a moment's memory. That? Oh, that is great-aunt Rose … She wrote. Oh, nothing you would have heard of; I don't think she was ever much read, even at the time; she just wrote. Novels, essays, verse – I forget what else; she just wrote away, as those Georgians did. Rather dull, I think. What besides? Well, I think she just went about; nothing special. There *was* some story … but it's all so long ago, I've forgotten. She ended poor, having outlived whatever market she had, poor old thing. Yes, she went on writing, but no one read her … she died poor, killed, I think, in an aeroplane smash; she learnt to pilot too old; she should have stuck to motoring. But she would learn to fly, and finally smashed a friend's plane and herself … silly, really. She had grown very tiresome before the end, they say. But look, here is someone more interesting …

It will be posterity's charming evening then, and theirs to pity, if they will, their pasteboard prisoners, as I now pity Aunt Geraldine with her mermaid's face and form, Uncle Frank who had to leave home so suddenly and so frequently, Great-Aunt Helen, of the rogue's face and little feather, who fell at the water-jump sixty years ago, Grandpapa General, who rode back with the Light Brigade, Grandmama, who had to be so often locking and unlocking her stores, Aunt Elizabeth with her forceps and her chickens, Aunt Amy rippling so elegantly from the waist down and marrying the curate who wrote tracts about the Eastward Position …

Poor figures I feel we shall most of us cut beside them, when the Albums shall imprison us too.

Arm-chair

> I love it, I love it, and who shall dare
> To chide me for loving that old arm-chair?

So, a century ago, defiantly enquired Miss Eliza Cook. Already, obviously, the sour and scornful denigrators of this article of furniture were busy with their cheap sneers, which one can only surmise to be based on envy. If Miss Cook's question were answered, one would find that the sneerers at the arm-chair (and they are many, in these days) were men who do not possess such chairs. They may be smart, modern men, whose chairs have arms of steel. They may be poor men; who cannot, perhaps, afford arm-chairs; who, having purchased one, possibly, on the Pay-Way system ('we never mention money here, Mr Everyman'), found it reft from them at the last owing to their too close adherence to this policy of reticent silence. They find themselves arm-chairless; they have to sit up straight on armless chairs, an embittering posture, or on the floor (an undignified one), or betake themselves to their clubs, where they find all the arm-chairs in chronic use by others, and are further embittered. So they sit down at one of the club writing-tables, on some hard, straight-backed seat, and, with a venomous eye roving round the room, proceed to write letters to newspapers about arm-chair critics, arm-chair pacifists, militarists, generals, reformers, statesmen, politicians, concert-goers, and the like. What they actually object to so strongly is arm-chair newspaper-sitters, who sit a clutch of journals as a hen sits eggs, without, for the most part, ever hatching out one of them, but if some callow chick of an idea should come cheeping out of the sitter's head and find its chirping way to public print, he is denounced by the arm-chairless as an arm-chair critic. Possibly such denunciations also come from civil servants and those who have to sit at office tables to do their stuff. These can ill bear that criticisms and suggestions about life and the world should be emitted by the comfortable, slugging it at ease in their arm-chairs, lolling and lounging, twiring through their long spyglasses at the scene which they with such bland and indolent effrontery criticize. No wonder that we who thus loll and twire rouse the wrath of those who must twire without lolling, those who have to do the work, and are peppered with the lazy fire from our arm-chair peashooters.

But we, calm and reposeful sedilians, do not resent such abuse or such envious contempt. We know that we have the best of it; that the most intelligent, as well as the easiest and most agreeable, criticism is emitted from the commodious depths of the easy chair wherein, *tranquillo animo*, we lie coiled in peace. (I speak as a female: for I am aware that gentlemen do not coil, but rather lie extended; this human law seems to apply also to bed.) Thus extended or coiled in our chairs, we vie happiness (as Evelyn wrote to Cowley about garden life, a far less comfortable affair) in a thousand easy and sweet diversions – 'not forgetting,' added Mr Evelyn, 'the innocent toils which you cultivate, the leisure and the liberty, the books, the meditations, above all the learned and choice friendships which you enjoy. Who would not, like, you, *cacher sa vie?*' And who could not *cacher* it with far more comfort in an arm-chair than in a garden? What happiness thus to

> waste away
> In gentle inactivity the day!

Many of us, like the gentleman Steele knew, 'fell into that way at the University, where the Youth are too apt to be lulled into a State of such Tranquillity as prejudices 'em against the

Bustle of that Worldly Business, for which this part of their Education should prepare 'em. As he could with the utmost Secrecy be Idle in his own Chamber he says he was for some Years irrecoverably sunk and immers'd in the Luxury of an Easy Chair, tho' at the same time, in the general Opinion, he passed for a hard Student'.

Fortunate gentleman. But there was no reason but his own averseness from such a path why he should not have been, in fact, a hard student, however deeply sunk, and even immersed, in the luxury of his easy chair. Books can pile the floor around the chair; dictionaries, histories, works of divinity, philosophy, and literature in all languages, can stand in the shelves within easy reach; pen and paper can lie on a table at hand, or slip down between the chair's cushions and its arms. In our arm-chairs we may join the mob of gentlemen who write with ease; wit can amble well, go easily; masterpieces can trickle elegantly and indolently from our pens; imagination, dandled, pampered, and stalled, can rise on spread wings and soar above Helicon, galloping among the seven planets, the firmament, and the empyreal heaven. What noble periods we conceive and pen; what stark and majestic lines, the starker in that our recumbent forms are so delicately stretched at ease.

Or music visits us, belling and stroking the ambient air, filling our room with linked sweetness, or with pure and complicated harmonies. Sometimes it will come from the Queen's Hall. Almost one can see that great assembly of listeners, sitting upright on hard chairs, afraid to stir or cough, straining forward to miss no chord, tier above tier of intent faces and rigid forms. While I am hearing the same sounds, or as near as makes no matter, reclined at ease in a warm and book-lined room, able to turn a switch and dismiss the whole affair when it no longer pleases. Does a soprano break out, shrilly tearing the air to tatters with a trilling scream? I turn the switch; she is gone; she troubles me no more than for one anguished second; peace and my arm-chair lap me about once more, like cloth of fine velvet of Turkey.

But it is not necessary, just because one sits in an arm-chair, to pass the noon of one's life, like the gentleman whose habits Steele deplored, 'in the Solitude of a Monk and the Guilt of a Libertine'. One may have company, either in another arm-chair, should they be so fortunate, or on some other kind of chair, or even on the floor. Let the company sit where it likes, or where it can. So long as I am in my arm-chair, I do not care where or how it sits. Conversation flows; what witty things we say; what creeds we demolish and erect, what characters and literatures dissect, what tales recount, what revolutions deprecate or predict, what hot battles fight, what conceits and fantastications fangle! We tire the stars with talking and send them down the sky; the stars, and the moon, and all the celestial bodies, for they have no arm-chairs, they wander, they labour, or they are fixed, all tiring conditions. But ourselves we do not tire; lying at ease in our chairs, nothing active or labouring but our tongues. Night, day, and the crystal spheres revolve about us; in our arm-chairs we shall for ever sit, triumphing over Death and Chance and thee, O Time.

But, alas, how rarely are they quite long enough in the seat!

Astronomy

The sand is cool to our bare feet, for the first time since breakfast. The sudden night has encompassed sea and shore, and, though they still hold the day's warmth, the sand no longer burns. It is a night for astronomy, the moon unrisen, the clear purple heavens thick inlaid with patines of bright gold. Look at the stars! Look, look up at the skies! Oh, look at all the fire-folk sitting in the air!

My father has set up the telescope, its three legs dug into soft sand, its questing proboscis peering inquisitively into the peculiar mysteries of the sky. We all look through it in turn, and see what we can see. We concern ourselves mainly with the major planets. We note that Mars is low and red, Venus brilliant, Jupiter enormous, Saturn triple-ringed and lackeyed by his myriad satellites, Mercury and Uranus negligible, Neptune not to be descried. (Or is not all this true of one night? Perhaps I confuse several.)

Then we spy on the fixed stars; we trace out the Great and Little Bears, find the Pole Star, the constellation of Cassopeia, the Great Square of Pegasus, Perseus and Andromeda, Capella and the Kids, the Pleiades, Sirius, Arcturus, Algol, Betelgeuze, Orion and his belt. But Aldebaran, Cygnus, Vega, Rigel, and a myriad more, I cannot, I am sure, identify. Can my father? Presumably, since he is, says our cook, 'proprio come il Signor Iddio, che sa tutto, tutto'. Alas, we are not like that. I perceive the heavenly bodies with the greatest difficulty: I lack siderial talent, with so much other. Still, I can find, after some search, the Bears and the Pole Star. For the rest, I say, with M de Fontenelle's Countess, I will believe of the stars all you would have me.

And look, the Milky Way! Even I can find that, with my naked eye. 'I wish you had a glass,' says M de Fontenelle, agreeing with my father, 'to see this ant-hill of stars, this cluster of worlds, if I may so call 'em. They are in some sort like the Maldivian Islands: those twelve thousand banks of sand, separated by narrow channels of the sea, which a man may leap as easily as over a ditch. So near together are the vortexes of the Milky Way, that the people in one world may talk and shake hands with those of another; at least I believe the birds of one world may easily fly into another, and that pigeons may be trained up to carry letters, as they do in the Levant.' This seems very probable, when one gazes up into that pale and beamy stream.

'The Galaxy,' says my father. 'From milk in Greek.'

How many stars in the Galaxy? No one knows; no one has counted.

Why not?

For one thing, they are not all visible.

Not even with the strongest telescope in the world, aren't they visible?

But my father is occupied with Sirius,

Suppose one discovered a new star? New stars are born, every now and then. *The Story of the Heavens* says so. Suppose one should find a little new star, just, just hatched, like a fluffy yellow chick thrashing out of its egg …

Father, what would you do if you saw a quite new star?

But my father, a modest man, whose profession is not astronomy, says that he would not know it for a new star.

Would Uncle Willie know a new star?

Probably.

Well, what would Uncle Willie do if he found a new star?

But my father is concerned with Jupiter and his satellites.

Venus slides, glittering and bland, down the sky to her bed.

A bright swoop down the western sky; a star shoots down,

like Lucifer from heaven, and plunges into the dark horizon of the sea, to join the floating lights that mark the fishing-boats and the phosphorescent shoals that spark in their wake. Look, look, a falling star! Has it fallen into the sea? Did it make a great splash where it fell? Would it sink a ship, if it fell on it?

No, stars do not fall into the sea, nor anywhere on earth. They career through space.

But they *might* hit the earth, mightn't they?

My father replies that this would be unfortunate.

Well, what would happen? Would it set us on fire? Would it kill us?

But my father is occupied with Saturn and his rings.

My mother once said that the great boulders of rock strewn about all up the bed of the river Teiro might be bits of fallen stars. My mother told us very interesting and wonderful things. She said that the white promontory of Spezia, which, on a clear day, we could see east of the Gulf of Genoa, was marble mountains. If we were to ask *her* what would happen if a whole star hit the earth, we should have a tremendous blaze and conflagration in a minute.

The moon is coming, cries someone; and, sure enough, a rose-gold haze flushes the eastern horizon, heralding the golden rim, like the segment of an orange, that will rise and rise from the dark sea until it is a whole orange climbing up the sky, to flood the night and dim the stars. My father quotes Ben Jonson, who was so wrong about Hesperus entreating the moon's light, for how should one of the sun's goddess lovers entreat the advent of another, who must dim her?

But, for our part, we welcome the moon, swinging up among silver flames, flinging her golden causeway across the bay to the ripples at our feet.

Astronomy is over. Like the monkeys and marmosets of whom Mutianus tells, we hop and dance beneath the moon.

A pig chase, we cry: for this pastime always concludes our astronomy. We race and chase about the brightening shore, up and down between the garden and the sea, in and out of the ripples that now glow gold as they curvet and spark, splashing lightly on damp sand. We flee and chase until we are as hot as if the moon were the sun, until we have no more breath to chase with or to flee.

At chasing and fleeing, I am as good as the next man; it is one of my stronger points. But deep in my heart there lies a shame; I am always the last to discern the Pole Star and the Bears. And sometimes I say that I see them without conviction, and fear, uneasily, that this may be an Untruth. Do the others really see these heavenly constellations as quickly as they make out?

Bakery in the Night

How sweet a waft of warm bakery breathes up from the nether world below the pavement, as I pass the baker's at midnight! All night they are at it, it would seem, making and baking that doughy substance which smells so much better in the making than ever it tastes when made. Fried fish is otherwise; it tastes good, but smells terrible when frying. That is one of the things about fish; it always smells ill – fishy, in fact – but tastes good, and not fishy at all. There would be few ichthyophagi if we judged fishes by their smell. Some bold and hungry experimenter must have ventured long since to disregard the fishy savour and try it in the mouth; he was rewarded, justified, and the tradition was established. The same with meat. But bread, poor enough stuff in the mouth, is delicious, when preparing, to the nose. Unfortunately this wears off after baking, and a fresh loaf smells of nothing in particular, while a stale one smells of mould.

But so delicious is this warm and bready odour that breathes up through a grating in the pavement that I pause entranced to sniff. For a moment I am persuaded that the bread I shall eat to-morrow will taste like this celestial smell; it will be manna, not mere bread. Nay, it will be ambrosia, such as is heaped on the tables of gods; it will be food for angels, for gourmets, for Lucullus at his solitary suppers. The sweet yeasty fragrance steals on the night, lingering on the air like the gentlest pretty insinuating tune. No wonder that men have sold their bodies and their souls for bread, if this is what bread is. Bread and circus games – the Romans were right in demanding these, in feeling that, together, they made the adequate life.

But, as I stand there and smell, strange unwelcome stories recur to my memory, of how bakers make bread. Has it not been said that, if we should watch them at it, bread-consumption would slump down, the staff of life would bend under us, and we should have recourse to potatoes and cabbage, rice, and even sago? It is the same, of course, with jam, with sausages, with veal. Better see no food prepared. Close the eyes, open the mouth, and say a grace that you were not there at the making of the pleasant finished product that slips so agreeably down your throat and into your system. And, if you come to that, what would your system look like, do you suppose, if you should have the misfortune to see *that*? It ill behoves us, with our insides, to be dainty about looking upon the manufacture of anything that goes into them; at its worst stage the object to be consumed can scarcely have presented so ill an appearance as does the place prepared for its reception.

Bathing

1 Off the Florida Keys

Over the pale jade-green shallows, a tiny breeze runs, ruffling the surface of the Florida Straits into ribbed glass, setting little ripples slapping against the mangrove-grown clumps of earth that enisle these strange seas. You may wade a mile out from the white beach, palm-fringed, of the Keys; wade towards Havana, ankle-deep, knee-deep, thigh-deep, waist-deep, breast-deep. Can one wade right across the straits to Cuba or Havana? I do not know: evening falls, and I have reached neither. Evening falls, and the sea, sunset-drenched, glows from green to rose, like gardens of ripening fruit beneath a glass roof. On the ribbed floor of sand gleam the coral forests: I stoop and break off brittle twigs and branches and flowers, as one gathers mushrooms or raspberries in a field. Through the forests dart slippery fishes, silver, coral, and turquoise, or striped black like little zebras; they glance through my hands. Here is a tiny goblin being in gleaming blue, with horns and a hump and goggling eyes; it is not fleet enough, and I cup it between my hands, and guide it to the nearest island, scoop a hole for it in the sand and fill it with water; it swims round and round, goblin eyes seeking escape; it feels its position acutely; it must be turned adrift again into the Florida seas, to join its goblin kind.

The boat that lies tethered to a mangrove tree on one of the islands is unmoored; one rows her back, while the others wade beside, shoving her over the sandy shallows, to beach her on the palm-fringed Key, where the evening breeze goes rustling among the star-shaped heads of slender, leaning royal palms, and the small waves shuffle sighing on white sand.

It has been a lovely bathe, an exquisite wade, an immersion, however partial, in enchanted waters. Nevertheless, of all the world's uneasy beds on which to tread, on which to sit, a bed of coral is the least deserving of that name. Of what is the marine cœlenterate polyps thinking, that he builds him of the skeletons of his tribe such harsh, such jagged arborescent beds for his habitation?

Rise, rise, and heave thy rosie head
From thy coral-pav'n bed ...

One is happy to know that the spirit was here mistaken, and that dear Sabrina, sitting under the glassy, cool, translucent wave of the Severn, was not sitting on coral, nor, as his excited fancy elsewhere tries to make out, on diamond rocks. We may be sure that Sabrina's bed and seats were of Severn mud, and fortunate she was that this was so. She would have said, I think, with Clive, and with all who have waded sandal-less off the Florida Keys, 'I have no desire for coral'.

2 Off the Ligurian Coast

The sea's warm edge sways lisping on hot sand, curling into tiny ripples, hissing, creaming, running delicately back. Wade in, take five steps in water as warm as a tepid bath, and the sharply shelving beach fails beneath your feet and leaves you swimming. Lapped in the clear, thin stuff, so blue, so buoyant, so serene, you can conceive no reason for ever leaving it. Strange element, on which you may lie stretched full length as on a bed, eyes closed, the sun hot on your face, wriggling your spread hands now and then like fins to propel you; or you may stand upright with folded arms, treading the sea with your feet; or hurl yourself through the water arm over arm; or dive down to the bottom of the deep, gather a handful of seaweed or pebbles, and shoot up. You may start swimming out to sea, heading for Corsica; swim and swim, until you are suddenly afraid you will meet a shark, and turn and race panicking for shore. Yes, there have been sharks in our bay; we have never met one, but we sometimes fear that we may.

Often we take out the canoe when we bathe. Three sit in the middle and one on each end; when it capsizes, we ride astride on its backside. Oh, pleasure, reeling goddess, I have spent much time with you, but I think that while bathing of an August afternoon in our bay with the canoe, we know you at your most reeling, your most zoneless. Such felicity seems to know no limit; measureless to man, it seems the pleasure of some celestial state, in which we swim and sport in the blue and heavenly inane, like the *putti* that leap through wreaths of flowers upon a painted ceiling.

Such pleasure, I say, like the pleasures of paradise, should know no term; it should endure for ever. But to our bathing a term is set. Unlike the children of the Italian *bagnanti*, we are summoned from the sea. We leave that lovely, that clear and celestial element, for thin air quivering with heat.

3 In the Cam

The birds wake me; many minds with but a single thought, they all break out singing at once; one does not know why. They wake me; they would wake the dead, if the dead lay where I lie, in an open arbour in a little wood by the river's edge. The river, pale and secret, slides past, between the green shadow of willows and the grey light of dawn and the white shining of the hanging may-bushes and the deep green of the waving weeds. It flows towards Cambridge, but will be long, at this rate, in arriving at that learned town, for it scarcely seems to move. Sluggishly the weeds wave, and with them the gold and white chalices with their broad-leafed saucers.

A phantom stream, a pale dream of green shadow and grey light. Alone in the dawn world, a pink climbing rose gives colour, a pure sharp note in a faint chromotone of greys.

The east too grows rose-pink, beyond the grey pricks of the willow leaves. Drowsily I lie, and watch the sun rise to the clamour of the birds. When it looks above the pollarded head of the large willow on the opposite bank, I shall bathe.

The river emerges from greyness into deep green colour and clear light. The sun tops the pollard. I throw off blankets and night clothes and slip from the bank into the cold stream. Spreading my arms wide, I let the slow flow carry me gently along through shadow and light, between long weedy strands that slimily embrace me as I drift by, between the bobbing white and gold cups and slippery juicy stems, beneath willows that brush my head with light leaves, beneath banks massed high with may, smelling sharp and sweet above the musky fragrance of the tall cow-parsley. Buttercup fields shine beyond those white banks; the chestnuts lift their candles high against the morning sky.

But suddenly there sprung,
A confident report, that through the country rung,
That *Cam* her daintiest flood, long since entituled *Grant* …
Is sallying on for *Ouze*, determin'd by the way
To entertain her friends the Muses with a lay.
Wherefore to show herself ere she to *Cambridge* came,
Most worthy of that town to which she gives the name,
Takes in her second head, from *Linton* coming in,
By *Shelford* having slid, which straightway she doth win;
Than which a purer stream, a delicater brook,
Bright *Phœbus* in his course doth scarcely overlook.
Thus furnishing her banks, as sweetly she doth glide
Towards *Cambridge*, with rich meads laid forth on either side;

And with the Muses oft did by the way converse ...
A wondrous learned flood ...

Possibly. But possibly also, by the mud of three centuries, a less pure stream, a less delicate brook now than then.

Beneath a hanging may-tree, a thin cheeping comes; a brood of baby moor-chicks has hatched in the night, and now swims out to explore the green and gold world, four small black balls behind their mother, chirping their excitement to the morning.

I splash up stream against the flowing weeds, scramble out and dry myself. The pure stream, the delicate brook, the learned flood, has a floor of soft mud, and is cold before the sun is high. I creep again into blankets, and would sleep the day in, but for the indefatigably cantiferous birds.

Bed

1 Getting into it

When I consider how, in a human creature's normal life, each day, however long, however short, however weary, however merry, circumstanced by whatever disconcerting, extravagant, or revolting chances of destiny, ends in getting into bed – when I consider this, I wonder why each day is not a happy, hopeful, and triumphant march towards this delicious goal; why, when the sun downs and the evening hours run on, our hearts do not lighten and sing in the sure and certain hope of this recumbent bliss. If it were a bliss less recurrent, more rare and strange, its exquisite luxury would surely seem a conception for the immortal gods, beyond any man's deserts. Even through the cold and sober definition given by the dictionary, comfort and anticipation warmly throb. 'It consists for the most part of a sack or mattress of sufficient size, stuffed with something soft or springy, raised generally upon a "bed-stead" or support, and covered with sheets, blankets, etc., for the purpose of warmth. The name is given both to the whole structure in its most elaborate form, and, as in "feather-bed", to the stuffed sack or mattress which constitutes its essential part. (A person is said to be *in bed*, when undressed and covered with the bedclothes.)'

What delicious memories and hopes do the quiet words evoke! A sack or mattress of sufficient size, stuffed with something soft or springy, raised generally upon a bed-stead or support, and covered with sheets, blankets, etc., for the purpose of warmth. Can well-being further go? Yes: for the purpose of even greater warmth, there may be a rubber bottle filled with hot water. Reflecting on, and still more, experiencing, this state of Olympian, of almost lascivious pleasure, how one pities Titania sleeping sometime of the night on her bank among thyme, oxlips, violets, and snakes, her only coverlet the cast skins of these reptiles, which serve us not for sheets but for shoes. She was but a fairy queen, and knew nothing of our soft human elaborations of comfort. 'Thou shalt lie in a bed stuffed with turtle's feathers; swoon in perfumed linen, like the fellow was smothered in roses.'

And to your more bewitching, see, the proud
Plumpe Bed beare up, and swelling like a cloud ...
... Throw, throw
Your selves into the mighty over-flow
Of that white Pride, and Drowne
The night, with you, in floods of Downe ...

That is better than the bank where the wild thyme grows; better, even, almost certainly, than the bed which Eve made out of flowers in the blissful nuptial bower, or than the roses that smothered the fellow. Not that down is necessary, or even desirable: a good hair mattress over box springs is more resilient, and as accordant to the frame as one can wish. The down can fill the pillows. The sheets are of smooth, fine cambric; not linen, which is heavier, colder, and less pliable, even when perfumed. Blankets should be according to season and temperature; it is well to have one or two in reserve, cast back over the bed's foot.

Climb, then, into this paradise, this epicurism of pleasure, this pretty world of peace. Push up the pillows, that they support the head at an angle as you lie sideways, your book held in one hand, its edge resting on the pillow. On the bed-head is a bright light canopied by an orange shade; it illustrates the page with soft radiance, so that it shines out of the environing shadows like a good deed in a naughty world. You are reading, I would suggest, a novel; preferably a novel which excites you by its story, lightly titillating, but not furrowing, the surface of the brain. Not poetry; not history; not essays; not voyages; not biography, archæology, dictionaries, nor that peculiar literature which publishers call belles-lettres. These are for day-time reading; they are not somnifacient; they stimulate the mind, the æsthetic and appreciative faculties, the inventive imagination; in brief, they wake you up. You will never, I maintain, get to sleep on Shakespeare, Milton, or Marvell, or Hakluyt, or Boswell, or Montaigne, or Burton's *Anatomy*, or Sir Thomas Browne, or Herodotus, or any poetry or prose that fundamentally excites you by its beauty, or any work that imparts knowledge. These will light a hundred candles in your brain, startling it to vivid life. A story, and more particularly a story which you have not read before, will hold your attention gently on the page, leading it on from event to event, drowsily pleased to be involved in such fine adventures, which yet demand no thought. Let the story amuse, thrill interest, delight, it matters not which; but let it not animate, stimulate or disturb, for sleep, that shy nightbird, must not be startled back as it hovers over you with drowsy wings, circling ever near and nearer, until its feathers brush your eyes, and the book dips suddenly in your hand. Lay it aside then; push out the light; the dark bed, like a gentle pool of water, receives you; you sink into its encompassing arms, floating down the wandering trail of a dream, as down some straying river that softly twists and slides through goblin lands, now dipping darkly into blind caves, now emerging, lit with the odd, phosphorescent light of oneiric reason, unsearchable and dark to waking eyes.

But what a small mischance can mar this clinic joy, this opulent bed of pleasure. Adam and Eve doubtless encountered pricks and thorns and crumpled leaves in their roseate couch, though we are reassured as to the completely unentomologous condition of the bridal bower. And our passible frames may meet, in some untended mattress, with a lump. Or, in some alien dwelling, beneath the roof-tree of callous friends, with coverings cold as charity, blankets scant and thin. The eiderdown, if eiderdown there be, may glide and slide to the floor, like a French *duvet*. The hot-bottle may leak. Your head may face the window, and the curtains be of white casement, with a gap between to admit the dawn. The bird of dawning may sing all night long. A clock may tick, and be too large to be shut in the wardrobe. There may be a thin, transaudient wall, and a snorer beyond it. Or a snorer in your very bed, or even a somniloquent. Worst of all, worse than any other clinic grief, almost too profound a grief to be so much as glanced at in a survey of pleasures, it is conceivable that the light may only be extinguishable by the door. I believe, nay, I assert with confidence and deliberation, having clearly in mind all other bedroom woes – such as hard mattress, flock pillows, scant covering, intrusive dawn, eoan bird-songs, disappointed or fatiguing love, companions lapped and chrysalised in robbed blankets and close-gripped sheets, and yet turning and ever turning still – I say with deliberation, that this is the shrewdest stroke of fortune, the harshest bedroom chance, a light only extinguishable by the door.

2 Not getting out of it

Infinite and interminable rivers of eloquence have run, singing and murmuring on this inexhaustible theme. It is probable that all has been said or sung on it that can be sung or said. Yet one is bound to contribute one's tributary, one's little stream of eloquence, to the flood which has flowed down the ages in praise of this great joy. The point is, once in the bed of pleasure, why get out of it? Humanity sees this point clearly every morning, yet, nearly every morning, obfuscates it, deserts the sheltering couch (where so much of the business of life might be transacted if we so chose, and at so much less cost of labour and distraction), and steps into the cold embattled world without.

How long wilt thou sleep, O sluggard? when wilt thou arise out of thy sleep? Yet a little sleep, a little slumber, a little folding of the hands to sleep ... Go to the ant, thou sluggard; consider her ways and be wise ...

Yes, but the ant's bed (even if the female ant does leave it as early in the morning as is here implied), is but a poor miserable resting-place compared with ours; the phrase 'to seek repose on an ant-bed' has been used as a synonym of fantastic mischoice. We must not be surprised if ants rise betimes, instead of replying, as we do, to those who rouse them, 'You have waked me too soon, I must slumber again'. Do not praise the ant's ready exsuscitation, but pity rather that entomological barrenness of invention which has never furnished this hard-worked insect with a really comfortable bed. Not for the ant the drowsy exit from delicious dreams to a world of soft down, box springs, and sheets that gentlier lie than tired eyelids upon tired eyes. Not for her (or him) the lively cup that disperses the somniatory clouds from the brain, the clean newspaper hot from the press, discreetly waiting to unfold its strange matutinal tale, the pile of letters, each throbbing with its little human message, each shut behind its enveloping protecting veil, which need not be torn asunder until, or unless, we choose – not these for the ant, waking on her stinging heap to another busy, bustling, onerous, formicarian day. Unhappy insect, motion-obsessed, for ever dragging, fetching, carrying, from one site to another, objects which are very well where they are, like those porters in Paris stations who can let nothing lie ... such labours she can scarcely begin too late in the day. Consider the ant's ways and be wise indeed, for her labour is like unto ours; we too are for ever dragging, fetching, carrying, changing, objects which are very well as they are … such labours we too can scarcely begin too late in the day. The advantage we have over the ant is that we know it; we have reason, she only instinct.

Lie back, then, among pillows and, gently yet firmly encouched, await the onslaught of the bellicose day, whose buffets jar less rudely those who take them lying down. Yield to the storm; venture not out into it, and it will pass,

Thou shalt have thy Caudles
before thou dost arise:
For churlishnesse breeds sicknesse
and danger therin lies.

Thus spoke a better lover than all those who have shouted to wake their ladies at dawn, Calling them slug-a-beds, pigs in straw, bidding them rise and dress and come a-maying, asking them why should they sleep when they have slept enough (what a question!), and, worst of all, telling them that their breakfast stays until they are up – water-gruel, sugar-sops, brown ale, and toast. A kind lover or husband would bring all these to the bedroom; an intelligent one would be consuming them there himself. After this meal (unless quite incapacitated by its various ingredients), you may lie and reflect on all the occupations and works which man has pursued in bed; how Milton therein composed much of *Paradise Lost*; how Dido and her court feasted Æneas and his warriors, and after supper listened to his mournful travelogue, all reclining on their couches; how emperors and dictators have lain on beds while damsels danced before them and made music; how Sir John Suckling practised and perfected in bed that card-playing by which he lived; how Hobbes did mathematics, drawing lines on his thigh and on the sheets; how generals have planned victories and ordered attacks; how the Kings of France received their ministers in bed and dispensed affairs of state; how Lady Mary Wortley

Montagu received poets, and Prime Ministers the news of victories; how men are born in bed, and frequently die there; how Samuel Pepys lay late with great pleasure, and Samuel Johnson lay all his life until noon or until two, purposing to rise at eight and telling young men that nobody who did not rise early would ever come to good. Indeed, so much of the world's business has been performed in bed, that even to begin to consider it will be a morning's work. Rise early and bed late, says a foolish old adage, but does not explain why you will be better out of bed than in. A thing too often forgotten is that, once you are out of it, you or some one else will have to make it. There was a certain man named Æneas who had kept his bed eight years, whom St Peter bade arise, and added that he was to make his bed. Æneas arose, and, we suppose, made his bed; but, after eight years of lying in it, this daily rising and making it must have seemed very strange, and we are not told how long it lasted.

Indeed, more should be done in bed than is (even more). We spend too many of these precious clinic hours in blind stupor, tenebrizing it like polar bears in winter. Going to bed is a nocturnal pleasure; but not getting out of it is a journal one, to be enjoyed with all the innocent ardours and relish of the day. Slug then in sloth, and languish in delights, while the day breaks and shadows flee away.

But the luxury of pleasure is marred, as time creeps on, by a bitter foreknowledge born of experience. Sooner or later some one of those who are under your roof, unless you have your roof all day to yourself, will enquire if you are ill, and, if you are well, at what hour you are proposing to rise. Why, in the name of all the great bed-lovers, should I be ill because I prefer to remain in so charming a refuge as my bed? Did Milton's daughters ask him if he was ill when he preferred to dictate from his bed? Was Dr Johnson ill? Were the French

Kings? No, I am not ill; I am merely philoclinic ... that is my answer, if I can but make it to her who arrives to clean my flat ...

Believing

Yes, I believe everything; you cannot tell me anything that I cannot believe.

That the forbidden fruit of Paradise was an apple presents no difficulties to me; nor that mermaids sing when combing their hair and swans when dying, that ostriches eat keys and a whale ate Jonah, that a remora can stay a ship, and the cockatrice, who is hatched by a toad out of the egg of a cock, slay a man by a glance.

All the reputed strange habits of birds and beasts I believe, even that little birds tell tales, unicorns love virgins, dragons are the faithfullest of pets, wild horses the most inquisitive, and yet the most uninformed, of quadrupeds, who still stick at nothing to drag secrets from people, but always drag in vain.

I believe (can you?) that

Slow *Boötes* underneath him sees
In th'icy *Isles*, those Goslings hatcht of Trees;
Whose fruitfull leaves, falling into the Water,
Are turn'd (they say) to living Fowls soon after;

and that

Rotten sides of broken Ships do change
To *Barnacles*; O Transformation strange!
'Twas first a green Tree, then a gallant Hull,
Lately a Mushroom, now a flying Gull.

And I believe in dowsing, and that anyone can divine water anywhere, whether it is there or not.

I believe in the Athanasian Trinity, and in angels; angels in heaven, on earth, and in the midmost air; angels with flaming swords expelling our parents from Paradise and obstructing Balaam's ass; French angels assisting the Allied armies at Mons and turning back General Von Kluck's march on Paris; Ulster angels crowding about Derry; Thomist angels crowding on needles; weeping angels distressed at what they see; guardian or tutelary angels steering our wayward course.

I believe that most things move the underjaw when eating, the crocodile not; that sirloins were knighted by an English king; that Diogenes lived in a tub, St Simon Stylites on a pillar, chameleons on air, salamanders in fire, mermen in the sea; that corpses bleed when their murderer approaches; that what I read in the newspapers is true.

I can be every man's gull, and am infinitely persuadable. For to believe greatly is to enlarge life's oddity; to teratologize and credit strange relations, to run open-mouthed after aniles, or old wives' tales, illustrates the world with coloured candles, whose queer and flickering flames quaver into dim hidden corners, suggesting the goblin tenebrios that lurk therein, defining little but denying nothing. The clear and garish lucence of the sceptical spirit I utterly reject: it is so dull.

And there is nothing left remarkable
Beneath the visiting moon …

That is what it ends in.

Give me a loud lie. Give me 'misse-stories, hisse-stories, by the old Serpent hissed and buzzed among superstitious men'; give me 'that babbling and fabling Abdias', who can tell me Ethiopian fables, and entertain me 'in a fools' Paradise situate above the highest mountains, with such delicacies as shew that Adam's children are still in love with the forbidden fruit'.

I promise you I will swallow all you give me, I will reject nothing, I will not strain at gnats, no, nor at camels neither. He over there, you say he is a werewolf, and prowls howling by night over Primrose Hill? I can well believe it; he has that air. That other, he is a spy for the Russian government, and that is where he gets all his money from. He instigates strikes; his pockets bulge with Russian gold. There are some Nazi spies here too; they track down and murder refugees. As for that group over there, they indulge in the wildest, the oddest debauches – you would scarcely believe if I should tell you. Yes, I can believe, but you could not … I can even believe that traveller from Bavaria, who last week saw a beautiful young man transformed into a goat.

I should like to sit in a coffee-house; one used to hear, from all accounts, the most ridiculous tales there. Everything was largened out of all reason and likelihood, like a flea under a magnifying glass, becoming thereby worthy of credence. But coffee-houses have degenerated, they are used now for rapid meals, and there is less time for tales. I am told that they still tell fine tales in taverns, and that after a short time in a tavern, a man can believe anything. Yes, but I do not need taverns; I can believe anything on tomato-juice.

It is good to believe so much. The only drawback is that I never have that fine truculent moment when I say to my informant, 'You lie'.

Bird in the box

He lives in elegant retirement in a house of dark tortoiseshell, behind an oval china door on which is painted a blue lake, a blue and pink sky, three transparent pink mountains, a rocky shore, three red-roofed houses, three slim bending trees, and two sailing-boats. A small lake paradise, you think, and wonder what it does there, so sweetly, gaily set in shining gold-flecked dark-umber shell. Then you lightly touch a spring, and lo, a miracle. The door of lake and mountains springs back, opening wide, revealing its inner side, on which winds a broad reach of blue water (lake or river?) with more pink mountains, more small red-roofed houses on the shore. This tiny china land and waterscape springs up from over a golden floor, a broidered mesh of woven flowers and leaves, like one of those enflowered golden meads in Paradise where, it is said, the blessed saints walk in bliss; and simultaneously there rises from this shining bed a bird. You will not credit this most extravagant sight, and I myself, as Herodotus was wont to say, am slow to believe it, but it is, nevertheless, the truth. An iridescent bird, a bird of shining blue and green, peacock-hued, tiny, he springs up, he flaps blue wings, he opens a small beak, he sings, turning this way and that, like a prima donna, against the oval background of pink mountains and blue lake. A stream, a fountain, of sweet pure lovely shrillness cascades into the air, unearthly, celestial, like the songs of angels which the blessed saints, walking on the golden floor, doubtless hear. This (approximately) is the tune that he sings:

And, having sung it, folds his wings and retires, lying suddenly, swiftly down on his side on the golden meadow, which opens to receive his small form, and the china door snaps shut on gold-broidered floor and vanished bird. The sweet echo of that piping cadence still lilts upon the silent air; I hold in my hand a mute shell box, dark umber, flecked with gold, inset with an oval door, the outside of a closed door, whereon blue lake and transparent pink mountains and slim trees delicately smile, lying firmly, reticently, over the strange secret within, over music fallen dumb and a blue bird sunk asleep beneath a flowery golden floor.

A bird of pleasure indeed, Like Walton's nightingale, he breathes such sweet music out of his little instrumental throat, that it might make mankind to think miracles are not ceased. He that at midnight (when the very labourer sleeps securely) should hear (as I have very often) the clear airs, the sweet descant, the natural rising and falling, the doubling and redoubling of his voice, might well be lifted above earth, and say, Lord, what music hast thou provided for the Saints in Heaven, when thou affordest men such music on earth!

My thanks are due to Miss Livia Gollancz, who patiently and skilfully took down this tune straight from the bird's beak – no easy task, with so rapid a performer.

And this makes me (as it made Walton) the less to wonder at the many aviaries in Italy.

So much for the bird of pleasure, of which very much more might be said. In brief, how infinitely am I taken with this agreeable cheat! Like the phœnix, like the sun, he sinks into his golden bed only to rise again. Call him, and he will return, singing his carol before his opened door, turning this way and that, with flirting wings, against china lake and hills – tirra lirra sweet sweet sweet!

But will there come a day when he does not come, when, though his door springs back, his gold bed holds him still asleep and stirless beneath its starry mesh? Or a day when he cannot get back, when, his song ended, he still stands poised as for flight, lacking power to fall sideways and sink into the floor, so that the little door shuts on him and crushes him as he stands? For at times he seems weaker, more tardy in his retreat, and you may glimpse him lying half sunk in gold, with the china lakescape resting lightly on his folded blue wing. Are he and the spell that bids him come and go immortal, or will the enchantment one day end, and leave only a box of dark and shining shell, with china door closed tightly over a golden mesh and a buried, songless bird?

Come, press the spring once more; make sure that he will come. Rustle, flutter, tirra lirra sweet!

Book auctions

It is a singular scene. Around the room sit and stand inner and outer circles of impassive men; each holds a catalogue, each a pencil. Another and still more impassive man enters, every few minutes, into the middle of the circle, holding up, for their critical, sophisticated, and supercilious stare, a book. None of them, it is apparent, think much of this book; it is, in each case, to judge from their expressions, a book that ought to go pretty cheap, a defective book, a book that, if they purchase it, will stand on their shelves unsold for ever. Sometimes it is several books; a lot: all poor.

Only one man in the room admires and likes these books; he is the presiding god, raised above the rest on a dais. He thinks very well of all the books; he likes books; he is a bibliophile, a bibliolater, even a bibliomaniac. He is, in brief, a bibliopole. He too, has an impassive face, but you can tell by his voice and his utterances that he likes books. He must feel lonely, presiding over this gathering of bored bibliophobes. Yet he conceals it; he addresses them in dulcet, persuasive accents, though not infrequently his tone gently conveys admonition and reproof, a kindly but shocked, 'Come, come, my dear sirs! Only five pounds for this admirable work! Come now, we all know better than that!' But he does not say it; except by the inflexions of his admirably modulated voice. Ever so slightly turning towards some unresponsive gentleman in the circle, he says, 'Guineas. Five guineas bid'. After that, with other slight glances round, 'Five ten. I am bid five pounds ten. Fifteen. Six Pounds. Guineas. Six ten, I am bid …'

As he speaks, his eyes turn to and fro, from one to another, as if he watched tennis. But none but he has spoken; none but he, one would say, has moved. By what silent telepathy has he divined from them their offers of these shillings of which he makes mention? Or does he invent them? Is he hypnotising these hard bibliophobes with his gentle, even tones, uttering his own hopes and counsels, like the still small voice of conscience in their ears, so that when at length he pauses, (why he ever stops, is not known; since he never gets any response, it cannot be that the moment arrives when he gets less response than before) when he at last breaks off, and murmurs that the book in question has been sold to such an one, for such a price, the individual mentioned accepts his destiny, half believing that he has indeed offered this preposterous sum for a book which he dislikes and despises. That little motion he made with his catalogue; the time he sucked his pencil; scratched his chin; blew his nose; twirled his moustache; jerked his head; crossed his legs; winked his eyes; performed any one of those thousand little actions by which humankind reacts to the encompassing universe; these must have committed him to this purchase, involved him in the payment of this sum so far in excess of the value of the book, or the lot of books, which seems to have passed into his possession.

Very well. Life is like that. He must accept his portion, and sell it, if he can, at a price a little more than that which he has given, if only he can meet a fool.

Thus (I imagine) these silent book merchants cogitate, as the books are, one after another, inexplicably knocked down to them.

Alternatively, have they actually intended, by the trifling nods and becks that have escaped them, to convey to him who can read their very thoughts the little advances which have mounted to such a sum? If so, it shows once more the perils of competition. The delirious excitement of rivalry which stimulates the horse to run ahead of the horse in front of him, stirs in the blood of these hard-bitten men, egging them on to offer, in emulous rage, sums which they never in cold blood would have paid over any counter. 'Ten shillings,' says (or indicates) Mr Robinson; 'fifteen,' the prompt repartee is hurled back by the flirt of Mr Smith's catalogue; 'twenty,' Mr Robinson, now roused, tilts his chair to convey; and 'guinea', replies Mr Smith's tilted hat. And so on and higher, in dumb but heated emulation, until one or other of the agonists comes to himself shaking his head as one who emerges from some strange delirious dream, and the disappointed, though calm, agonarch awards the prize to his rival.

Meanwhile, while these contests of giants rage about me, I sit rigid and stirless, benumbed, beclumpsed and dull. I dare not move nor breathe, nor lift my eye to encounter, perhaps, that roving eye which is so extreme to mark the least motion, so alert to interpret it. There is a book I should like to buy, but it is not due yet; we are only at number 532, which is called *Coleoptera of the British Islands*, and should I but uncross my knees, it would be mine, in five volumes, with coloured plates. They have reached twelve and sixpence. 'Anyone bid fifteen?' That commanding, probing glance passes over me.

> My nerves are all chain'd up in Alablaster,
> And I a statue; or as *Daphne* was
> Root-bound, that fled *Apollo*.
> Fool, do not boast,
> Thou canst not touch the freedom of my minde
> With all thy charms …

'Fifteen. I am bid fifteen'… By me? Quite possibly … no, he looks elsewhere; the *Coleoptera* are knocked down to a bookseller on whose shelves I shall triumphantly see its five volumes, its coloured plates, reposing in unwanted redundance, because that unguarded bookseller coughed at the crucial moment.

Off they go again. 'Five shillings bid ... Seven and six.' ... What is this? The enquiring eye is on me; I realise that I have hiccupped. 'Ten ... twelve and six ...' Someone else must have hiccupped too, for the eye passes to and fro between me and another; the thing has become a rally. I have hiccupped again; that makes fifteen shillings. Seventeen and six, twenty ... my colleague in distress must be cured, for he does not raise my last. 'Twenty. I am bid twenty shillings ...' I shake my head, in denial of this assertion; it is useless. 'Twenty shillings I am bid ... Sold for twenty shillings.' The book is mine; I look at my catalogue and see that it is a French book about Venus ... Yes, and about Eunuchs too ... Quite definitely I cannot, no, I will not take it home; I will explain to the clerk afterwards ...

The auction proceeds. Soon it will reach my book – the *Bucaniers of America*, 3rd edition, 1704. How greatly I desire it! Surely I can win it, seeing that, despite all my struggles not to do so, I won Venus and the Eunuchs.

'640.' It is held up before us; I see its stained title page; felix culpa, fortunate stain, that will keep it within my means. 'Fifteen shillings,' says the auctioneer. My hiccup was cured, apparently, by the shock of acquiring Venus, but I flick my catalogue, meaning 'Seventeen and six.' What is this? He does not see me; he looks towards some haggling bookseller who has blown his nose; he says, 'seventeen and six', but not to me. I too blow my nose; the word is now 'One pound', but it is the word of the dumb Mr Robinson, who has tilted his bowler hat to the left. 'Guinea,' I mutely cry, flapping my catalogue like a signal of distress. He will not look, he passes by; he observes Mr Jones to scratch his cheek, and says 'Twenty-five'. I am as a desperate castaway on a lone island, signalling vainly to ships that steam unheeding by, picking up other castaways from other islands, but never me. In vain

I flap my catalogue, cough, clear my throat, cross and uncross my legs, jerk my chin. The *Bucaniers* are flung to and from between Mr Jones and Mr Robinson in mute, tense rally and return. 'Thirty. I am bid thirty …' Mr Jones is slackening; he performs no more little actions; he slumps in his chair; the game is to Mr Robinson. I cannot endure it; I spring to my feet. That chaste and muted hall is rent by a cry. 'Two pounds.'

The crude and raucous vocality of my bid shocks the mute multitude to surprise. The auctioneer at last looks my way; impassively he murmurs, 'I am bid two pounds. Going for two pounds.' He rakes Messrs Robinson and Jones with enquiring eyes; he decides that their gestures are those of bored negation; they have lost interest in the *Bucaniers*, and are thinking about something else.

'Sold for two pounds.'

The *Bucaniers* are mine.

But I should have said thirty-five. The *Bucaniers* were not mounting by ten shilling steps. The delirium of auctions turns the brain.

Booksellers' catalogues

How lightly, softly, insinuatingly, they arrive, flipping through the letter-box, alighting like leaves on the passage floor; green like leaves of spring, red or brown or orange like leaves of autumn, or white like drifts of snow; but each folded neatly and precisely in a wrapper of thin or stout dun-coloured paper. I will not open them; I will not slit that concealing jacket that protects me from the song of these luring sirens; like Odysseus and his sailors, I will be deaf and blind. I will cast them, as I cast without a pang all the other catalogues of merchandise that arrive in my home, unopened into the waste-paper basket.

That small, orange-red being, the colour of a street beacon, in its stout paper jacket – I gather it up to fling it into the basket. Two inches of orange-hued catalogue protrude from each end of the wrapper, closely printed; odd, how booksellers seem always short of paper, so that they have to use every inch of even the covers of their catalogues for their lists of wares. What shows on the two inches of double column visible above the wrapper is:

1063 [**Utterson** (E N)] Select Pieces of Poetry; republished principally from Early Printed Copies, in the Black Letter, *with woodcuts*, 2 vols in one, 8vo, *half morocco, t e g, uncut*, 8s 6d [J6]   1817

1065 **Vergil** (Polydore) English History, from an early translation, Vol I, containing the first eight books, comprising the period prior to the Norman Conquest, edited by Sir Henry Ellis, sq 8va, 4s 6d [J1]   1846

1066 **Viccars** (Joanne) Decapla in Psalmos, sive Commentarius ex decem Linguis MSS et impressis Hebr, Arab, Syriac, Chald, Rabbin, Graec, Roman, Ital, Hispan.

1076 **Weekly Entertainer** (The); or Agreeable and Instructive Repository, containing a Collection of Select Pieces both in Prose and Verse; Curious Anecdotes, Instructive Tales and Ingenious Essays on different subjects, Vol 41–42, 2 vols in 1, 8vo, *old boards, calf back* (two pp torn), 12s 6d [G16]   *Sherborne*, 1803
With an index to Vol. 41. Short accounts of Ancient English Sports, Balloons, Cockfighting, Origin of War, Rebellion in Ireland, etc.

1077 — Ditto, Vols 43–44, 2 vols in 1, 8vo, old boards, calf back (no index), 10s [G16]   *Sherborne*, 1804
Late Rebellion in Ireland (continued), Origin of April Fool's-Day, Trial for Bigamy, Ceylon, St Domingo, etc.

And below the wrapper:

be another habitable World in the Moon, with a Discourse concerning the possibility of a Passage thither. Unto which is added a Discourse concerning a new Planet, tending to prove that 'tis probable our Earth is one of the Planet, 8vo, *fourth edition, old calf, binding stained and wormed*, 7s 8d   1684

1083 **Zoology**, – **Moufet** (Thomas). Insectorum sive minimorum animalium theatrum. Fol. **First Edition**. *Old calf, badly broken, title page missing, £1 10s*   1634

1084 — The Silkewormes, and their flies: lively described in verse, by T M a Countrie Farmer, 4to. **First Edition**, *rebound in calf. Pages stained, £1 5s*   1599

My dear Bishop Wilkins and my dear Dr Moufet, looking up at me from parallel columns. It is apparent that I cannot waste-paper them without a look; I have the greatest regard for them both, the insectophile French physician, and the mathematical, ingenious, speculative Bishop of Chester, who so happily pursued his mechanical, astronomical, and philosophical researches throughout wars and tumults, and got so prosperously, so discreetly, through the Civil War, Commonwealth, Protectorate, and Restoration, ending a Bishop and a member of the Royal Society; who, after the Restoration, 'stood up for the Church of England, but dislik'd Vehemence in little and unnecessary Things, and freely censur'd it as Fanaticism on both sides'; for, in truth, his mind was up among the moon and planets, or speculating on how men might best fly, or thinking out levers, screws, wheels, pulleys, and wedges. This book here will be, of course, *The Discovery of a New World in the Moon*.

The wrapper is slit and cast off. One may as well mark the *New World in the Moon*; no harm can come of marking it. And, now that the catalogue is opened, it would be foolish not to run an eye over the rest of it, just to see what is here. There may be another Bishop Wilkins.

There *is* another Bishop Wilkins – *Mathematicall Magick*, 1680 edition. How fortunate that I opened this catalogue, for I have been wanting a cheap *Mathematicall Magick* for months.

And here is a modern reprint of John Maplet's *Greene Forest*. As I know of no other edition since the sixteenth century, I may as well mark it, though I remember its introduction to be foolish and sentimental, and of the 'quaint old Maplet' type. Better is Burnet's *Sacred Theory of the Earth*, Third Edition, review'd by the Author, broken back and damaged boards, 1697. And William Shipway's *Campanalogia; or, Universal Instruction in the Art of Ringing, in Three Parts: to which is prefixed an Account of the Origin of Bells in Churches, with the Principal Peals in England*, cr. 8vo, orig. boards, nice copy, uncut, 1816. Not that I need it: quite definitely, I do not need it at all; still, I will put a tick against it, in case I wish to refer to its title again.

1104. Yonge (C.M.) *Der Erbe von Redcliffe, aus dem Englischen* ... Vol. I only, Author's Own Copy, 5s., Leipzig, 1856, Dear Heir of Redcliffe: I should like to see how your flashing eye and curling upper lip would go in German; but I will not; it would be desecration; *Der Erbe* shall have no tick.

Nor shall any of these modern first editions. Why does anyone prefer a first edition of a modern book to a later one? I am told that this is one of the diseases that one cannot hope to understand unless one suffers from it. It is, I presume, called protophilism, or even protomania. Sufferers from it keep, perhaps, the first white stone they see when out walking, or the newspapers for the first day of each month, or the top button off each of their coats, or the first stamp out of each stamp-book, or the programmes of the first nights of plays, or the firstlings of the infant year. Jehovah collected firstborns, alike of men, beasts, and plants, saying, 'They are mine', so the instinct has high and ancient origin.

There are a number of firstlings in this catalogue. They are pathetically cheap. Ezra Pound, D H Lawrence, *John Halifax, Gentleman*, Jerome K Jerome, *The Way of an Eagle*, and a company of others, many of them 'nice copies', and all about three shillings apiece. Does anyone buy them? I could, for my part, read lists of modern firsts for ever, and remain as full in purse as when I began; I never feel 'they are mine'. I could wish that catalogues contained nothing else, and were not, instead, alive with more perilous seductions.

How these lure one down the page! We are arrived at the P's; PEZRON (M) *The Antiquities of Nations; Englished by Mr Jones*, 8vo. calf, stained, 1706. PLAYS. Samuel Foote, calf gilt, cracked, label missing, 8s 6d; 1799. PLINY. *Naturall Historie of C Plinius Secundus. Trans.by Philemon Holland, very worn* ... POLWHELE (R) *The Influence of Local Attachment with respect to Home*, joint cracked, 4s 6d. *POPISH CRUELTY EXEMPLIFIED in the various Sufferings of Mr Serres & several other French Gentlemen, done into English by Claud D' Assas*, calf, a few leaves Stained, 5s 6d, 1723 ...

And so down to Zola and Zoology, the former of which seems to remain a bore, even in a catalogue, while the latter is so enticing that to read the names of its dryest manuals is a stimulant.

A stimulant: yes, the word is apt. To read these catalogues is like drinking wine in the middle of the morning; it elevates one into that state of felicitous intoxication in which one feels capable of anything. I must control myself, and not write to booksellers in haste: there must be a gap between the perusal of the catalogue and my postcard. Drinking, said Dr Johnson, should be practised with great prudence; one must have skill in inebriation. A man without such skill will undertake anything ... I will wait until the effects are worn off, and then write a postcard sober, temperate, moderate, brief, restrained ...

But, while I wait, those more intemperate than myself will have rushed in and bought *Mathematicall Magick*, the *New World in the Moon*, the *Theatre of Insects*, and the *Silkewormes*. It is obvious that I cannot wait. Probably I should telephone ...

I need a new bookshelf. I am short of money. I could have read all these books in the British Museum; some of them even from the London Library. In short, I am sober again. But I am glad that I was drunk.

Bulls

How agreeable to watch, from the other side of the high stile, this mighty creature, this fat bull of Bashan, snorting, champing, pawing the earth, lashing the tail, breathing defiance at heaven and at me, crooning in ignoble rage (for rage is always ignoble when both causeless and ill-directed). How mighty are his sinews, how stout and fierce his horns, how fiery his nostrils, how strong and huge his thews! Did he that made the lamb make him? He is a very king of cows. One sees him roaming the great prairies, lord of a herd, rounded up by cowboys with cracking whips.

> That lordly Bull of mine …
> How loudly to the hills he croons,
> That croon to him again!

And now here he stands, so near and yet so far, his heart hot with hate, unable to climb a stile.

But suppose that, using his horns as battering-rams, he should rush at it and break it down?

Candlemas

The parroco came before each Candlemas Day to bless the house. He would walk about it, sprinkling holy water, and he would bring each year a tall and lovely candle of entwined and multi-coloured wax, which he had blessed. We had, too, a number of little candles, made of long spirals of coloured wax twisted close and coiled up like a snake, to be uncoiled as they burned down. They were red and green and yellow and blue, and of great beauty. We took them out with us for our Candlemas picnic, which consisted of oranges, a few preserved fruits, dates and prunes, and fragments of rolls. This feast we took with us along the Savona or the Genoa road, or along the river, or up the hill path behind the house, that climbed, stony and steep, past the carob-tree to our rock houses. Arrived at these craggy piles and promontories, we sat down, lit our coloured candles, and stood them on stones. Rearing slim necks to heaven, they burned, frail and flickering golden buds, while we gnawed bread, sucked oranges, kept the exquisiteness of preserved fruits and French plums for the last *bonne bouche*, and, having finished all, but being still loth to cease, plucked myrtle berries and so prolonged the feast. Some of these were black and plump, almost sweet, others immature and sharp. At any stage, they were better than juniper berries, which dried the mouth.

Thus we kept Candlemas, looking over a wide blue bay through a pink shimmer of almond blossom, while the town below made festa, and a procession wound, harshly chanting, through the deep and narrow streets to Santa Caterina's pink church at the hill's foot. In the still and resinous air our candle-flames burned like little tulips, the flower elongating as the stem dwindled. Thrifty, we would not unwind all the coils and burn them out. The feast done, we extinguished the tapers and put them by for future use. The Candlemas festa thus kept with pious rites, the rock houses became castles to be besieged.

But we had an annual Candlemas difference of opinion with our father, for we thought Candlemas should be a holiday from lessons. Not so he; and he won. So Candlemas Day was wasted until the afternoon.

Canoeing

A great curve of smooth blue Mediterranean spreads between my frail bark and the distant line of shore. I slip down an azure orange, a swelling and limpid mountainside; I perceive about me what one has always heard, that the earth is indeed a ball. I can still just, when I turn my head and look, spy the bay, the shore, the town, the church towers, the house on the shore to the bay's east, nestling beneath and in front of a jagged line of piney, terraced hills and of the wild running steeps of higher Apennines behind these. But a few minutes, a few strokes of the paddle, and all but the hills will be sunk, vanished, drowned below the rim of the round world.

I turn again and look: the town, the shore, are gone; I am alone with a blue horizon ahead (beyond lies Corsica, but I shall not see that island), the mountain rim of the bay behind, a long jut of soft indigo grey (Savona) thrusting out into western sea and sky, the further and fainter blue point of Genoa lying twenty miles east, bounding the great bay, and beyond that Spezia, pale and shimmering as fairyland, for there, so one has been told, are marble mountains.

On the ocean's rim flies a far ship with spread sails, like a gull. I am alone; I navigate uncharted seas, where the known stars are laid asleep in Tethys' lap; where neither birds can instruct to any near shore, nor any birds in the main Ocean to be seen; where without the compass all things are out of compass, and nothing but miracle or chance can save or serve. I am of the great company of hazardous mariners who brave the deep; I am Captain Cook, Columbus, Cabot, Magellan, Raleigh, Drake; I am Jack, Ralph and Peterkin exploring round their Coral Island; I am an officer of the Royal Navy, sent out on a lone mission to spy out slavers, pirates, French or

Spanish men-of-war; or I seek treasure left absent-mindedly on a small island long since, and the secret chart, yellow with age, without which I can never arrive there, lies folded against my breast.

I am the first that ever burst into this silent sea. Perils beleaguer me on every side. There a sharp fin pierces the smooth surface like a sail; a white belly gleams as a giant shark turns on its back. He rushes on me through the deep, with open jaws: one lurch of his body beneath my canoe, and it and I would be hurled out of the water, and down again into that ravening mouth. Only one thing to do – the trick learned of the Coral Islanders: I wait until the monster is close, wait until he turns on his back, then, with a mighty thrust, insert the end of the paddle between his jaws. He threshes about in the water; the canoe is swirled round, as I cling fast to the paddle: but before long he chokes and sinks down into the deep, a corpse, fortunately spewing forth the paddle before doing so I am saved; but I believe that his widow and little ones, his infuriate and formidable bereaved (sharks being very family fish), are not far distant, and may at any moment apprehend the situation and give chase. It behoves me to be wary.

Also, that sail on the horizon is, beyond doubt, a pirate sail: if it should sight me, I am lost. And at any moment I might be surrounded by canoes fraught with savages. There are mermaids too, and mermen, leaping and diving, shooting up from the bottom of the monstrous world to spy and peer at the gallant young sailor in his frail bark. To entertain me, they strike their harps with a most melodious twang, and sing sea chanties. Here too are flying-fish, and there is that leviathan; he even spouts; every marvel of the perilous deep displays itself before the explorer's sophisticated and unastonished eyes.

Of a sudden the deep heaves and swells; the canoe lurches up and down. I am dismayed and astonished, I reel to and from like a drunken man. For a ship bears towards me; a real ship, a steamer in full tilt, rushing towards Genoa; in her wake the white foam flies, the furrow follows free; she disturbs the ocean with her passing, and like a cockle-shell my bark rocks. Peril assumes the sterner face of reality; pirates, mermaids and sharks vanish into blue sea and air; I toss alone in a canoe on the heaving main; she may overturn. Often enough she overturns nearer shore, when the waves run high or the crew are restless; that makes no matter, for we sit on her bottom and navigate her upside down. But to overturn alone, far out on the round sea's curve, out of sight, out of swimming distance, of land; perhaps to sink – that is another matter. As to sharks, they exist; one was thrown up on the beach near Cogoleto lately; a man bathing off Albissola was once killed ... Sharks are real, and the canoe is lurching up hills, valing down valleys, bobbing and leaping like a porpoise or a cork.

The ship passes on her way; the heaving sea's long roll lessens, little and little, until the blue level which is really a curve spreads again from east to west, from north to south.

But fear has looked in, chill phantom among golden dreams. I no more desire to paddle south into the boundless main, into the Ligurian sea towards Corsica, for ever sliding down the curving world, further with every stroke of the paddle from my home bay. I paddle shoreward quickly, as if a shoal of monsters of the deep gave chase; I climb the blue glass ball again, slipping higher and higher up its limpid side, until below the hills the coast road appears, and the little many-coloured town, curved around its bay, arises like a drowned city, a lost Atlantis from which an ocean drops, exposing it once more to view. Detail appears; churches, pink or yellow or striped black and white; the stone archways that lead from town to shore; palms, oranges, lemons, eucalyptus, luxuriantly topping garden walls and burgeoning on terraces ('from whence,' as Mr John Evelyn, coasting the Riviera, wrote, 'might perfectly be smelt the peculiar joys of Italy in the perfumes of orange, citron, and jassmine flowers, for divers leagues seaward'). And now I can perceive the fishing-boats and nets lying on the sands; and the square red house beyond the town, with the slope of beach running down from its garden to the sea's edge.

Land; safety; port for the sailor home from the sea; the end of an adventure. The angelus ringing across the bay; hens clucking; the lisping and hissing of tiny waves on sand; the late afternoon soaking hills and shore with golden heat. Gliding in to shore with the ripples, stepping out into warm, knee-deep water, dragging the canoe until she rests on dry beach. Voices that plain like gulls – 'It's not fair, taking her out alone and keeping her out all that time. We're going a voyage to the rocks ...'

Chasing fireflies

Each midsummer eve, after dark, we would go on a firefly walk. The way started through a little orto, where a vine trellis arched over a shadowed path, and orange- and lemon-trees bordered it, standing against white walls and filling the velvet night with sweetness, as the frogs in every little reservoir and ditch filled it with melody. Beyond the orto, the path climbed up between terraces, where the olive trees cast delicate black shadows on the moonlit stairway, and orange and lemon groves still perfumed the night. Among them, and all about the myrtle shrubs and juniper and little pines, capered and leaped the fireflies, flying between the cold moon and the earth. They pranced and danced, they twinked and blinked, they sparked, they larked, they burned like flying stars, like leaping gems, and after them we sped beneath a huge golden moon, scrambling up rocks, jumping down terraces, plunging scratched hands into juniper bushes, standing still against sticky pine-trunks to tempt the brilliant creatures near. Too rarely our cupped hands closed on a spark and held it, while it blinked at us shyly, on and off, like a lighthouse. Not to all was it given to catch a firefly; it was an event, a triumph; to hold one was to hold a magicking imp, that now burnt like a star, now darkly brooded, a sullen insect without joy.

'If you find any pretty insects, keep them in a box,' Dr Browne of Norwich wrote to his son in France. So also did we desire to do. But authority was against us; we were given to understand that in boxes our fireflies would pine, extinguish, and die. So we released the lucent sparks; they fled to join the host of dancing candles that bespangled the hills.

In the midsummer moonlight, with enormous golden stars empatining a violet sky, and these tiny bright ones skipping among black shadows about the lemon-sweet, frog-sung mountains, the world on St John's Eve was incredible yet familiar, like worlds known in dreams.

But they never would let us stay out in it all night.

Christmas morning

Christmas woke me early, in the small dark hours, as if someone had touched me on the shoulder and said, Wake up, wake up, it's Christmas. I woke up and it was dark, and would not be Christmas for hours. I crawled to the foot of the bed, to where it hung on the painted iron bedrail, the large woollen stocking that had yawned so emptily overnight, but now so stiffly, bulkily, swollenly bulged. It might not be opened until daylight, but I felt it outside, pinching and poking its various protuberances, from the square cornery one above the knee to the round one in the toe that might be an orange or a glass witch-ball. Shivers of ecstasy curdled my blood as I fingered and felt; my hair stared, my skin goosed, my pulses hammered in heart and head. It was Christmas Day. However often I whispered it, I could scarcely credit so strange, so preposterous, so heavenly a fact. Christmas Day had indeed arrived. But how could it really, actually, in point of fact, have come, and I in bed as usual, in the same red flannel pyjamas as on any other night? Yet Christmas Day must come; one had long expected it, and here it was. Perhaps it was a dream.

But of a sudden the still dark was shaken and shattered and a-clamour with bells. Not the gay sweet chiming of an English church peal, but harsh, clanging, iron, tremendous, a very roar and tumult of noise. The great Roman brick tower of Sant Ambrogio in the large piazza outside the windows, the striped black and white tower of San Domenico in the small piazza up the street, the more distant, but patronal, Santa Caterina along the sea road beyond the town, the church of the Collegio up the hill path, the chapel of the convent school, all with one accord awoke to Christmas morning and clanged their summons to Mass. They were insistent, commanding, almost menacing. English bells, sweetly and uncertainly tumbling as they chime, seem to sing, *Come along to church, good people if you please, come along to church on Christmas Day.* These bells cry, *Venite, venite, il Signore v'aspetta, levatevi pronto, pronto, e fatte il dovere.*

But to me they only shouted, *Christmas Day! Christmas Day!*

Soon the piazza and streets were alive with hurrying feet, and with such resonant cries as Italians emit even between bed and Mass.

I crawled back under the bed-clothes and curled up to wait for Christmas Day. When it should be held to have fully arrived, we should all assemble on one bed and open the stockings. To me, lying in the clanging dark, forbidden to go and wake others before it was light, the propitious and blest day seemed half the night away. How foolishly the others slept, oblivious of the jubilant occasion!

Full little thought they than
That the mighty *Pan*
Was kindly come to live with them below;
Perhaps their loves, or els their sheep,
Was all that did their silly thoughts so busie keep.

Whatever it was, and regardless of the bells, they slept like pigs in straw.

Church-going

1 Anglican

How dignified, how stately, how elegant, with ranks of tapers wavering gold against a dim background, while boys' voices lift the psalm *Audite hæc, omnes* high above the pealing organ to the high embowed roof, to linger and wander there among ten thousand cells. Through the windows richly dight, slant crimson, violet and deep blue rays of October evening sunshine; it touches the round heads and white surplices of little singing boys; it glints on the altar, dimming the tall, flickering flames, gleaming on the heads of thoughtful clergymen who listen to the quire's chant. *For he shall carry nothing away with him when he dieth: neither shall his pomp follow him. For while he lived he counted himself an happy man: and so long as thou doest well unto thyself, men will speak good of thee. He shall follow the generation of his fathers: and shall never see light. Man being in honour hath no understanding: but is compared unto the beasts that perish ...*

The soft and melancholy chant dies on a falling lilt. The clergy, quire and people sit down in deep oak seats, all but the lector, who rustles to the lectern, adjusts his pince-nez, and says gently, 'Here beginneth the first verse of the sixth chapter of the Book of Micah. Hear ye now what the Lord saith: Arise, contend thou before the mountains, and let the hills hear thy voice ...'

The musical Eton-and-Cambridge monotone, just not parsonically pitched, strolls on, relating the Lord's controversy in the mountains with his people. I turn the pages of my Prayer Book, read the charming rubrics, read the Preface, of 1662, so gentlemanlike, so suavely urbane. *It hath been the wisdom of the Church of England, ever since the first compiling of her Publick Liturgy, to keep the mean between the two extremes ...*

And then, Of Ceremonies, why some be abolished and some retained ... *And moreover, they be neither dark nor dumb ceremonies, but are so set forth, that every man may understand what they do mean, and to what use they do serve ... And in these our doings we condemn no other Nations, nor prescribe anything but to our own people only: For we think it convenient that every Country should use such Ceremonies as they shall think best to the setting forth of God's honour and glory, and to the reducing of the people to a most perfect and godly living ...*

Meanwhile, the Eton-and-Cambridge voice is gently putting searching inquiries, becoming reluctantly menacing. *Are there yet*, it asks, *the treasures of wickedness in the house of the wicked, and the scant measure that is abominable? Shall I count them pure with the wicked balances, and with the bag of deceitful weights? ... Therefore also will I make thee sick in smiting thee, in making thee desolate because of thy sins. Thou shalt eat, but not be satisfied ... Thou shalt sow, but thou shalt not reap; thou shalt tread the olives, but thou shalt not anoint thee with oil, and sweet wine, but shalt not drink wine ... That I should make thee a desolation, and the inhabitants thereof a hissing ...*

It has grown too violent, this mountain controversy. *Here endeth the first Lesson*, and so to the Magnificat. One feels that it was time.

These violent Hebrews: they break in strangely, with hot Eastern declamation and gesture, into our tranquil Anglican service, our so ordered and so decent Common Prayer. A desolation and a hissing: those are not threats that our kindly clergy like to quote, even against those of their flock who have abominable scant measures and wicked balances. Milton railed against 'the oppressions of a simonious, decimating clergy', but, though they cannot help (since they must live) being decimating, they are no longer so simonious, and are a kindly race.

As to these services, which they long since so gracefully adapted, so fitly, beautifully, and ceremoniously translated and assembled, they are, as Sir John Suckling pointed out three centuries ago, fit for the attendance of even the fastidious Cato, who was disgusted by those of his own age and country. 'Then,' complained the shocked Sir John, 'the Ceremonies of *Liber Pater* and Ceres, how obscene! and those Days which were set apart for the Honour of the Gods, celebrated with such shews as *Cato* himself was ashamed to be present at. On the contrary, our Services are such, as not only *Cato*, but God himself may be there.'

Or so, at least, we hope. No doubt the Romans hoped too that Liber Pater and Ceres were present with them at worship, and that their lectisternia were enjoyed by the reclining and feasting deities. Be that as it may, and whatever the gods may think of it (and one must endeavour not to fall into arrogance in this matter of divine attendance at our worship), for my part I greatly admire and enjoy the Anglican order.

Though of course there is, from time to time, a sermon … But it seems that this cannot, in any Church, be helped.

2 Roman Catholic

Is it because they happen to be the earliest in my memory, that the churches in a small Italian fishing-town still seem to me to be the very concentrated essence of what we mean when we say 'church'? Or is it one's mediæval heritage, from the centuries that stretch back through time, through ages of mystery, of what our civilised Anglican Prayer Book calls dark and dumb ceremonies, of harsh chanting in dog-Latin, of swinging censers that smother the musty air and human odours with drifting clouds of aromatic sweetness? From whatever cause, when I think 'church', I am back in a great, cool, dim, pillared interior, shut from a sunlit piazza by heavy leather door-curtains, clouded with drifts of that agreeable smoke which, while it ascends to heaven, fortunately perfumes all about it, and which we have always so rightly and wisely offered to our gods. Indeed, those churches which do not do so probably make a tactical error which no audible or visual beauty can redeem. Amid these fragrant clouds we advance, past the stoup of holy water which, thinks my mother, needs more frequent changing than it gets, past the notice on the wall which pleads, alas how vainly, 'Per l'onore di Dio, e per l'igiene, si pregono di non sputare', into the dim interior, full of scraping wooden chairs, standing men, and old women kneeling as they mutter over their beads. One of these interrupts her orisons to put out a gnarled brown hand to my mother, murmuring mechanically *Ave Maria, piena di grazia*, un soldino, signora, per l'amore di Dio. *Santa Maria, Madre di Dio, prega per noi peccatori, adesso e nell' ora della nostra morte*'. We kneel on chairs, our chins resting on their backs, and listen to that nasally monotonous chanting which seems to be the most widely and long approved tone in which to address one's God. Anyhow to me it seemed, and seems, to have a certain fitness and rightness which less primitive accents lack. It seems the voice of the whole world at worship; a black savage, an Australian aborigine, would surely feel at home with it, as with the fragrant smoking spices and gums, and the gaudily clad wax or plaster figures who stand in niches round the church, some cruelly transfixed with swords or arrows, some enwreathed with paper flowers, but all with patient eyes upturned to heaven, and all with rows of candles guttering about them. A charming hagiary; I could not then, I cannot now, hear them scorned without resentment. Often one or another of them would be carried by a procession, on his or her festa, out of church and all round the town, and then they appeared to greater advantage than ever. Those adorable processions: I can scarcely admit to the status of a real religion a church which does not have them. A church, like a monarchy, must be potentially and occasionally processional, must show itself for worship and jubilee in the open, must at times be peregrinating and agoral, and wind, rich in pomps and gauds, through marketplace, street and town. Pomps and gauds, chanting and sweet smells, ceremonious adoration and mystery – if these be not the fit circumstance and habit of worship, the worshipping world has for many thousands of years erred.

At all events, when I say 'church', I am incense-shrouded, wax-saint-surrounded, kneeling on a high-backed chair on an uneven stone floor much *sputato*, among neighbours who tell their beads and have eaten garlic, and the primitive, eternal chanting drones on before a gaudy high altar, where peasant priests, richly vestured, genuflect, advance and retreat in stately measure. From the sun-baked piazza without come the voices of men, who, in order not to waste their time are waiting for the essential moment to enter, and meanwhile are lounging outside the drogheria, or hitting a ball through hoops. And, through and beyond this male clatter, there whispers, sighs, and lisps the delicately turning edge of the summer sea, running lightly up the sand, drawing back, rustling like a cicada's wings.

But see, one of the priests is in the pulpit; he is preaching about *l'inferno*, its horrid and enduring torments. Well, that too is primitive; one hears in it the rolling thunders of the Christian Church down the ages, the awful fulminations, denunciations, miniations, of saints, popes, councils, prophets, and poets, who have never scrupled or boggled at fiery damnation, or at the horrid picture of Satan and his tailed minions at work. Like pomp and ceremony, hell also has always been part of religion. Anglicans have forgotten it, have gently, rationally, and fastidiously damped down and blurred over that fiery scarlet patch in the cosmography of religion, turning it into a vague cloud which they call the unsearchable and incalculable mercy of God. You will hear no hell-fire sermons from them; and when one of the creeds formulated by Councils in less delicate ages speaks with zest of without doubt perishing everlastingly, there is an Anglican agitation to have it omitted from services.

But there is no such squeamish humanitarian nonsense about Roman Catholics, and to this day you may hear from Irish and Latin pulpits the genuine old-world sizzling of frying souls, which gives such zest to being still above ground, such determination to make a good end.

The sermon is over; the preacher descends; for a moment one hears again that rustling, sighing whisper from the seashore, before the chant of Christian believers sings above it: *Credo in unum Deum, Patrem omnipotentem, factorem coeli et terræ visibilium omnium et invisibilium* ...

3 Quaker

The seventeenth century meeting-house stands in a dell in a beech-wood; it is built of mellowed, lichened brick, with latticed windows and whitewashed walls and a gallery running round. Outside the clear glass windows green beech waves, and dark green holly sharply twinkles. The door stands open, and through it sounds the singing of birds, the call of a cuckoo, and the running, leaping, and chattering of squirrels. The Friends sit in stillness, waiting on the Spirit, who will presently move some one to rise and speak. For my part, I shall not be ill-pleased should the Spirit move no one this morning, except the squirrels and the birds and that distant hen who would appear to have produced an egg.

But the Spirit is, as usual, stirring. The caretaker of the meeting-house gets up; he speaks about the happy birds, mentioning also the more agreeable among the insects, such as butterflies, who, says he, are also happy. He refers to the cuckoo, who so soon must fly, with that intelligence bestowed on him so amply by the Lord and so profitably used throughout his English trip, to warmer lands. Happiness: taking no care: this appears, perhaps naturally, to be the caretaker's ambition; his view is that happiness is widely experienced among the feathered and the winged, and that the reason for this is that they take no care, but trust in the Lord. He even appears to be interpreting the piping parliament among the trees as a meeting for worship. Can he be right? And do birds believe, and tell one another, that human beings are happy? And do we perhaps exaggerate the carefreedom of our plumy fellow-creatures, who obviously have their troubles, some of them more troublesome than those which normally visit man? Squirrels, for example ... Still, it gives pleasure to the caretaker, a generous and unenvious man, to think that birds are happy and take no care.

He resumes his seat, having left with us these interesting speculations, over which we meditate for a while, until the Spirit moves again. This time we have a little talk about the importance of making our wills, lest we be cut off intestate, thus causing trouble and confusion among our survivors. The speaker must, I think, be a solicitor. He speaks well: we make mental notes: *Will: make it at once.* He is a more practical man than the caretaker. The caretaker cannot, surely, much approve his advice, for his own was to live like the birds, looking not ahead, but trusting that the Lord would arrange. The birds do not make wills. That is one of the points about Meeting – you get all points of view. The next is that of a kind-faced woman, who has been sitting surrounded by children, whom she has been successfully pacifying and rendering innocuous for half an hour and has now led out and set free. Returning to her place, she speaks about children. One wonders again, why do children, so attractive in life, become in discourse so uninteresting? Perhaps people say the wrong things about them ... They become, on the tongue of this kind woman, strangely like the birds of the caretaker – happy, care-free, trusting, very religious. In another moment, one feels, she will be saying that those cheerful voices receding through the woods are raised in the praise of God. But no; she does not go so far as that. She is either a mother or a school teacher, and knows children better than the caretaker knows birds. Still, the children of her discourse are shadowy little cherubs, simple-minded, almost winged; by no means the stormy, questioning, imagination-haunted, earthy, ingenious, gluttonous, perverse, exciting and excited little creatures that we know. Those who thus think of children set one wondering at what point the Great Change occurs which turns them into the so different adults that they become. The children they envisage would have been approved by Pelagius, for they have no original sin; they seem ready to die straight away, like a child by Charles Dickens, and wing their way to heaven.

After this, a speaker is moved to talk of living by conscience. He is practical, idealistic, spiritual, ethical, stirring. He makes it seem, while he speaks, almost possible that humanity should live in such a strange, unusual manner. He brings righteousness into the foreground ... Is this where most churches fail? If they would give religion a rest and concentrate on ethics, who knows what odd results might follow? When the Friends, as they frequently do, speak thus, one understands the disturbing and unwelcome emotions of dislike that they used, in less tolerant centuries, to arouse, so that all the warring churches, Anglican, Roman Catholic,

Presbyterian, Anabaptist, and the rest, were united when they saw, heard of, or thought of Quakers, by a common and fervent desire to whip them, to set them in stocks, to brand them with hot irons, to fling them into dark cells for life. How many a meeting, in this very house, has been held in the shadow of these fearful intentions! They seem still to lurk in the beech woods, to be creeping along the deep lane, the constable with his posse of men coming to catch the Quakers red-handed at their damned conventicling blasphemy, to arrest them and hale them off in chains to the magistrate, there to be sentenced to the whip, the stocks and the gaol. The rustling squirrels, the leaping rabbits in the undergrowth, they are the steps of spies, the tramping of armed men, coming to seize us in the name of the King, the Church, and the Laws.

Still, if we live according to the implanted light of conscience ... that is what the quiet-voiced speaker is saying ... Even in gaol and the stocks we could, we suppose, do that – if indeed we could ever do such an extraordinary thing ... But, anyhow, what an idea! Much better sing psalms, hymns, anthems, swing censers, praise the Lord. It is time that I slipped out of this meeting, into the woods.

4 Unitarian

It is certainly ugly, with its varnished deal seats and green paint. What a pity that those who believe on the Trinity have secured all the best churches! Still, there must be some temporal penalty for those who cannot thus think; not so long since, they used to burn them, and we know, from the Athanasian creed, in what predicament they will find themselves after death. Green painted hot water pipes and varnished yellow deal are, doubtless, their punishment in this life for gainsaying that long line of theologians who have, with no uncertain voice, instructed them through nineteen centuries on the tremendous Triune Mystery. Similar, indeed, is the punishment, in this country, of most of the dissenters from Ecclesia Anglicana, who seldom seem to be able to build good churches for themselves. (Westminster Cathedral is a notable exception.) Anyhow, this Unitarian chapel is a sad ugly place, and must pain its thoughtful, earnest, attentive worshippers and the pale, eager young minister who is preaching about the barren fig-tree. He is concerned about this fig-tree; the story of how it was cursed and sterilised for evermore troubles him; he cannot see that it was a right way to behave to an innocent tree; perhaps he has a fig-tree of his own at home. That Trinitarians should have related and believed such a story down the ages throws for him an unfortunate light on the mentality of Trinitarians down the ages.

But this was, for him, not necessary. He, and we, already knew that Trinitarians down the ages have been like that. We have found our way to a purer, a more tolerant, a more rational faith. The pleasure of enjoying this, of being so rational, so tolerant, and so pure, lifts our hearts and swells our voices as we sing our monotheistic hymns, from which all references to the Holy Ghost have been expunged. In our kindly voices rings that superiority which comes from never having burnt Trinitarians, Tritheists, or atheists, nor whipped Quakers; no, nor wished to. The first Arians may, it is true, have committed a few excesses against Athanasians, but that was merely because they got out of hand in a hot climate. Since then, all has been with us sweet reasonableness, kindness and light. Photinians, Macedonians, Sabellians, Socinians, Ebionites, Dr Martineau, all our so rational predecessors hover around us, a small but intelligent cloud of witnesses, delighted that their heresy, so long abhorred, persecuted, despised, is at length permitted to express itself freely in a green and yellow chapel smelling of hot water pipes.

There was a period in my youthful career when I used to think, if one could believe at all, it would be in the Unitarian God. It seemed so easy, so comparatively reasonable ... But, alas, the Unitarians undid themselves with me by their architectural and ritual inadequacies. Nevertheless, there is a very pure and intelligent atmosphere about their worship, and they are very right to see through the fig-tree story.

Cinema

Never a dull moment! From a bright foyer we descend in darkness down a slope lit by the flashing torches of fantastic elves, dancing ahead like wills-o'-the-wisp until they settle, pointing us to seats in the middle of an eagerly gazing row of persons, past whom we push, to subside into plush chairs and eagerly gaze too. There is a news reel on; ships are being launched, royalties visit cities and are met by mayors; football is played in the rain before vast crowds, tennis flashes by like lightning, and is repeated in slow motion, horses race and leap, troops walk past with that jerky gait peculiar to animated photography, Signor Mussolini, roaring wide-mouthed like a bull of Bashan, harangues the people of Italy; all is bustle and energy. One feels that ours is a busy world, wherein humanity scuttles about like ants, each bearing his little burden. It is not very like the world which we see about us; still, it is a little too like to be really good entertainment, and we are pleased when it abruptly ceases and the screen burgeons into the colour and fantastic nonsense of a Silly Symphony. This is what films ought to show us; they should assist in the process of apotheosising the absurd. This is, indeed, what they do throughout, even when they mimic life, and this is why I prefer them to flesh and blood miming on the stage, which is often so near life as to be tedious. This flat, two-dimensioned moving photography can never be at all like life; it is the most charming, the most bizarre, the most ludicrous convention. See how flowers ring bells and sing, how trees turn into forest demons, how hares play lawn tennis, leaping over the net to take the ball they have served! And, the Silly Symphony over, the Big Picture begun, how the photographs representing persons run about, emitting, in metallic, hollow voices and the lilt of the Californian tongue, the most improbable remarks. Those young British officers, trained at Sandhurst and pursuing their vocation on the Indian frontier, have obviously profited by a career of film-seeing, for they speak the purest Hollywood. So does the little Scottish minister, which is stranger, for he lived before films were. So too does that Roman Empress, and the proud patrician Marcus, but that is all right; if you translate the speech of foreigners, it may as well be into American as into English. The remarkable thing is that any of these photographs should speak at all. It is like women preaching, or dogs walking on their hind legs.

See how that daring young man leaps from his aeroplane in mid air, sailing in his parachute so as to alight on the roof of the house in Chinatown where the gangsters have the girl tied up. Can you beat it? Certainly not on the stage; probably not in life. That is the beauty of the films; they expand life, puff it up into a ludicrous, incredible, magnificent balloon, set it soaring through space, cut loose from the ropes which tie it down to fact. Then, how well they photograph raging seas, glaciers, deserts, mountain peaks, penguins, grasshoppers, and wild beasts prowling through jungles. Battles, too; here are Waterloo and Plassey in little, terrible with battling elephants and upping Guards. Had Shakespeare known of such a way of miming Agincourt, how he would have rejoiced! And in what unearthly, horrid and transparent shapes would his ghosts have revisited the glimpses of the moon, in place of the too solid flesh in which perforce dead Cæsar and King Hamlet stalked the boards and stalk them to this day. As to his fairies, in what elegant and dainty minuteness would Titania and Oberon meet and square, while their elves for fear crept into acorn cups and hid them there.

There is, to be sure, one thing that moving photography should never attempt; that is to portray serious and actual human drama, the relations between human creatures. Indeed, why should they? These we can see all about us in life, and very weary of them we get. To be confronted with them again on the screen would be too much. Indeed, I seldom am so, since I choose my films with care. They should be funny, fantastic, exotic, anything they like, but not human. Love they should shun like the devil; it is not for photographs, however animated, nor for mechanically recorded voices, however Hollywood, to mime this universal terrestrial passion. Let the films know their business, and lead us tip-toe through strange fantastic realms, soaring above the clouds, burrowing in the bowels of the earth, galloping across cactus deserts among mesquite and Gila monsters, pursued by Sheriffs, zig-zagging in wild and rickety cars pursued by the constabulary, grappling with monsters of the deep or of the trackless jungle, wooing humour with the suave voice and face of Mr Laughton, the impassivity of Mr Harold Lloyd, the rolling eyes of Mr Cantor, the improbable legs and the impossible figure of Mr Jack Hulbert and Miss Courtneidge, the imbecility of Mr Ralph Lynn, the glitter of Miss Lynn Fontanne. Once they stoop, or attempt to stoop, to realism, they are undone, these wonderful contrivances. Heavens above, is there not enough realism in life, that our moving photographs should ape it?

Come away: a gripping drama has begun. Out, past still eagerly gazing rows; out into the night. If we must have gripping dramas, we prefer to see them in the world at large, where, alas, they are all too common. Our comic fairyland falls shattered about us at so crude a trumpet blast. We will adjourn to the Café Royal and consume sandwiches and bock.

Clothes

How handsome it looks, my new dress, fresh from its maker's hands! How elegant, how eximious, how smug, how quaintly fashioned, how all that there is of the most modish! How like other people I shall appear when I wear it! With what respect they will regard me, saying one to another, Look, do you see that woman? She knows how to dress; she is in the mode; indeed, she looks very well. I think I have at other times seen her in dresses three, four, even five years old, altered, as she believes, but not really, to the discerning eye, altered to matter, for they still remain of their epoch, and insufferable to people of good taste and modern outlook, now that there is such gaudy going and such new fashions every day. But to-day she really has a new dress, and a good dress; to-day she really is a Well-Dressed Woman. I like its cut, do not you? And the colour is precisely right.

This is how (I trust) they will speak to one another of me and of my new dress, when they see it. How I shall prank it among them, 'loitering up and down, peacocking and courting of myself'. I shall feel as Adam felt when Eve made him (after, of course, their great and disastrous removal) a medley coat of feathers.

> Eve, walking forth about the Forrests, gathers
> *Speights, Parrots, Peacocks, Estrich* scatt'red feathers
> And then with wax the smaller plumes she sears,
> And sows the greater with long white Horse hairs...
> And therof makes a medly coat so rare
> That it resembles *Nature's Mantle* faire,
> When in the Sun, in Pomp all glistering,
> She seems with smiles to woo the gawdy Spring ...

> Then on he puts his painted garments new,
> And Peacocke-like himselfe doth often view,
> Looks on his shadow, and in proud amaze
> Admires the hand that had the Art to cause
> So many severall parts to meet in one,
> To fashion thus the quainte Mandilion.

I shall feel as the serpent must feel in her new skin, as the barrel-organ monkey in his new red jacket and cocked hat. Strange, what a singular effect the body's outer wrapping has on the mind, how it elevates or depresses the termless spirit of man, exalting it to preen its feathers among the plumy angels, abasing it to creep the earth with meanest worm.

Foolish questions have been asked about this matter by philosophers and moralists since human beings began to put foolish questions at all. Dr Watts, for example, inquired.

> Why should our garments, made to hide
> Our parents' shame, provoke our pride?
> The art of dress did ne'er begin
> Till Eve our mother learn'd to sin.
>
> When first she put her covering on,
> Her robe of innocence was gone;
> And yet her children vainly boast
> In the sad marks of glory lost.
>
> How proud we are! how fond to shew
> Our clothes, and call them rich and new!
> When the poor sheep and silkworm wore
> That very clothing long before.
>
> The tulip and the butterfly
> Appear in gayer coats than I;
> Let me be drest fine as I will,
> Flies, worms, and flowers, exceed me still.

And, 'Have you', Crœsus, adorned in his pomp and glory, inquired of Solon, 'ever seen a goodlier spectacle?' 'Yes,' said Solon, 'cocks, pheasants and peacocks.'

Why, in short, the philosophers and moralists desire to know, should we that are earth, ashes and dust prick up ourselves so peacockly? They are but seldom answered, since the earth, ashes, and dust is too busy pricking up itself to pause to reply to foolish questions. But the answer is apparent. Why does the crow emplume itself with gaudy borrowed quills? We that are so mean and plain cannot face our fellows without extraneous decking. Were we modelled out of crystal, jade and turquoise, of the lucent milky moonstone and the orient pearl, were we even fashioned like the small birds and pretty beasts, no adornment should we need or use. But nature has not thus privileged man. 'If' (as Montaigne remarks) 'we impartially enter into judgment with our selves, we shall find, that if there be any creature or beast less favoured in that than we, there are others (and that in greater numbers) to whom nature hath been more favourable than to us. *A multibus animalibus decore vincimur.* We are excelled in comeliness by many living creatures: yea, of terrestrial creatures, that live with us. For, concerning those of the sea, omitting their figure, which no proportion can contain, so much doth it differ, both in colour, in neatness, in smoothness, and in disposition, we must give place unto them: which in all qualities we must likewise do to the airy ones ... Such as most resemble man are the vilest and filthiest of all the rout: As for outward appearance, is the Monkey or Ape:

Simia quam similis, turpissima bestia, nobis!

as for inward and vital parts, it is the Hog. Truly; when I consider man all naked (yea, be it in that sex, which seemeth to have and challenge the greatest share of eye-pleasing beauty) and view his defects and manifold imperfections, I find we have had much more reason to hide and cover our nakedness than any creature else. We may be excused for borrowing those which nature had there-in favoured more than us, with their beauties to adorn us, and under their spoils of wool, of hair, of feathers and of silk, to shroud us.'

To shroud us … melancholy word. Remember,

Soon the grave must be your home,
And your only suit, a shroud.

Consider,

Green as the bay tree, ever green,
With its new foliage on,
The gay, the thoughtless, have I seen,
I pass'd – and they were gone.

Read, ye that run, the awful truth,
With which I charge my page;
A worm is in the bud of youth,
And at the root of age.

Having thus remembered and thus considered, I will go out to my party in my new dress, gratulating myself that at least, if no handsomer than the ape, the hog, and the hippopotamus, and rather less so than the ant-eater, I have more wit than they, for I can, if not make, anyhow cause to be made, and assume, a flattering garment.

Cows

Seen close, you would appear to have every fault but one. You are preposterously bovine, you are cornigerous ruminants, you chew cud and let it dribble from your moving jaws, you stand in ruminating herds by stiles and gates, trampling the grass until it seems like the field of campaign at Passchendaal, fit for ducks, not men, to tread; you listlessly emit that pale, unencouraging fluid which we offer to sick persons and young children and cats, and from which strong men and women turn in disgust; you pursue, with lowered horns, my dog. You are not beautiful; you are far from clean; and the melancholy cries with which you rend the evening skies are like steamers that take the ocean, or sirens in a fog.

What then is this strange pleasure that I take in your uncouth forms? What makes, as I approach you across the next field, my heart leap up as who beholds a rainbow in the sky? Analysing it, I discern it to be a pleasure of sex. I have said that you have one virtue; my pleasure lies in perceiving it, in recognising that, whatever you may have looked like from far, you are but cows after all.

But, alas, some of you are mothers: little ones run at your sides; and it is of mothers alone among she-creatures that there is any truth in the otherwise preposterously mendacious statement that the female of the species is far deadlier than the male.

Departure of visitors

An exquisite peace obtains: a drowsy, golden peace, flowing honey-sweet over my dwelling, soaking it, dripping like music from the walls, strowing the floors like trodden herbs. A peace for gods; a divine emptiness.

> Fair Quiet, have I found thee here,
> And Innocence, thy Sister dear!
> Mistaken long, I sought you then
> In busy Companies of Men …
> Society is all but rude
> To this delicious Solitude.

The easy chair spreads wide arms of welcome; the sofa stretches, guest-free; the books gleam, brown and golden, buff and blue and maroon, from their shelves; they may strew the floor, the chairs, the couch, once more, lying ready to the hand. 'I am afraid the room is rather littered …' The echo of the foolish words lingers on the air, is brushed away, dies forgotten, the air closes behind it. A heavy volume is heaved from its shelf on to the sofa. Silence drops like falling blossoms over the recovered kingdom from which pretenders have taken their leave.

What to do with all this luscious peace? It is a gift, a miracle, a golden jewel, a fragment of some gracious heavenly order, dropped to earth like some incredible strayed star. One's life to oneself again. Dear visitors, what largesse have you given, not only in departing, but in coming, that we might learn to prize your absence, wallow the more exquisitely in the leisure of your not-being.

To-night we shall sleep deep. We need no more hope that you 'have everything you want'; we know that you have, for you are safely home, and can get it from your kitchen if you haven't. We send you blessing and God speed, and sink into our idle peace as into floods of down.

But you have unfortunately left behind you, besides peace, a fountain pen, a toothbrush, and a bottle of eye lotion with eye bath.

Disbelieving

I believe very little: you will have to tell me something excessively credible before I believe it. Do not come to me with your ghosts, crystals, palmistries, cards, creeds, miracles, scandals, rumours, gossips, and all the little news of the town; your new moons, black cats, and piebald horses I cannot away with. Is there an earthquake in the Barbadoes, an eruption in Sicily, a war in Abyssinia, a revolution in Spain? It is possible: but I do not see them, and have heard such tales before.

I have a friend who cannot believe in atrocities. All her life she has heard of atrocities, and earnestly sought them when travelling abroad (for it is abroad that atrocities occur), but she has been always disappointed, for she has never found one. She was once told (says she) of a Balkan atrocity exhibit, a woman of whom it was reported that Bulgarian atrocities seen and suffered by her had made her mad, so that she was kept in an asylum, a permanent exhibit. My friend, thinking, 'Here is a veritable atrocity at last', made a pilgrimage to the asylum and asked to see the woman, but found her quite sane, only annoyed by her confinement. So now, when she hears of atrocities, she always thinks of this woman whom atrocity had not driven mad, and rejects them sadly. If you offer her past atrocities, such as those of Nero and Caligula, she rejects them too, feeling that Suetonius was unreliable. I do not go so far as this friend of mine; the atrociousness of human nature has not, I must conclude, been always without its vent. For my part, I decimate atrocities, which leaves me more than enough.

But, concerning most relations made to me, I consider, as Sir Thomas Browne held of the digesting of iron by the ostrich or sparrow-camel, that the negative seems most reasonably entertained. Or anyhow, whether reasonably or not, the most easily. Tell me what you will of earth or heaven; with Montaigne, I feel that we should say most times, there is no such matter.

It makes me feel agreeably aloof, not to be imposed on by all those strident, thundering events of which I hear, not to be taken in by rumour-mongers, magicians, gossips, quacks, moon's men, old wives' tales, 'puerile hallucinations and anile delirations', and, in fact, the whole rumour of the humming world.

But sometimes a thought troubles me, and I ask myself, should I, many centuries back, have been numbered with those who denied the Antipodes, and the rotundity of earth? Of these Bishop Wilkins complained, mentioning among them Chrysostom, Austin, Lactantius, the Venerable Bede, Lucretius, Procopius, and the voluminous Abulensis, together with many Fathers, and with Herodotus, who wrote, 'I cannot choose but laugh, to see so many men venture to describe the earth's compass, relating those things that are without all sense, as that the sea flows about the world, and that the Earth itself is round as an orb'. While Lactantius exclaims, 'What are they that think there are Antipodes, such as walk with their feet against ours? Is there anyone so foolish as to believe that there are men whose heels are higher than their heads, that the plants and trees grow downward? What shall we think, that men do cling like worms, or hang by their claws as cats?' with much other pleasantry such as the ignorant and unbelieving use.

I must beware, then, of too wide and too deep an incredulity, and remember that there are many things yet hid from us, and that really everything is extremely peculiar.

Doves in the chimney

The voice of the turtle is heard in my chimney. It is the prettiest soft low crooning in the world, like the soughing of wind in a pine wood, or the low moan of seas imprisoned between rocks. When first it stole into my room, as I sat reading there, I thought I had been Steele's pastoral lady friend, Mrs Cornelia Lizard, 'whose Head was so far turned … that she kept a Pair of Turtles cooing in her Chamber, and had a tame Lamb running after her up and down the House. I used all gentle Methods to bring her to her self …'

But no: I am more fortunate than Mrs Cornelia, not only in that I am lambless, but in that my pair of turtles (if pair they are, and not a mourning widow turtling it after her mate), have not taken up their abode in my chamber, but have, it seems, made them a nest in my chimney. Yes, my chimney is a pigeon-cote, a culver-house, and in it the kind turtles sit and coo, and answer to each other's moan. I like to think that there are two turtles, that my turtle is not bereaved. And yet, to have so chaste, so musically mourning a widow at hand, would also be charming. 'As a turtle-dove did I chatter, and as a dove did I mourn'; melancholy ordinance of nature, that this otherwise oblivious bird, so unlike the elephant that she forgets practically everything immediately, including her young the moment they have been taken from the nest, and the peckings and unkindnesses of her husband, and all wrongs done her, should remember and mourn her mate until death. Even the widowed cock mourns, winging him to some withered bough, or to some friendly chimney. But who shall say why he mourns? Basil wrote that the eating of vipers, a favourite food of theirs, gives turtles a pain, until they can find some marjoram to heal it. They will find no marjoram in my chimney, and so they mourn there still.

But no; I believe that turtles have been misjudged, and that the gentle crooning which has been taken to indicate grief actually, even in the solitary bird, expresses a tranquil pleasure in existence. I like to think this, for I have (who can other?) a great esteem for this amiable bird, so kind, so passing chaste, a messenger of peace, an ensample of simpleness, clean, plenteous in children, follower of meekness, friend of company, forgetter of wrongs, nicely curious, carrier of letters, emblem of the Holy Ghost. I will not suppose that my chimney-cole culver is a sad widow; she is the most constant pretty cooing turtle, and doubtless a happy, if forgetful, mother, sitting upon an ill-made nest up there and crooning to her unborn turtlets. Her voice is so sweet, so comforting, so heavenly, it would convert the sceptical *jeune homme de Dijon* himself, did he hear it as I hear it now, rising, murmuring, falling, dying, melting away to start again – croo, croo, croo.

My chimney is a hospitable lodging for turtles. But what is their fate when they make their home in chimneys which are funnels for fire and smoke? Do they flit away, forgetting their turtlets, at the first alarm, to build in the next chimney? Or do they remain, faithful birds, amid the choking fumes, until, like the Phœnix and the Turtle, they enclosed in cinders lie?

Driving a car

To propel a car through space, to devour the flying miles, to triumph over roads, flinging them behind us like discarded snakes, to rush, like Mulciber, from morn to noon, from noon to dewy eve, a summer's day, up hill and down, by singing fir woods and blue heath, annihilating counties and minifying kingdoms – here is a joy that Phaethon, that bad driver, never knew. Phaethon, like us, was inebriated with rushing (as he fondly thought) through the air, intoxicated with pride in the great and hazardous car he drove, deeming himself a speed king. He believed himself to be doing his circuit of 583 million miles in twenty-four hours, or about 25,000,000 mph. That is to say, had the sun really been rushing daily round the earth, that is about what it would have had to do, though it is possible that neither Helios nor Phaethon actually knew the mileage. Anyhow, as we now know, Phaethon was not really moving at all; it was the earth that was moving, and Phaethon crashed simply from nerves.

The same might be said of all the charioteers before the present age; they thought they were speeding, but were really scarcely moving at all. Nero fancied himself as a driver: but what was Nero doing? At the most, about fifteen. Bishop Wilkins much praised for their swiftness certain chariots with wheels and sails that were, said he, driven over land by the wind at a rate far exceeding the swiftness of ships on the sea. Such chariots sailed, he said, over the great smooth plains of China; and there was one at Sceveling in Holland, which that eminent inquisitive man Peireskius travelled to see, and would ever after talk of it, saying that its passengers did not feel the motion of the wind that drove them, since they travelled with equal speed themselves; men running before it seemed to go backwards, and things which seemed at a great distance were presently overtaken and left behind. Grotius was very copious and elegant in the celebration of this invention, and Bishop Wilkins inquires, what could be more delightful than to make use of the wind, which costs nothing and eats nothing, instead of horses. In two hours' space, says he, the Sceveling chariot would travel two and forty miles. So, after all this fuss and travelling to see it and excitement on the part of English bishops and the eminent inquisitive Peireskius and the copious elegant Grotius, the thing could only do twenty-one.

The fact that our grandchildren, nay, our children, will soon be talking with similar contempt of us, rather adds to than detracts from our pleasure. The cars that we send hurtling over the earth by the touch of a foot on a knob are but at the beginning of their race with time and space; we drive slow and clumsy embryos. But they are swift enough to delight us, as with open throttle and hands lightly on the wheel we scud the roads, watching the needle mount, slipping past those other cars which unfortunately also scud the roads and impede our view.

All is bliss; we hum songs of triumph, as all charioteers have, even when they have been ignobly dragged by the brute creation, instead of by a drop of volatile spirit and a rotating engine, which is so obviously far better. Our song is chorused by the little chirping squeak of the door handles, the faint rattling of the windows, the less faint humming of the engine, the running of the wind. The scenery is doubled in charm by being seen at this rate; it flashes by with the vividness of a string of jewels, glimpsed, admired, and gone. How tired we should get of it were we afoot, trudging along with pack on back! One should not give scenery the chance to fatigue one. Seen thus, it will glow in the memory like a fairy land scarce trodden, awaiting one's return.

The serpent in this Eden, the canker in this lovely bloom of speed, is (need one say it?) the other vehicles in our road. And particularly in the middle of our road which is where cars, horse-carts, and cyclists love to travel. But, did all travellers keep, as they should, to their near side, driving would be too like heaven for sinful man below. As it is, when our time comes to go, when we fall in turn to the juggernaut, we may hope to be translated to some paradise traversed by great fair roads, to each soul a road to herself, along which her car shall dash at some supramundane speed, hugging (for souls shall be made perfect) the near border of thymey Elysian grass.

Easter in the woods

A delicate shimmer of greenery flickers, a light veil, over purple and brown, and starry blackthorn and wild cherry-blossom riot, in flights gay and white like angels, over wood and hill. How the copses, all enverdured with larch and birch and thorn and springing beech, climb the steep brown hillsides, running down to cowslipped dells and banks, while at their feet the marshy bottoms, gold-starred with kingcups, lie! Standing here, my feet deep in brown beech leaves, on Wheatham Hill's steep shoulder, I can see the high hangers, copses, valleys, commons and farms, for miles around. There is the long, circling hanger called, in its different curves, Oakshott, Juniper, and Happersnapper, lying coiled, like a great snake of beech and oak, holly and birch, and alder, on the heights above Higher, Middle, and Lower Oakshott Farms; there are Moore's Copse, Cheesecombe, Cherrycombe, lying about Oakshott Stream to the north; in the nearer distance burgeon those three pretty copses, Roundabout, Hazel Holt, and Naps. While to the south writhes the wild steep Shoulder-of-Mutton hill, all embeeched, and edged along the ridge, where the wood breaks into bare grass gnarled with wind-bent thorn-trees, by the little deep-set path of Cockshut Lane. Eastward, in the near distance between the meadowy valley below these woods where I stand, and the running line of high moor and forest beyond, Wheatham Farm lies on its hill; its hens have laid Easter eggs, and their cries of content float to me through the soft still air, striking their own exotic galline note in the merry Easter concert that pours from the greenwood. What plumy people sing in every grove! What whistling, what warbling, what chiff-chaffing, what lyric sopranos and coloraturas, what shrill sweet zest! Could humanity but sing like this …

But I am waiting and listening for a voice overdue, a voice as yet unheard by me this year. Will it come to-day? The stage is all adorned and set for the entry of this monotonous but enchanting performer; here is blossom and greenwood, soft sunshine and blue shadow, light breezes and sweet air. But he tarries still. The stone-chat ejaculates, sharp and bright, from the furzy common; the wheat-ear nods and flirts and says 'Chak chak'; the ring ouzel sings, wild and gay, doing, no doubt, his marriage dance in the patch of moory grass above the wood; the blackbird, already settled, a householder, mellowly and with prosperous dignity whistles a tune; the nightingale jugs, the robin warbles, the wren twees, the goldcrest (or is it a long-tailed tit?) zee-zee-zees, the Dartford Warbler pittews, the hedge-sparrow chirrups, the linnet trills. At least, this is what I believe that I am hearing; the sum of it, anyhow, is the finest merry melodious canticling you can hear in a Hampshire Easter week.

And then, from the brown heart of Roundabout Copse, breaks the cry, high, far and clear, of the roving bully who is just arrived for his season of pleasure and increase in these islands after his African tour, and carelessly brags the freedom of himself and spouse from household cares, from the tedium of domesticity, from the trouble of parenthood, from the monotony of monogamy. The cuckoo is a witty bird; hearing his gay, cool, exultant cry, one hails once more the eternal pleasurist. They know how to live, these cuckoos; they rove, they love (briefly, but effectively), they breed, they procreate, they lay their cheerful Easter eggs singly in homes of eggs like-hued, relying, with a confidence justified by the inherited experience of ages, on the frail intellects and kind hearts of non-cuculan birds; and so away to the greenwood they hie, having thus made ample and painless provision for a progeny they have no notion of ever seeing again. Family business thus brilliantly disposed of, all spring and summer stretches before them for song, riot and debauchery; and why in the world their name has been taken by humanity as a synonym for stupidity, passes conjecture. Wise birds; intelligent, unscrupulous, cynical, sensible birds, wearing their freedom like a panache, crying it like a witty brag. They seem to me to have a Renaissance touch, to be like Medici princes and popes, luxurious, clever, conscienceless, getting the better of simpler, better men and women, looting the world of its pleasures and giving in return only their own insolent enjoyment. Life is no trouble to cuckoos; *solvitur cantando*. Their gay boast rings over the April woods like bells, ringing in the merry summer. First far, then drifting nearer, from Roundabout to Hazel Holt, from Hazel Holt to Naps Copse, and so across the dell to Wheatham Hanger, and then all over and about the wood, *cuckoo, cuckoo, cuckoo*, so negligently, boldly gay, as if they mocked, as well they may, the chorus of little warblers, the future foster-parents of their, as yet, unlaid young. *Cuckoo, cuckoo, cuckoo*! the cry drifts westward, away and away towards Juniper Hanger. Follow it through the greening woods, up sweet dim twisting paths, among the alders and the great bare budding beeches and the young slim beeches springing green, rustling through the deep brown pile of the beech carpet (laid last autumn, and overlaid with the green running pattern of agrimony), by ancient chalk pits and blown bare ridges hawthorn-grown, across the deep grass track of Old Litten Lane, and so to the wild sweep of Juniper Hanger, where it climbs above the Oakshotts against a shifting, sea-hued sky. The cuckoo is away now, following his private ploys somewhere in Happersnapper woods, but he has left the spring behind him, its gay bravery and the eternal dip-and-come-up of the dauntless, resurrecting Easter world, with its cowslips, its singing, and its dancing sun.

But now the blue distances deepen to violet; rain sweeps across the Oakshotts from Selborne way, and patters light drops on the beeches. Decoyed from wood to wood by the teasing gay bird, as if by the tee-heeing pixies, I am left now deserted by it as by these, with the Easter rain pattering on holt and hanger, and the chorus of good little birds warbling and weeting on every bough.

Eating and drinking

Here is a wonderful and delightful thing, that we should have furnished ourselves with orifices, with traps that open and shut, through which to push and pour alien objects that give us such pleasurable, such delicious sensations, and at the same time sustain us. A simple pleasure; a pleasure accessible, in normal circumstances and in varying degrees, to all, and that several times each day. An expensive pleasure, if calculated in the long run and over a lifetime; but count the cost of each mouthful as it comes, and it is (naturally) cheaper. You can, for instance, get a delicious plate of spaghetti and cheese, or fried mushrooms and onions, for very little; or practically anything else, except caviare, smoked salmon, the eggs of plovers, ostriches and humming-birds, and fauna and flora completely out of their appropriate seasons, which you will, of course, desire, but to indulge such desires is Gluttony, or Gule, against which the human race has always been warned. It was, of course, through Gule that our first parents fell. As the confessor of Gower's Amans told him, this vice of gluttony was in Paradise, most deplorably mistimed.

We shall never know what that fruit was, which so solicited the longing Eve, which smelt so savoury, which tasted so delightful as greedily she ingorged it without restraint. The only fruit that has ever seemed to me to be worthy of the magnificently inebriating effects wrought by its consumption on both our parents is the mango. When I have eaten mangoes, I have felt like Eve.

> Satiate at length,
> And hightn'd as with Wine, jocond and boon,
> Thus to her self she pleasingly began.
> O sovran, vertuous, precious of all trees
> In Paradise, of operation blest ...

And like both of them together:

> As with new Wine intoxicated both
> They swim in mirth, and fansie that they feel
> Divinitie within them breeding wings
> Wherewith to scorn the Earth: but that false Fruit
> Farr other operation first displaid ...

And so on. But, waking up the morning after mangoes, one does not feel such ill effects as was produced by that fallacious fruit when its exhilarating vapour bland had worn off. One feels, unless one has very grossly exceeded, satiate, happy and benign, turning sweet memories over on one's palate, desiring, for the present, no more of anything. The part of the soul (see *Timæus*) which desires meats and drinks lies torpid and replete by its manger, somewhere between midriff and navel, for there the gods housed these desires, that wild animal chained up with man, which must be nourished if man is to exist, but must not be allowed to disturb the council chamber, the seat of reason. For the authors of our race, said Timæus, were aware that we should be intemperate in eating and drinking, and take a good deal more than was necessary or proper, by reason of gluttony. Prescient and kindly authors of our race! What a happy companion they allotted to mankind in this wild animal, whom I should rather call a domestic and pampered pet. How sweet it is to please it, to indulge it with delicious nourishment, with superfluous tit-bits and pretty little tiny kickshaws, with jellies, salads, dainty fowls and fishes, fruits and wines and pasties, fattened and entruffled livers of geese, sturgeon's eggs from Russia, salmon from the burn, omelettes and soufflés from the kitchen. I have always thought the Glutton in *Piers Plowman* a coarse and unresourceful fellow, who, on his way to church and shrift, was beguiled merely by a breweress's offer of ale.

(How ungenteel Mr H W Fowler must have thought her, and all of her century and many later centuries, for using this word, which he so condemns, for beer!) The Glutton asked, had she also any hot spices? and she assured him that she had pepper, paeony seeds, garlic, and fennel. And with this simple and unpleasing fare, Glutton was content, and made merry globbing it until night. Glutton was no gourmet, no Lucullus. Nothing recked he of rare and dainty dishes; nothing out of the ordinary entered his imagination. Not for him the spitted lark, the artful sauce, the delicate salad of chopped herbs and frogs.

There are some sad facts concerning eating and drinking. One is that the best foods are unwholesome: an arrangement doubtless made by the authors of our being in order to circumvent gluttony. It is a melancholy discovery made early by infants, and repeatedly by adults. We all have to make it in turn, only excepting the ostrich. No doubt the Lady in *Comus* made it later, after she had more fully grown up, though as an adolescent we find her remarking, sententiously and erroneously, to the enticing sorcerer,

And that which is not good is not delicious
To a well-govern'd and wise appetite.

Even the untutored savage knows better than this. They of Dominica, said Antonio de Herrera, that elegant Castilian chronicler of Spanish travels in the West Indies, they of Dominica did eat, one day, a Friar, but he proved unwholesome, and all who partook were ill, and some died, and therefore they of Dominica have left eating human flesh. This was a triumph for Friars, which must be envied by many of the animal world.

Another sad comestive truth is that the best foods are the products of infinite and wearying trouble. The trouble need not be taken by the consumer, but someone, ever since the Fall, has had to take it. Even raw fruit was, to the exiles from Eden, hard to come by.

> Their meanest simple cheer *(says Sylvester)*
> Our wretched parents bought full hard and deer.
> To get a Plum, sometimes poor Adam rushes
> With thousand wounds among a thousand bushes.
> If they desire a Medler for their food,
> They must goe seek it through a fearfull wood;
> Or a brown Mulbery, then the ragged Bramble
> With thousand scratches doth their skin bescramble.

And, did they desire anything better, they could not have it at all. Slowly they learned, we suppose, about planting seeds and reaping ears and grinding flour and welding it into that heavy substance we call bread. Rather more quickly, perhaps, about the merits of dead animals as food, but how long it took them to appreciate the niceties of cooking these, we know not. That is to say, no doubt the students of the history of man know, but I do not.

Once learnt, this business of cooking was to prove an ever growing burden. It scarcely bears thinking about, the time and labour that man and womankind has devoted to the preparation of dishes that are to melt and vanish in a moment like smoke or a dream, like a shadow, and as a post that hastes by, and the air closes behind them, and afterwards no sign where they went is to be found.

Still, one must keep one's head, and remember that some people voluntarily undertake these immense and ephemeral labours, for pay or for a noble love of art even at its most perishable, or from not being able to think of a way of avoiding it. All honour to these slaves of baked-meats: let them by all means apply themselves to their labours; so long as those who do not desire to prepare food are not compelled to do so. If you are of these, and can get no one to cook for you in your home, you should eat mainly such objects as are sold in a form ready for the mouth, such as cheese, bread, butter, fruit, sweets, dough-nuts, macaroons, meringues, and everything that comes (if you have a tin-opener) out of tins. If you can endure to apply a very little and rudimentary trouble to the matter yourself, eggs are soon made ready, even by the foolish; bacon also. I would not advise you to attempt real meat; this should only be cooked by others; so should potatoes.

But, whatever has been prepared for you, and whoever has had the ill chance to prepare it, there comes the exquisite moment when you push or pour it into the mouth, What bliss, to feel it rotating about the palate, being chewed (if this is required) by the teeth, slipping, in chewed state, down the throat, down the gullet, down the body to the manger, there to find its temporary home. Or, if it is liquid, to feel it gurgling and gushing, like the flood of life, quite down the throat with silver sound, running sweet ichor through the veins. Red wine, golden wine, pink wine, ginger beer (with gin or without), the juice of grape-fruit or orange, tea, coffee, chocolate, iced soda from the fountain, even egg nogg – how merrily and like to brooks they run!

My subject runs away with me: I could, had I but time and space, discourse on it for ever. I could mention the great, the magnificent gourmets of history; I could dwell on the pleasures experienced by Lucullus, Heliogobalus, those Roman Emperors, those English monarchs, those Aldermen, who, having dined brilliantly and come to sad satiety, had their slaves tickle them with feathers behind the ears until this caused them to retire in haste from the table, to which they presently returned emptied and ready to work through the menu again. These are the world's great gluttons; to them eating and drinking was a high art.

But they are beaten by one Nicholas Wood, a yeoman of Kent, who, in the reign of James I, 'did eat with ease a whole sheep of 16 shillings price, and that raw, at one meal; another time he eat 13 dozen of pigeons. At Sir William Sedley's he eat as much as would have sufficed 30 men; at the Lord Wotton's in Kent, he eat at one meal 84 rabbits, which number would have sufficed 168 men, allowing to each half a rabbit. He suddenly devoured 18 yards of black pudding, London measure, and having once eat 60 lbs weight of cherries, he said, they were but wastemeat. He made an end of a whole hog at once, and after it swallowed three pecks of damsons; this was after breakfast, for he said he had eat one pottle of milk, one pottle of pottage, with bread, butter, and cheese, before. He eat in my presence, saith Taylor, the water poet, six penny wheaten loaves, three sixpenny veal pies, one pound of sweet butter, one good dish of thornback, and a sliver of a peck household loaf, an inch thick, and all this within the space of an hour: the house yielded no more, so he went away unsatisfied ... He spent all his estate to provide for his belly; and though a landed man, and a true labourer, he died very poor in 1630'.

And this is the third snag about good eating and drinking.

Nevertheless, expensive, troublesome, and unwholesome though it be, it is a pleasure by no means to be forgone.

Elephants in Bloomsbury

Can it be true, or do I dream? Driving at dead of the night (if the night is ever dead) through Tavistock Square, can it be that I discern in the street before me a herd of elephants? Large, grey, tranquil, accompanied by a man with a little stick, I think that I see them pad along the Bloomsbury streets, swinging their heads, their trunks, this way and that, enjoying the air of the cool summer night. Slowly I drive past them; they do not seem concerned. I leave them behind; I see them mirrored in my glass, padding, wagging, pompous, serene, wreathing their lithe proboscis to make me mirth, as if they trod their native jungle tracks.

Native? Were elephants, after all, not native to these islands once? Did they not roam our tangled weald and jungled swamps, trumpeting blithely one to another as cows in pastures trumpet now? Have they, perhaps, never quite vanished, and do they still pad out on a summer night to take the air, tramping round our pleasant squares, breaking off boughs from the trees in the gardens and munching them, one little eye ever open for their bitter foe the dragon? Does the she-elephant go seeking in vain for the mandragora tree, that her husband may eat thereof and turn to her and give her the little elephants which she, never (it is said) he, intermittently craves? And when these little creatures are due, does she pad Thamesward, along the Embankment, seeking steps down into the river, that she may bear them in water, safely out of reach of the dragon? And do the herd go thither always to drink? for they drink not wine, we are told, except in war-time, when they like to get drunk, but will suck up whole rivers of water, and it must be muddy, for they will not drink if they see their own shadow therein.

I recall other things I have heard about elephants: how they hate mice, love sweet flowers, which they will go gathering in baskets, and will not eat the food in their stables until they have decked the mangers with these fragrant nosegays and herbs. I recall how chaste they are, how never there is adultery among them; how they love and defend their young; how, though like to living mountains in quantity, no little dog becomes more serviceable and tractable; how the African elephant has such an inferiority complex that if he do but see an Indian one he trembles and hurries past, by all means to get out of his sight.

I think of their patriotism, how they love their own countries so well that they will not go abroad unless their rulers swear a solemn oath that they shall return; and, even after this, and however well entertained they be with meats and pleasures abroad, they will always weep. The elephants I have just passed were not, I think, weeping; they must, therefore, be native to this land.

I remember how, when they have eaten a chameleon by mistake with their leaves, they will die unless immediately they take a wild olive; how they are so loving to their fellows that they will not eat alone, but invite each other to their feasts, like reasonable civil men; how the troglodytes take them by leaping on to their backs from trees and shooting them with arrows dipped in serpent's gall; how at the new moon they come together in great companies and bathe in rivers and lout one to another, and teach their children to do likewise; how if they meet a man lost in the wilderness, they will draw themselves out of the way, not to affright him, and then will pass before him and show him his road; how they will face and overthrow troops in battle, but will flee from the least sound of a swine; how, like the unicorn, they love young maidens, and when these sing will come and listen until they fall asleep.

Other of their amiable habits come to my mind: how they are excellent linguists, and understand human tongues; how they remember their duties, delight in love, glory, goodness, honesty, prudence, and equity; how religiously they reverence the sun, moon, planets, and stars; how they can learn the most ingenious tricks, such as climbing up ropes and sliding down head first, and flinging darts into the air.

Yea (if the Grecians do not mis-recite)
With's crooked trumpet he doth sometimes write.

Great dancers they are too, though sometimes in a somewhat rude and disorderly manner; and marvellous bashful, and die easily of shame; it does not do to make game of elephants; they never, as is well known, forget. I recall also how great conquerors have always used them – Hannibal in the Alps; Alexander; Bacchus, who charioted over India behind a pair of them; Pompey, who returned, similarly encharioted, to Rome after the conquest of Africa, but his elephants failed to pass two abreast through the gates.

All these feats and characters of elephants I recall, and more beside, as I drive home through the bland, lit streets of London. Elephants become, as I brood on them, so wonderful, so all that I admire, looming heaven-high, far more than brute and little less than god, that by the time I reach the British Museum I am sure that I never saw elephants straying free in Tavistock Square. They were ghosts, dreams, no more flesh and blood than the two lions who guard the Museum's back door. I think of them as the historian of Ophirian travels thought of elephants in Peru. No Elephant said he, could come into Peru but by miracle, the cold and high hills every way encompassing being impassable to that creature. Yea, said he, I aver further than an Elephant could not live in Peru, but by miracle. For the hills are cold in extremity and the valleys without water, whereas the Elephant delights in places very hot and very moist. But I deserve blame, he concludes, to fight with Elephants in America, which is less than a shadow, and to lay siege to Castles in the Air.

Less than a shadow. Perhaps my nocturnal elephants in Bloomsbury were, after all, no more than that. Nevertheless, I swear they moved, mighty and gentle and elephant-grey, swinging heavy heads and wreathing lithe trunks, across Tavistock Square an hour before the midsummer dawn.

And really, if the London traffic problem is going now to be complicated by elephants, heaven alone knows where it will all end. We shall be having dinosaurs next.

Fastest on earth

When I return to my parked car, I often find on it, attached to the wind-screen or window or lying on the seat, a square of paper bearing the printed boast, 'Fastest on Earth'. I should like to keep it there, a visible testimony to my car's prowess, as I roll through the streets, that other cars, yes, and even omnibuses, may yield to me and my Morris pride of place in the Hyde Park Corner scuffle, at the Marble Arch roundabout, and dashing up Baker Street. 'There goes,' they would say, 'the Atalanta among cars; see how it swifts along, passing all others; it travels post, it shoots through space like a star, or would, were it not held up by other traffic and by policemen; it is the car of Mercury himself, make way, make way!' The dogs would bark, the children scream, up fly the windows all, and every soul cry out, 'Well done!' as loud as he could bawl. 'She carries weight, she rides a race! 'Tis for a thousand pound!' And still, as fast as I drew near, 'twas wonderful to view how in a trice the turnpike-men their gates wide open threw. Gongs would sound, police shout, all would be uproar and pursuit.

The very thought of going thus tagged and bragged, intoxicates, weights my foot on the accelerator, speeds my swift course around St James's Square.

But see, he who tagged me hastens up; he appears to desire remuneration. He is also informing me that I have left my car in his park for over two hours. 'Fastest on Earth' indeed, when I cannot even hurry out of the square quickly enough not to be overtaken by one of its covetous and curmudgeonly guardians. So much for his label; I scatter it to the winds.

Finishing a book

It is done, it is over. This litter of papers that has got in my way, taking my time and my space and my energy, intruding on my leisure, for so many months, this horrid mess of nonsense which I call a book – do it up in brown paper, send it away to its publisher, let me see it no more. Let me not look ahead. For the moment, I have rid me of its foolish presence, and that is enough.

Leisure spreads before my dazzled eyes, a halcyon sea, too soon to be cumbered with the flotsam and jetsam of purposes long neglected, which will, I know it, drift quickly into view again once I am embarked upon that treacherous, enticing ocean. Leisure now is but a brief business, and past return are the days when it seemed to stretch, blue and unencumbered, between one occupation and the next. There are always arrears, always things undone, doubtless never to be done, putting up teasing, reproachful heads, so that, although I slug, I slug among the wretched souls whom care doth seek to kill. But now, just emerged as I am from the tangled and laborious thicket which has so long embosked me, I will contemplate a sweet and unencumbered slugging, a leisure and a liberty as of lotus eaters or gods. As for books, never more will I write one; nay, I have done, you get no more of me. Is there none other way by which I may sustain a life, own a roof-tree, a bed, a board, a car, a few clothes? Must I depend on these accursed labours, these toils that never cease?

Forget them. This last bundle of them has taken to itself wings like a dove; it will flee away and leave me at rest.

But, alas, it is a homing pigeon; it will return to me, typed words turned into print, bristling with even more errors, even more solecisms and follies, than when it left my hands. I shall struggle laboriously to amend it, send it away once more, and it will again return to make a fool of me in the end.

Fire engines

How they dash by, car after car, brave in scarlet, imperious with clanging bells, fraught with an army of courageous brass-helmed men! What calm and placid-seeming beings! And yet they must be seething, beneath that tranquil exterior, beneath those bright helmets, with more than all the excitement of those who go to look at fires, for they are pyromachs, they will wage a fearful war with ravening flames, they will run up ladders and rescue human beings, furniture, and cats from incineration, they will turn on a hose and deluge rooms and buildings with cooling, quenching streams, watched from all sides by a gratified populace and a busily recording Press.

All this, at least, is what I suppose that they mean to do when they arrive at the destination towards which they are so rapidly and impetuously proceeding, admitting no obstacle, ignoring traffic signals, ringing an imperious peal which sends cars, omnibuses, pedestrians, cyclists, yes, even horse-vans, those stately, marching monarchs of the street, scuttling out of their way.

So, one imagines, did the chariots of Roman Consuls dash imperiously, clatteringly, through Roman streets, scattering Roman citizens as the white herds on the mountains and in the chestnut-shadowed gorges scatter before wolves. Did the Roman citizens, thus scattered, gaze on the speeding chariots with applause and exultation in their hearts, with that joyful yet lachrymose emotion which is caused by the sight of rapidly speeding brass-helmed men with coiled lengths of hose, jangling bells as they hurry flame-ward in flame-hued cars? No; our emotion must be more pleasurable, for it is fiery in origin; paradoxically, it is pyrolatry which causes us to delight in these pyroletrous engines and men.

Not only pyroletrous but panolethrous, for their scarlet cars of Juggernaut mow down all that cannot expeditiously enough fly from their path, and one of them has grazed my car's newly painted wing. I make no protest; they would not heed me were I to do so. They are out on a practice run and no casualties shall give them pause.

Flattery

How rare, how sweet they fall, these honeyed words, these golden bells that stroke the listening air! O Flattery, thou coaxing, heav'nly maid, thou com'st too seldom to seduce and soothe. How amiable are thy feet as thou drawest nigh, how bright and insincere thy smile!

Sometimes the post brings thee. Perhaps an American professor has written me a kind word; he is learned as well as good-natured; he seems to know what is good in literature. Perhaps it is, instead, a kindly unknown, living in the English provinces. What a clever, well-educated man! What a sympathetic, intelligent woman! How different from some others! Here is someone who admires my poetry; another who thinks my essays well expressed; even my novels well conceived, with passable plots. Their words are sweet as honey in the mouth. An author there are few to praise should save and keep these copious and elegant celebrations of her merit: keep them, and show them one day to those contemners, those heapers of gratuitous obloquy, who write tasteless and tactless books pointing out how deficient in literary merit and personal worth practically all authors are. Here, Mr Blank (I shall say), is the real truth about me, which you, who have apparently omitted to read the majority of my works before pronouncing on them and on me, have so blindly overlooked. What about this, pray, I shall boast to the reviewers of my next book, when they find it insubstantial and facetious, or pedantic and dull, or sadly trivial and unconvincing. I would like you to know (I shall say) what this learned professor thinks of me, and this excellent gentleman from (or perhaps still in) Yorkshire, and all these ardent young students who desire to write a thesis on me in German, Italian, French and Scandinavian universities. (This is not a form of flattery that pleases me, as these young innocents all request lengthy and informing answers, and, though from me they receive no answer, they remain, on account of their projected theses and their tender years, a little on my conscience. It is obvious that they write to all authors. Has any so far answered them, poor nit-wits?)

Flattery. That great call, to which every sentient being down the ages has responded. Gods, men, women, children, beasts, and birds; how readily these have fallen into the snares spread for their feet, the while they spruce themselves and smirk and smug, tripping it along life's highway, toes barely touching the earth, as if they were indeed puffed up with these agreeable gases until they have acquired the levity of balloons. For a very little, they would leave the earth, and soar away into the skyey sphere, still smiling and smirking like cherubs among the buxom clouds. 'Vix humum tetigit pede,' wrote Milton of his proud and dreaming youth; scarcely did he touch the earth with his feet; and so these happy ones who live with flattery. The sweet inebriant only comes my way on occasion, and stays not long enough to obliviate that negligence which is man's normal earthly portion. I would that it were otherwise. I would wish to go companioned and beleaguered by flatterers telling their sugared lies, like those Italian gentlemen whom one meets in trains. 'Come è bellina, simpatica, graziosa!' Charming voices murmur in one's memory, like honey-bees among clover. How comely and how elegant you appear, how fitly garbed, how altogether worthy of esteem. Nor man nor woman did I ever see, at all parts equal to the parts in thee ...

'Think'st thou,' asked Silvia disagreeably of Protheus trying to please her, 'think'st thou I am so shallow, so conceitless, to be seduced by thy flattery?' 'Nay, Sir,' says Dr Johnson, 'flattery pleases very generally. In the first place, the flatterer may think what he says to be true: but in the second place, whether he thinks so or not, he certainly thinks those whom he flatters of consequence enough to be flattered.' In the third place, he has a kindly desire to please them, and they are churlish indeed if they be not pleased by his amiable intentions, his delightful cozenage. Look on the pleasant fellow's picture, sketched three centuries since by the observant but hard-to-please Dr John Earle.

'He will commend to you first what he knows you like, and has always some absurd story or other of your enemy ... He will ask your counsel sometimes as a man of deep judgment ... and whatsoever you say, is persuaded ... A piece of wit bursts him with an over-flowing laughter, and he remembers it for you to all companies, and laughs again in the telling. He is one never chides you but for your virtues, as, you are too good, *too honest, too religious...* It is a happiness not to discover him, for as long as you are happy, you shall not.'

Certainly I shall not. By all means flatter me; be kind and courteous; hop in my walks and gambol in my eyes; feed me with apricocks and dewberries; nod to me and do me courtesies, fool me to the top of my bent, for I enjoy it.

Though, alas, it makes the unflattering world at large seem more hard, chilly, and malicious than ever.

Flower shop in the night

How it glows, golden lit, empty of people, mysterious and dumb, behind curved glass that is as space bending unseen, that melts into the still, thin air, guarding what seems to the deceived eye unguarded and free to the touch. Still and bright and strange, like a deserted fairyland, like Eden after its erred denizens had been outed, like a palace garden whence queens have fled, gleams that ordered and enchanted space, blossoming like a greenhouse in the dead of the night. Golden baskets are piled high with pink roses; crimson roses riot in curious jars; hydrangeas make massed rainbows beneath many-coloured lights; tall lilies form a frieze behind, like liveried, guarding angels. Among the flowers are piled exotic fruits, pears and pines and medlars, little round fruitlets from China; clusters of purple grapes, asparagus in close formation, pressed together like sardines reared on end.

It is all very lovely, this gleaming vision of the night, so still, remote, and bright, entranced behind its unseen glass, as it were a water garden deep planted in green seas, lit by the phosphorent illumination of a thousand fish. And look, it has glass tanks of fish, coral, and sea horses, softly shining in each corner, sending faint light over the flower garden from below, while brighter lights illustrate it from the high walls.

It is a scene so exquisite and so strange that it might be a mirage, to melt away before the wondering gaze. We will leave it, while it is still clear and brilliant; turn away and walk down the cold, empty, and echoing street, looking not back lest that bright garden be darkened and fled like a dream before dawn.

Flying

I am in the cockpit of the Klemm two-seater of my friend. I am helmeted, goggled, strapped in. There was recently a man not strapped in, says my cheerful friend, as he takes his place behind me, who got left in the air two thousand feet up when the plane dropped in a pocket. The man followed, quickly but inaccurately; he reached the earth first. So it is better to be strapped in.

We taxy (odd word for it) over green pastures and turn into the wind. The starting light shines in the tower, the throttle is opened full, the engine roars. Faster and faster we go, bounce once or twice, and suddenly are off the meadow, in the air, rising up, climbing th'aerial height with eager haste, winging it like the mounting lark, scaling the steep ascent of heaven like the saints, eager to be above the clouds. What height now, I shout through my telephone to the pilot behind. About a thousand, he calls back. To be above the clouds we must climb two thousand more.

Still we fly sunward, like Icarus the rash. We are in the clouds now, pushing through them, flying blind. I, in my intrepidity, am unmoved by this; the pilot does not share my nonchalance, as he believes the heavens to be cluttered with hidden aeroplanes practising from the school. The clouds are cool and wet; when we emerge from them the wind-screens are seen to be soaked and dripping, as if we had been in a storm of rain.

We are above them now, winging through a heaven of sunshine, with cushiony billows floating below, a feather bed for the gods, a range of snowy mountains, a forest of giant white trees, a pride of fairy castles, a gibbering of gliding, shrouding ghosts, a field of ice. Through rifts and chasms we catch glimpses of a distant earth, laid out green and hedged, like a chequer-board.

How high now?

About four thousand.

We speed along through radiant space. Enormous bliss, as Milton would say.

How fast? I call.

About a hundred miles.

It does not feel that, with only thin air for resistance. A car travelling at forty seems faster. Until you put a hand outside the wind-screen; then the whole weight and force of the heavens rushes storming against you.

We are nosing downward now; we shall soon be below the clouds again; we fly earthward, as the Archangel Raphael flew from heaven.

> Down thither prone in flight
> He speeds, and through the vast ethereal sky
> Sails between worlds and worlds, with steady wing
> Now on the polar winds, then with quick fan
> Winnows the buxom air; till, within soar
> Of towering eagles, to all the fowls he seems
> A Phœnix, gazed by all as that sole Bird ...

What does Raphael, what do all the archangels, angels, seraphim, cherubim, principalities, dominions, and powers, what do all the gazing fowls, think of our Klemm two-seater, so bravely soaring the heavens with golden wings outspread? One supposes them used to it by now; it is not a phœnix, not a strayed archangel, but just one among a flight of those great noisy birds that now disturb heaven's peace.

But to us it is a dream come true; never a man, woman, or child down all the ages but has dreamed of thus soaring and winging it through space, has conceived and desired what Bishop Wilkins called such volant automata. Though, as he said, the common desire has always been for wings fastened immediately to the body. That was Dædalus his manner; indeed, says the Bishop, it has been frequently attempted, not without some success. There was the English monk, Elmerus, about the Confessor's time, who did by such wings fly from a tower about a furlong; and so another from St Mark's steeple in Venice; and Busbequius speaks of a Turk in Constantinople who attempted something this way. Mr Burton doth believe that some new-fangled wit ('tis his cynical phrase) will some time or other find out this art. Though the truth is, most of these artists did unfortunately miscarry by falling down, and breaking their arms or legs, yet this may be imputed to their want of experience, and too much fear, which must needs possess men in such dangerous and strange attempts. Those things that seem very difficult and fearful at the first may grow very facile after frequent trial and exercise. And therefore he that would effect anything in this kind must be brought up to the constant practice of it from his youth, trying first only to use his wings in running on the ground, as an ostrich or tame geese will do, touching the earth with his toes; and so by degrees learn to rise higher, till he shall attain unto skill and confidence …

And so much for flying like a bird, with wings attached to the body. But the mathematical Bishop preferred a flying chariot, which seemed to him altogether as probable and much more useful. It would be serviceable, said he, both for making discoveries in the Lunary World, and for the conveyance of a man to any remote place of this earth; as suppose to the Indies or Antipodes. How right he was!

Pull the stick towards you, calls the pilot (for there is a second stick in my cockpit, which I am now and then allowed to manipulate).

I pull, very gently; up goes our nose, seeking heaven.

Now push it from you.

We point earthward; it is like riding a bucking horse, his head and his heels up by turns. Then sideways; we bank, and all the chequered face of earth tilts up, now left, now right.

Now, says the pilot, we shall side-slip.

We move crabwise, leftward, more steeply than before, towards earth. So this is a side-slip, of which one has always heard. It is definitely agreeable.

We are now only about three hundred feet up, nearing the aerodrome, facing into wind. We nose down, drift slowly over a hedge. Green pastures rush up at us; the earthly sense of speed returns; we land at forty. The wheels touch ground; the stick is pulled back, bringing the tail to earth, dragging us to a standstill after a seventy-five yards' run. We taxy back to the hangar.

Climbing out, I look up and see dark birds with spread wings zooming between earth and heaven. Was I too there? Did I so soar, sail between worlds and worlds, winnow the buxom air, gazed by terrestrial eyes?

It is a pity that one feels after it a negligible but a just noticeable trifle of giddiness. Do the fowls of the air also so? It is said that some fishes are sea-sick, even after all these æons ...

Still, enormous bliss.

Following the fashion

I have a dress with puffed sleeves; the skirt is very long and full; about ten yards of silk, I think it took. It hangs in the wardrobe, taking a lot of room, because of the sleeves.

I have shoes with high heels; about three inches, I dare say. I can wear them if I want to.

I think I shall change my Morris, and get a small stream-lined green thing, and look smarter in the streets. It will not be so good for touring, but it will look better.

I may paint my nails red; or green, if that is coming in.

I shall write my memoirs, I think. I shall bring in every one I know, and have an index, so they can find themselves and their friends. There are plenty of things I can say about them. If they do not like it, they can lump it. It will serve them right, for having met me.

I may write a book about contemporary writers, too. They won't like that either, the things I shall say about them.

I can write tough-guy stories. What I mean is, I can write stories like this:

She was a grand girl. You're drunk, she said. But I wasn't so drunk, either. I mean, I'd had a few, but I could see straight; and I could hold the wheel. I had the headlights on, too. To hell with those lamps, she said, and switched them down. Do you want to dazzle everything on the road, she said, so it rushes into us? You're nuts.

She was a grand girl. You're a grand girl, I said, and I switched on the big lamps again, and I held her waist with my left, and hugged her up to me close, so as I felt her warmth. That's the style, I said, and I saw the needle get up to sixty. Oh, you're crackers, she said. Driving like hell with the big lamps on and necking me with one arm. How to-night'll end, she said, I don't know. I really don't, do you? Like most nights end, I guess, said I, and that's when comes the dawn. Aw, you're crazy, said she. I told mother I'd be in by four. Well, you won't be in by four; maybe by eight. That's time enough for breakfast, isn't it? I know a swell place down the river. Oh, for heaven's sake, said she; we shall never get any place at this rate. And what must she do but start grabbing at the wheel, crying out I was all over the road. And so we were, after she started grabbing. Then she screamed out, and something hit us and we slewed right round.

There was the hell of a mess on the road. One of those little Austins, it was, and all crumpled up, and a man and a girl all crumpled up too. There was blood and glass and things around. But my Buick had only buckled a wing.

See here, I said, we can't do a thing. We'd best get on. She was being sick in the road; the blood had turned her up, I think. That and the shock. And seeing those two …

Here, I said, come on out of this. We can't do a thing. I put her in the Buick, and slewed around again and drove off. There was something banging loose, and I got out to look; it was the number plate, so I wrenched it off and took it inside. We didn't have the headlamps on now; the off one was smashed, anyway, by that bloody little Austin. I drove away. The steering was a bit funny, too. She never stopped crying and talking, it made me tired. Women can't get this: when a thing's done it's done. That's a thing no woman can ever get. They can't let it be. Hell, did I want that bloody little car to muscle into us that way? Aw, forget it.

All the time as I drive I seem to hear that damned radio saying, in its polite Oxford-Cambridge voice, 'Before the news, there is a police message. Between two and three on Sunday morning an Austin seven car came into collision with another car, which apparently failed to stop …' Failed nothing. I did stop, see? I stopped, and saw there wasn't a thing I could do, so I went on again.

Oh, to hell with your noise …

✕

Yes: I could write a story like that if I liked. Perhaps I will. Fine magazine stuff. What I mean is, a magazine would take it.

And I can write tough-guy poetry. A magazine would take that, too. I can write poetry like this (I call this one *To the Barricades*):

Mr Jiggins goes to the circus.
(The girls, the hoops, the clowns, the seals, the hoopoes.)
He has donned his Harrow tie,
But Borstal was his alma mater true.
He meets Mrs Fortescue-Fox,
With a jade cigarette-holder, long and green like
                asparagus or a dead woman's fingers
Or the pale weeds swaying in the duck-pond,
But never a sprig of rue.
You're so handsome, where you going?
Don't know where I'm going, where I am, where you are,
where the sweet hell anyone is.
(Forward to the barricades! To the barricades –
                    where else?)
Ohé! Ohé! mes brave petits! the fat is in the fire!
εἰς τὸ πῦρ εκ τοῦ κἀπνου.
As Lucian pointed out, things can always be worse.
Pink and stout he was, pranked out with rings and gold
chains, he was.
What a fool he looked!
Dites donc, monsieur, si qu'on irait se coucher,
                    n'est-ce pas?

Festinare nocet, tempore quæque suo qui facit, ille sapit.
In fact, no hurry.
(March, march, march, the feet of a thousand men
marching as one. No hurry?)
They trample like artillery in my head.
Allons, allons, faites donner la garde!
But Mrs Fortescue-Fox,
Unable to wait, flung herself upon the obdurate rocks.
Life is like that.
'But never mine,' Mr Jiggins cried.
And up washed the running tide,
Flowing up, casting corpses on the slimy beach,
Casting statues, casting coins, casting mermen and
mermaids and old bowler hats.
Ting-a-ling-a-ling ring the bells of hell; where you bound
now?
Allons, companions, we march to the barricades.

In the grey dawn of yesterday
We wipe away all tears: – perhaps.

There's another I call *Petrol Pumps*. But that's longer, and I
won't print it here. It's fine magazine stuff too.

I like being in the fashion.

I may join the Communists.

Or I may write a novel a million words long, and very
strong; the longest and strongest novel of the season.

The trouble about the fashions is, there are too many going
on at once, and you can't follow them all.

Sometimes I think I will give them all up, and just be
dowdy.

Fraternal

In how gentle and civilised an adult group we sit about the room! We talk, we read, we listen, we discuss, argue, contradict; but we are polite, considerate, forbearing: we behave, on the whole, grown-up. At meals, we pass things about; we help one another to food; we do not care who gets the most. We listen to one another's stories; we respect (within limits, and with considerable dissension) one another's opinions; we admire one another's several experiences and lives. We are assembled from far places; behind one of us is a background of hot Indian plains and rice swamps, of prowling snakes and tigers, of rice-devouring brown men. Behind another, prairies roll, skis and sledges glide over snow-bound plains, pine-clad mountains guard great lakes, moose and coyotes and gophers leap. Each trails behind him or her the clouds of a separate environment, a strange and different life.

You pass me honey: you do not watch how much of it I shall take. For all you observe, I may take it all, and there will be none left for any one else. Time was when you would have said, 'That is too much; leave some for the rest of us'. Time was when we should have eyed one another's plates with the zealous justice of the savage, feeling that good things should be apportioned in equal shares; we approved Miss Edgeworth's Frank, bidden by his papa to divide the sugared cake into equal parts and weigh them with scales.

The years roll back: a curtain lifts. I am no more in a drawing-room among adult beings having tea. I am seated at a table, among my savage kind; a nurse presides, feeding us with bread and butter. One eats the crumb; one arranges the bitten crusts in a circle under one's saucer, out, so one hopes, of sight. One tilts one's chair back on its hind legs, rocking to and fro.

'Now then, Miss R, don't tilt your chair.'

'But A is tilting his. May A tilt his chair?'

Telling tales. We do not tell tales of one another now …

Some one is licking the treacle from her bread.

'Now then, Miss J, that's not pretty. How often have I told you? … *Master W!*'

Master W, in mood of ill-timed levity, has flung his bread and treacle at the ceiling. To our delight, it sticks there for a moment, before falling down. It leaves on the ceiling a sticky golden-brown smudge. Master W is in trouble.

What undignified, what compromising situations have I seen you all in, brothers and sisters! Suspended head downwards from the knees from trees, like monkeys by their tails; rolling like barrels down green slopes to lie at the bottom and vomit; crawling along the top of a high wall to inhale the drain-trap placed (surely oddly) thereon; sitting astride on an overturned canoe at sea; slithering bare-legged up and down a rope; prone in impassioned sobbing on the floor; rolling over and over in angry wrestling; pulling hair, pinching, fisticuffing, hiding books under chair-cushions, as a dog buries bones, that no other may have a turn of them. You, sitting reading there with your pipe, I remember your seizing my book and flinging it out of the window, that I might desist from reading. You, who do not smoke, I remember how you and I took the cigar tops cut off by uncles and smoked them; how we all trooped to the village toy-shop and bought Woodbines, and smoked them sitting in a row on the pig-sty roof. I could repeat the precise order in which we each met defeat at this pastime and retired. Yes: I remember all of you in the most ridiculous positions …

We cannot hide from one another: we know too much. We know one another's faults, virtues, catastrophes, mortifications, triumphs, rivalries, desires, and how long we can each hang by our hands to a bar. We have been banded together under pack codes and tribal laws. The remembered jungle is behind us, with its pleasures and pains, its follies, adventures and jests.

Jests: yes. We share a comic background, that could never be explained to others. A chance word may touch a spring set deep in the common stock of memory, and loose on us a joke, a surge of laughter, that is out of all proportion to the word uttered, for it rises from those deeps where forgotten and remembered jokes lie tangled in a giggling past. Giggling is the word for the excessive, the uncontrollable mirth that shook us when young, that shakes us even now when together, and to which no other has the clue.

Contradiction is moderated. Argument, which still rages on every topic, political, theological, literary, sociological, factual, has grown more complex; it no longer tails off into the bald competition in endurance of 'it is', 'it isn't', 'it is', 'it isn't', 'it is'. Activity has dwindled: no more do we sally forth to climb roofs or trees. Manners have improved: no more do we track passers-by along the street in furtive detective-formation, registering clues in hissing whispers as we go. We behave civilised, even when in a pack. But pack jokes remain. They may be no better than other jokes; they are often worse. But they are jokes by themselves, and are among the marks which distinguish the pleasures of fraternal association from any other.

Getting rid

Life is one long struggle to disinter oneself, to keep one's head above the accumulations, the ever-deepening layers of objects, of litter (for so I call those objects which I do not want), which attempt to cover one over, steadily, almost irresistibly, like falling snow. The danger is (one has heard) that one is lulled to sleep beneath the drifts, and will not (so also one has heard) wake again, but lie for ever besnowed, buried, unable to stir. Courage, then: fight the insidious, the deadly drifts while there is yet time; up and scatter them to the winds, tear them to shreds, fling them into dustbins, into the street, anywhere, and stand up free and disencumbered to abide the next storms.

If one had the wisdom to cast out litter as it arrives each day, one would not have these mighty periodic disencumberments; one would live more easily; but one would miss that tremendous, that spacious, sense of easement which follows a great clearance.

Tear them up, then, those piles of letters which you have never answered, nor will. Are you not born free? Shall anyone with a pen or a typewriter, a stamp or two, and some stationery, have the power to assault you, to bully you, to tear your precious time and your frail brain and attention, so sorely needed elsewhere, to shreds by making you answer his letters? You do not, I am sure, write to all and sundry asking them this and that, requesting them for time, for gifts, for attention to some business in which you, but not they, may chance to be interested: you give them credit for having their own interests, their own work, their own lives and schemes. You let them, in fact (I hope), alone. But how unusual this abstention appears to be! Letters arrive for you; pamphlets,

newspaper cuttings, books, discursive remarks, al! manner
of suggestions and requests. There they lie, reproachful piles,
awaiting your attention.

If only you had a secretary ... But I take it that, like most
of us, you have not a secretary. Even if you had, you would,
I suppose, have to give her some indication of how you
wished her to deal with the manifold topics opened up by
your correspondents. But you have not even a secretary. You
would, should you attempt to cope with the situation, have
to find stationery, stamps, words, forms of courteous refusal,
idle chat, turn off from your typewriter the paper which
waits those laborious stampings and stammerings which it
is your profession or your pleasure to make on it, and with
which you are already so far behind time, and replace it by
one piece of notepaper after another, on which you imprint
the date (if you can call it to mind) and the disgusting word
'Dear', and then pause to collect the kind of words apt to the
distracting occasion. By the time you have done all this, your
somewhat weak (it is probably somewhat weak) intellect will
be all-to scattered and depraved, and you will find it hard
to turn it again on to its proper tasks. Imagination, after its
efforts to find words of polite and idiotic refusal, thanks, and
regrets, will lie down fatigued, and boggle when set at its
customary courses. You will have to give it a rest, and take
the car out instead.

No; you were better not to tackle those piles. Let them
lie and grow. But, one day when the reproach of the great
unanswered becomes too heavy a burden, or when your
groaning writing-table is so deep ensnowed that it holds
no room for anything you may desire to keep on it on your
own account, then rise up, either calmly or in noble rage,
and destroy. Shovel the litter into some deep bin; let the
scavengers, those kindly, cocked-hatted men, carry it hence,
to the great pits and furnaces which shall receive it, and

transmute it into the rags whence it came. Eternal process of to-ing and fro-ing, from rags to paper, from paper to rags: whether is the worse condition? A few minutes ago you would have said paper. But now, having rid yourself of papers, you turn, strong and collected, in calm of mind all passion spent, to deal with rags.

Rags! How these encumber cupboards and drawers, hanging on hooks and on pegs, relics of earlier ages, which to be seen abroad in now were very shame, even if they were not so riddled and devoured by those gluttonous lepidoptera who make your cupboards their home. On most occasions, no doubt, you are wearily acquiescent in this; one look at the cupboards or drawers, and you turn away back to more normal and congenial employs. And quite right too.

> Neglected heaps we in by-corners lay,
> Where they become to worms and moths a prey,
> Forgot, in dust and cobwebs let them rest,
> While we return to where we first digrest.

But, now, heartened and strengthened by your victory over the papers, you face the rags, you fling them out, you decide that no claim of old affection or habit shall induce you to wear them again, to clean, to mend or to tolerate them. And, as for leaving them where they are, is it your duty to feed that tribe of greedy stolephage insects who have come unbidden to your table? Experience throughout the ages has shown that you may safely leave that to their Creator. Remove, then, their food; brush and shake it; tie it up in bundles; it is for the Poor. If the Poor reject it, as well they may, it can return to the transmuting furnace and boilers, there to be encharted once again. One day you may be throwing it into your waste-paper basket; and hanging in your cupboards for the moths those letters which you have just now so triumphantly flung for a while out of your life.

This getting rid is a kind of intoxication; be wary lest it carry you too far. Do not lay rash hands on all the letters, all the journals, all the garments, that you see lying about. You may want some of them again. Exercise moderation in destruction, that heady lust.

And when you have finished, you will sit down, happy, victorious, and rid, while the enemy creeps on again, seeping in through every crevice, surrounding and submerging you with relentless, unpausing advance. Your pleasure in victory is brief, and haunted by the imminence of future defeats. For riddable litter comes on like the sea, and there is no staying it. Even in prison cells, they say, litter enters and must daily be removed. It is our mortal heritage, and a losing war against nature that we wage.

But, for the moment, those letters, those newspapers; are gone. Thus far, we are, for the moment, one up on nature, that sinister, wily, and determined harridan, against whom civilisation wars perpetually and, for the most part, in vain.

Hatching eggs

Actually, I do not know that hatching is the right word, for I never, by human warmth, delivered any chicken from its shell. Neither would 'sitting on' be correct, for that was not the method adopted. I suppose incubating is the word. Anyhow, the pleasure lay in hope and dreams, never in consummation. We carried our eggs on the person by day, under the pillow by night. Only one at a time, and when it broke we began on another. They were mostly laid by hens, but once I found a duck's egg in the road, huge and pale green. How far it might already be advanced towards the duckling stage, I had no means of knowing; but I adopted it forthwith and stowed it away in the front of my sailor frock, the largest and proudest of the eggs on the persons of a family at the moment a prey to acute eggomania. There it lay, in that repository designed by heaven for carrying about oranges, books, rabbits, and kittens, so that the wearing of sailor suits, male and female, made a family inclined to thinness bulge in front as if they had been reared on some rich health food. My egg lay, I think, alone, and handkerchief enwrapped; when tree or rock climbing was indulged in, it was removed and carefully laid in some snug cache.

For how many days I nursed this greenish and pregnant treasure, this shrine of a fluffy golden being who should emerge in the fullness of time, who should owe its happy waddling life to me, I know not. They were glorious days, if few. I walked and gingerly ran, dream-wrapped; I was with duckling, and must walk warily. When in the slippery paths of youth with heedless steps I ran, the bouncing against my bosom of my duck-to-be recalled me to the cautiousness of prospective motherhood.

How I would love it! It would be my dandling, my nestlechick, my pet. With my own hands I would teach it to swim, to run, to jump (for we were accustomed to organise hurdle races for our pets, of whatever species). Mine would be the swiftest duck e'er entered for the stakes. It would accompany me everywhere, sitting on my lap at meals, at lessons, bathing with me in the sea. How, too, it would love me! Why does the duckling love her so, people would ask, as of Mary's lamb. Well, she loves the duck, you see, they would reply. And was I not giving it life, tending it, sacrificing for it other pleasures? Should it not, when it came to perception, gratefully quack, with Joseph Addison,

> Unnumber'd comforts to my soul
> Thy tender care bestow'd,
> Before my infant heart conceived
> From whom those comforts flow'd?

Thus I mused in my maternal meditations, moving delicately about house, shore, road, hill-side, my hands often crossed over my breast as in some holy picture. I felt safe, guarded, protected, with my dear and perilous burden; a thousand liveried angels lackeyed me, and I knew that this time a duck would be born. I would often take out the egg and put my ear to it as to a shell, to listen for faint cheepings, which I sometimes fancied that I heard. I wondered what would happen if it should hatch by night, beneath my pillow … Suppose that I were to wake one morning and find a smothered duckling, whose cries had failed to wake me? But we had been told that chickens and ducklings usually hatched by day, so this chance seemed remote.

The end came, as usual. The liveried angels went off duty, and with heedless steps I ran across the slippery stone floor of a room, and fell prone on my chest. A horrid smash, and my pet flowed away, sticky, addled, smelling of the corruption of all mortality, and past return were all its dandled days.

In the ensuing mess and bitterness of baulked hope, my one and chilly comfort was that there had never, it seemed, been duck life in that shell. I had not been with duckling, only with egg; and with stale and ancient egg of date incalculable. My nestlechick had been but a fluffy golden vision, conceived in the pregnant rovings of my brain, never by duck and drake in sweet communion linked. It had been the child of my doting dreams alone. But, while they lasted, what doting and what dreams!

Heresies

I know how the great heretics felt; I can enter into their fervorous assertions, their obstinate denials, their ingenious and fantastic inventions, their wild day-dreams concerning the world, the heavens and themselves. I can share their triumphant firmness in error, which would keep them ergotising sleepless through days and nights, frapling one against another, pro and con, across some seeming-small but bridgeless gulf which yawned between them and their opponents; I know the proud self-confidence which, after all these eager ergotisms, so often sent them heaven or hellward encharioted in flames.

More, when I recall some of those peculiar heresies which have down the ages made men and women feel so strongly, argue so fiercely, slay and die with such a ruthless calm, I feel in myself a responsive pleasure in nearly all. There must have been something in these strange delusions, I tell myself, that they inspired such confidence. Indeed, they have a quality of persistence which discovers them to be deeply rooted in human nature; scarce one in past centuries that you will not find echoed to-day; scarce one which I do not find re-hereticised in my own soul, at one moment or another, for the soul has its days and moods.

I am often pleased, for instance, to be an Origenist, as have been so many amiable men, and to think that there shall be no man damned, but all saved at the last, including the Devil himself. There are moments when I like to be Eustathian, to look on marriage as sinful, and wish, with Sir Thomas Browne, that there were some more delicate way to populate the world; other moments when polygamy captivates me, and I desire, with the Anabaptists and Mormons, that everyone should wed to the top of his bent. On hot days in the south I am Adamite, and wish to stroll abroad clad only in what Jeremy Taylor called rustick impudence; when skies are cold and sad I turn Manichee and hate the flesh. Often I am Pelagian, and vainly talk against original sin, boasting the potency of man's will to virtue; or I embrace Arianism, Socinianism or Photinianism, defying Athanasian thunders. How frequently am I one with the Fraticelli, their partiality to not too monotonous affections, their distaste for manual labour; or the Dulcinists, who combined with these errors the repugnance felt by the Waldensians for the clergy, for the cult of the saints, for the rights of property, and for the indissolubility of marriage.

Often too, I belong to the Agonyclites, and will not kneel; I like to be Collyridian, Messalian, Quartodeciman, semi-Pelagian, in turn; I will even experiment in Partial-Diluvianism, and maintain that the Flood left parts of the earth's surface uncovered; I will participate in a hundred of those enthusiastic and fanatical errors which are a heritage from our audacious, speculating, and so wrong-headed fathers.

These damnable and damnèd tenets are charming to hold, these poisoned streams sweet to the palate. That humanity, so imperilled by hereticide, so close to ravening lion and crackling flame, could be so ingenious and so determined in straying from the true path, is not strange to him who peruses human history. That Montanist and Donatist, flung into the same arena by Emperors to encounter hungry Christianophagous animals, should turn their backs on one another with expressions of distaste and advance into the jaws of different lions, resolved not even to be joined in martyrdom, is natural enough to him who is familiar with odium theologicum. For heretics too, have their portion in the heritage of this great odium; while in the grip of one heresy I condemn and abominate the others as if I were a partridge in a cage. (*Like as a partridge taken and kept in a cage, so is the heart of the proud*. Ecclesiasticus 11.30.)

Hot bath

A hot bath! I cry, as I sit down in it; and again, as I lie flat, a hot bath! How exquisite a vespertine pleasure, how luxurious, fervid, and flagrant a consolation for the rigours, the austerities, the renunciations of the day. All day I have moved about in chill air, in fog, in bitter and annihilating blasts, in inclement elements for which the tender human frame, contrived for the balmy airs of Eden, was never made. I have sat upright in a chair and tapped with stiff fingers on a typewriter; I have wrung numb thoughts and words out of a frozen brain, transmitting them on to paper in a gellid trickle; I have walked through chill murk and contagious fogs, with sore eyes and throat, every breath a pain, the grime of a great ennebuled city choking pores and lungs, the mazed world a darkness and a doubt, the round red sun extinguished, quite put out. I have, in brief, suffered angry winter's chiding tongue and dark brief day.

And now the bath; and now hot water gushing lavishly from a chromium tap into a white porcelain bed, spreading thin and clear, then verdurously bubbling round green and piney bath salts, assuming the tinge of a glasshouse full of ferns, or of tropical forests. Soaked in green light, with two small red ducks bobbing about me, I lie at ease, frayed nerves relaxed, numbed blood running round again on its appointed, circular mortal race, frozen brain melting, thawing, expanding into a strange exotic efflorescence in this warm pine forest. Bare winter suddenly is changed to spring,

And on old Hiems' thin and icy crown
An odorous chaplet of sweet summer buds
Is, as in mockery, set …

Like those Japanese paper flowers which gently unfold and bloom in bowls of water, thoughts and dreams burgeon, the mind puts out boughs and sprigs of blossom and ripe fruits, inebriating and enticing the charmed soul. Music seems to sound: is it that music of the spheres which only (so we are told) the chaste ear hears, or is it some strayed mermaid? Or does the dandled brain itself dream harmony, drowned in warm sweetness like a tropicked ship? The waters lap gently about the almost submerged island; sirens sing, the lotus flower opens, naiads move in rhythm, genius flows like wine, poems, tales, and pictures create themselves, swim in heavenly brightness, and dissolve. I am in the Golden Age; in Paradise; in the Fortunate Isles; in the gardens of the Hesperides and of Alcinous; in the floating gardens of Montezuma. I lie in Eden's bower, among odorous gums and balsams, or in a lake that to the fringed bank with myrtle crowned her crystal mirror holds, while universal Pan, knit with the Graces and the hours in dance, leads on the eternal spring. So, lulled in these flowers with dances and delight, I drowse entranced.

The Emperor Commodus is reported to have had a hot bath seven times a day; and who can blame him? Rich women have bathed themselves in milk, sometimes in the milk of five hundred she-asses at once. But water is better, for milk, if hot, would form a skin. The slimy touch of that white, crinkly skin on one's own ... but perhaps the rich women's slaves kept the milk bath in continual motion, so that no skin could form. Fear of skin must have been the shadow that hung over those rich women's baths. The shadow that hangs over mine is the fear of cooler water, dread lest the hot delight running from the taps should grow temperate, tepid, neither hot nor cold, to be spewed out of the mouth. That will be the end: it is already the end: the warm bower cools, its flowers fade, its songs die; the water, which I ruffle and splash to warm it, chills moment by moment.

Still I sojourn here, alone and palely loitering, though the sedge is withered from the lake and no birds sing. For I sent the bath towel to the wash this morning, and omitted to put out another. I have no towel.

Ignorance

1 Of one's neighbours

No, I do not know the names of anyone in this street, these flats, this square. No, I do not know who Mrs Miller is, or where she lives. This flat is my flat, and quite self-contained; I do not know my neighbours. Pride and self-containment swell me; I keep myself to myself, and wish you to know it. Who and what is this Mrs Miller, that you should suppose I know of her? Has Mrs Miller the run of my home, or I of Mrs Miller's? The savage pride of the cave-dweller surges in me. No, I know nothing about any of the other caves, thank you. Their inhabitants are probably despicably uncivilised, and, for all I know, keep parrots. You will have to find out their names for yourself.

What? Something has happened at Mrs Miller's? There has been a burglary, a murder, a fire? The police are here, and do not know which door to break down? Alas, it is too late for me to be concerned with that now; you should have told me at once. How can I now conduct you to Mrs Miller's door and share in the fun? You must ask someone else, and next time you ask me anything, kindly state your reason first.

2 Of current literature

No, I am afraid I have not read that either. It is good, you say? I am sure you are right. But I have no time for all these novels and things. I cannot imagine how you make time for them. You find they are worth it? They do not *look* good. Not that I see them; but they do not sound good, from the advertisements and reviews. Not that I read advertisements and reviews. I like to keep myself clear from all this second-rate stuff. Am I not afraid of missing something good? Well, I feel that the danger of reading something bad outweighs that risk. Yes, as you point out, I contribute to current literature myself. But then I scarcely *read* my own stuff, after all. And the point is, I get money for writing it. If anyone gave me money for reading, that would be another matter.

Yes, I am going off on Monday for a month in the country. You were going to give me some of your review copies, did you say? But now you will sell them instead ... Oh, well ...

3 Of gossip

They have quarrelled? No, I had not heard. I never hear about people's quarrels. And Daphnis and Chloe are to divorce? I had not heard that either. You hear all these news; I do not. No one tells me; I am too busy to inquire. It is better not to know; it avoids embarrassing moments. When I meet people, there is no subject I need to avoid; I can say anything. It is better so. It would be so tiresome not being able to mention Phyllis to Chloe, or Corydon to Daphnis, just because there are entanglements. After all, is not all life one long entanglement, and is it worth while to inform oneself about every knot? It is so much simpler not to know. And such things are not really interesting. Human beings being what they are, affections, animosities, meetings, partings, intimacies, estrangements, libel actions, occur all the time; to keep *au fait* with them would tax the most alert mind and take all one's time. As for me, I am happiest among my books.

You are going? But I thought you had something to tell me ...

4 Of wickedness

Can you understand wanting to act like that? I must say that I cannot. What I mean is, I am no saint, heaven knows, and I have my faults as much as anyone, but when it comes to things like that, one simply cannot enter into them. For instance, I can lose my temper, and say hasty things, but when it comes to real delight in cruelty, such as Nero's, or Caligula's, or the Nazis', or our ancestors', I simply cannot begin to understand it. Nor wanting to make marks in other people's books. Nor taking books and not returning them. Nor stealing stockings. And all this pornography one hears of. It never comes my way. One hears of books, of films, of postcards, of pictures, but I never see any. No doubt I am very ignorant. Bishops seem always to contrive to see improper films. They must have an excellent information service; of course, bishops cannot afford to be ignorant. What a time they must have!

But I see you think me a prig. That is the worst of ignorance; people either think you stupid or a prig. Probably both.

5 Of one's pass-book

This, I presume, is my pass-book, returned by the bank after being made up. I shall not open it; I shall put it away in a drawer as it is. It is one of those many books which are better unread. Am I Pandora, to open an odious box and set cares flying loose to sting me? Why should I depress myself by looking at all those figures, and the ridiculous sum they write in pencil at the end? I suppose they will tell me when they do not care to cash my cheques any more, and until then I shall go on drawing them, and shall not brood. The Bible tells us not to worry, but to take no thought for the morrow. If I were to begin poring over my pass-book (I cannot imagine why my bank should always give it a capital P and B, as if it were so desperately important) I should be paralysed, I could not live at all. Every mouthful would choke me; I could not so much as buy the means of subsistence, such as National Benzole or Shell, without hesitation and pain. While as for a wash and polish for my car, or a shampoo and set for my hair, I should cut them out altogether. And go nowhere, and see no one. I have anguish enough already at quarter days, what with rent and gas and electricity and telephone and bills, and that insolent income tax twice a year. If I were to read and remember my pass-book, it would be worse still …

So I do not read it. I walk in trust, hoping that I am still well on the hither side of indigence, and that my estate will prosperously endure. I spend, I consume, I commune with the angels, I live, I turn to rude facts a genteel and well-bred back.

The day will come. My landlord, the Gas Light & Coke Company, the Borough Council Electricity Department, the Controller of the London Telephone Service, the Income Tax Inspector, the very milkman, will all one day receive back from their banks cheques marked R D. I shall be run down, run out of my estate, finished. However then I may strive after Ignorance, that tranquil maid, I shall not be permitted to dwell with her again. Perhaps, if I were to open and read this sealed book now …

> Yet ah! why should I know my fate,
> Since sorrow never comes too late,
> And happiness too swiftly flies?
> Thought would deny my paradise
> No more! Where ignorance is bliss …

Enough. Return the thing to its drawer.

Improving the dictionary

On a blank page at the beginning of the Supplementary Volume of my Dictionary, I record emendations, corrections, additions, earlier uses of words, as I come on them in reading. Ah, I say, congratulating myself, here Messrs Murray, Bradley, Craigie, and Onions are nearly a century out; here were sailors, travellers, and philosophers chattering of sea turtles from the fifteen-sixties on, and the Dictionary will not have them before the sixteen-fifties. And how late they are with estancias, iguanas, anthropophagi, maize, cochineal, canoes, troglodytes, cannibals, and hammocks. As to aniles, or old wives' tales, they will not let us have this excellent noun at all.

Thus I say to myself, as I enter my words and dates. To amend so great a work gives me pleasure; I feel myself one of its architects; I am Sir James Murray, Dr Bradley, Sir William Craigie, Dr Onions. I belong to the Philological Society; I have delusions of grandeur. Had I but world enough and time, I would find earlier uses of all the half million words, I would publish another supplement of my own, I would achieve at last my early ambition to be a lexicographer.

If there is a drawback to this pure pleasure of doing good to a dictionary, I have not yet found it. Except that, naturally, it takes time.

Listening in

Who would have thought it? I press a switch, and my room is full of the clamour of voices from strange worlds, a thousand fantasies of calling shapes and airy tongues, on sands and shores and desert wildernesses, that may startle well but not astound the virtuous mind ... The coconut harvest is gathered in Malaya; tobacco is planted in Nyasaland, tea in Ceylon, timber hauled in Oregon, ship-loads of daffodils languish on Scilly quays while high seas rage, herds of reindeer trek across Canadian snows, and hearty voices from America strive to greet us above the rushing noises of the severing Atlantic. Or small, flat, twanging voices sound, telling us about Art, about Architecture, about Currency, crossing the 't' in often, dotting the 'i' in opposite, speaking of *de*fects, figyures, ideels, currencee, dwelling fondly on those shy syllables in English words which are meant to be seen and not heard, and are only put in to make spelling more difficult. Or Youth prophesies in sad tones that the future will be quite different from the past, Eskimos sit naked in their igloos and spear whales in Hudson's Strait, and the sky parades before us its marching regiments of planets and of stars. Had I time, I should listen to all of it, and know, very soon, everything, even the prices of fat cattle.

Then the music. How delicious to sit at ease and hear, without visible orchestra, this harmony that rains upon the ear. It might be, it very possibly is, that heavenly symphony, that music of the spheres to which Pythagoras used to say that the celestial universe revolved in tune, unheard by practically every man but him, for none but he was pure enough, Plato added sirens to the orchestra, seating one of these on each celestial orb and causing her to sing, so that at the honey-sweet chorus gods and men marvelled. It must certainly be so, said Milton, endorsing this delightful celestial concert, for the spheres would have long since wearied of their rotatory labours, had they not had music to sustain and encourage them. Other poets support this.

> The turning vault of heaven formèd was,
> Whose starry wheeles he hath so made to passe,
> As that their movings do a musicke frame,
> And they themselves still daunce unto the same.

The lark can hear this music, the nightingale too, and so should we, but for our grossness. It is

> the heavenly tune, which none can hear
> Of human mould with grosse unpurged ear.

Milton blames Prometheus, who robbed us of our innocence; others have put it down more to the error of our first parents, who are said to have been, until they fell, so tele-visionary and tele-audient that they could both see and hear the farthest, faintest star. Anyhow, and for whatever cause, we are now too sunk in brutishness to hear these heavenly harmonies. If our souls were pure, chaste, and snow-white, as was formerly that of Pythagoras, then should we hear that lovely rumour of the circling stars; or so they all say.

But what? Do I not hear the very sound? Does it not steal in ravishment upon my ear? What other than the rotating spheres and their melodious sirens can make these unseen harmonies? Have I indeed won the reward of a blameless life and become, like Pythagoras before me (and a few birds), celestially audient, cœlo-tuned? So, indeed, it seems.

> So dear to Heav'n is Saintly chastity
> That when a soul is found sincerely so,
> A thousand liveried Angels lacky her …

And in cleer dream and solemn vision
Tell her of things that no gross ear can hear.

This must be what is occurring to me. How gratifying; how delightful. How Plato's Er would have envied me: he only speculated on the spheral music; he never heard a note of it. Perhaps one evening I shall hear a bat squeak. Meanwhile the celestial orchestra performs for me.

then listen I
To the celestial Sirens harmony,
That sit upon the nine enfolded Sphears …

But what is this? What shriek tears the soft air to quivering shreds? Heaven, who has given me such signal favours, protect me now, for a soprano has broken loose upon the divine orchestra, and her savage cry rends the evening peace as if a cat shrieked upon a roof. This is no siren, but rather some Fury, busy about her barbarous and vengeful tasks. So shrieked the Erinnyes, pursuing Orestes for his unnatural crimes, so the Harpies, gobbling the food of poor Phineus as they flew down black winds.

A soprano! What terrific cataclysm of nature gave tongue in such sort, what shrill and squawking bird was slain long since by huntsman, so that the race of men were condemned to have among them for ever its voice in human female shape? Procne remetamorphosed, and returning from her chelidonian adventures with more than chelidonian voice wherewith to plague Tereus and all mankind for their sins. That singing sea-maid on a dolphin's back to whom Oberon listened from his rocky promontory, and to hear whom certain stars shot madly from their spheres, sang, it is sure, in a sweet contralto, smooth and shadow-haunted and creaming as the long run of waves into a deep green gully, or the humming of summer winds in a pine wood. Not a star would have deserted its own rotatory and siren music for a soprano. It fills the air with barbarous dissonance: but only for a moment. A touch, and it abruptly falls on silence. I turn a knob, and am in France; a cascade of sharp and throaty Gallic patters in my ears,

Who would have thought it?

But far be it from me to close on a note of pure content. Sopranos are all very well, and so are trombones and xylites and all such barbarous noises, for I can quickly rid myself of them. But not so with all airy abominations, for some of these are inserted out of due place, in the midst of news which I desire to hear. Such is the case with cricket, Cricket is, I understand, palatable news to some; they hang on bat and ball, on test match, ashes, and wicket; and, reading on news-posters in the street such catastrophic and momentous head-lines as 'ENGLAND FALLS', their hearts fall too. Very good: I would not grudge them their news. There is, at the end of the News Bulletin, a section entitled Sport. It is in this section that the results of games played with balls are announced, and those who do not desire to hear these may switch off at the word 'Sport'. But too often cricket rises surging out of its place like a river in flood, breaking its levees, rushing out of Sport into the main news, so that, having heard about the weather, and settling down all agog for the odd tale of European events, I hear instead the odious word Cricket complacently uttered, and followed by a drab tale of balls flung and hit, runs run, inningses declared, and players in or out. And how can I switch off this dreary stuff, when I know not at what moment it will end and give place to news that I might want to hear?

I submit that this is not fair play, not (to use its own foolish phraseology) cricket. What I mean is, you might as well put the Italian-Abyssinian crisis in the Sport section. Better.

This must be mended. It is rousing up and down England an ugly feeling of resentment. We are a patient people, but our patience has limits, as our monarchs and other rulers have from time to time found. This business of misplacing the news items may be the rock on which the British Broadcasting Corporation will founder.

Logomachy

Strange! The quiet and sunlit garden, in which, but a moment since, we lay enwrapt in post-prandial dominical peace, affably exchanging sugared and drowsy comments on delphiniums, Marxism, Hitlerism, religion, literature, landscape, and life, has suddenly become a Whipsnade, noisy with the howls, snarls, chatterings, gibberings, trumpetings, roarings, yappings, of creatures who differ concerning words. Someone spoke of pornography – what more natural, what more inevitable, a topic, since it connects with Marxism, Hitlerism, religion, literature, landscape, life, and probably delphiniums? In brief, it connects, they say, with everything; someone had been sent a boot and shoe catalogue between whose lines it lay, or so it seemed to her, like *foie gras* between bread in sandwiches. Be that as it may, we spoke, still drowsy and still sugared, still post-prandial and still dominical, of pornography. And a very amicable course the conversation would doubtless have pursued on this congenial topic, but that we discovered that we did not agree as to the meaning of the term. Two schools of thought arose: one held that the word, if correctly used, must imply pleasure given, or intended to be given, to the readers of the pornographic narrative or discourse or what not; the other that the intentions of the writer were irrelevant, and that pornography was, quite simply, what the Greek word means, always provided that sufficient wealth of detail was supplied. The battle raged; one school accused the other of putting a gloss on the word, the other retaliated with charges of having an etymological mind, of pedantic insensitiveness to accepted shades of meaning. Other words broke in; we spoke of phenomenal, of litotes and meiosis, of the derivation of ilk (someone erroneously conceived it to come from the Latin *illic*), of anthropophagi (someone erroneously maintained that these should properly be human), of erotic, of melodrama, of prelate, presbyter, and priest, of highbrow, of a dozen more such contentious points. The garden rang again with our logomachy, with our loud ergoting pro and con. All were conceited, scornful, happy, crying ha-ha like the war-horse charging in battle. There is poetomachy, bibliomachy, angelomachy, theologomachy, gastromachy, erotomachy, a hundred other strifes; of them all, logomachy is the most absorbing, the most calculated to fill with sound and fury a pleasant Sunday afternoon.

But, during a moment's pause, I recollected how logomachs have been disapproved of, scornfully entreated, regarded as petty squabblers and unworthy quibblers, out of tune with the infinite, out of place on Parnassus. I recalled John Milton, how, in a Cambridge oration, he railed against logomachia. *Has argutiolas*, he coldly exclaimed, *inanes quæstiunculas*; these quibblings, these empty little questions. And, 'It is abundantly clear how little these trifles lead to integrity of life and cultivated manners, which are the greatest good. This logomachia neither contributes to the general welfare, nor in any way to the honour and profit of our country. Two things most advance and ornament a country – fine speaking and brave action; but this litigious battling of discrepant opinion neither instructs in eloquence, inculcates prudence, nor incites to brave deeds'.

And that, to be sure, is the main thing, is it not?

'Away, then,' continued John Milton, 'with these Cunning chatterboxes ...'

He must have been right. Nevertheless, as the word-battle swells up around me, I cannot help thinking that it does, after all, incite to some eloquence.

Meals out

1 On the roof

Shut the attic skylight door; that is right. Do not let us put our toes through such tiles as we can conveniently avoid; there was some trouble last time the Brave Alpine Climber Band was on the roof. We will encamp in the valley between the two smoking peaks of Etna and Vesuvius. Here is the rucksack; it has five oranges, seven rusks, three bottles of ginger pop, twopence worth of pear drops, and a mug. And a packet of Woodbines, in case we feel brave enough for a smoke. Only no one must be sick on the roof; it would be too disgusting. Anyone who means to be sick must get through the skylight first, or else swarm down the gutter pipe into the yard.

The BACB is enjoying its well-earned meal. It has climbed far to-day, and got very dirty and rather scraped. Pass round the mug; bang in the glass stoppers of the pop bottles, and do not let too much run fizzing over the roof. Turn and turn about; Climber Nansen's turn is lasting too long. Have we finished? All but the pear drops and the cigarettes. We will now sit astride on that gable, or rather that mountain ridge, and suck the former and smoke the latter.

A fine view indeed. The yard lies spread beneath us, and the stable and barn and outhouse roofs lift their peaks and gables around us. We see the kitchen door, and the kennel, and the wall that divides the yard from the fruit garden and the lawn. We can see right over this, and over the holly hedge into the lane and the great field that slopes down beyond it. We can see the fields even beyond that; the corn-field with the footpath running through it, and the reapers at work, the large elms that hide the lane to the village. The universe simmers before us in a hot August drone. We are drowsy in the sun. We have a pear-drop in one side of the mouth, a Woodbine in the other. We suck; we smoke. Climber Nansen pales, spews out his pear-drop, drops his Woodbine, reclines. You had better, Climber Nansen, get back through the skylight before it is too late. Crawl away quickly; quicker, can't you; I am crawling behind you; with me it is nearly already too late. All things are with God, but He must not permit anything to occur on the roof …

2 On the pavement

The Café-Restaurant Garcia has an orange and blue striped awning outside it, shading the pavement from the sun and the moon. Beneath it we sit at our table; we sit on, long after we have ceased to dine, drinking coffee, sipping cognac, eating lumps of sugar, smoking, talking, looking at the plaza with its elegant ordination of palms, oranges, and lemons, listening to the band which plays there. Mexican gentlemen and ladies stroll about, sit and drink at tables, twang musical instruments. It is balmy, it is warm, the night smells of lemon trees. There is a yellow ochre cathedral at the other side of the plaza, built by Spanish missionaries four centuries ago. The houses round the plaza are the houses of old Spain. Beyond them rise against the violet sky the dim serrated peaks of Mexican mountains. I eat oblongs of cane sugar, dipped in the cognac of my companion. Brandy-sugar: it sweetens and burns the blood, sets the night to a merry tune. The band has stopped, but the Mexican gentlemen still twang strings, and there is singing.

Hey, mozo! Otro aguardiente! Y mas azucar.

New Year's Eve

Walking in the fields on the last of those brief, chill and gentle afternoons that run the old year out, I felt the cool damp air of Hampshire, sweet with fir and heather, stir about me like cold wings. The sky loomed greyly over the purple-brown line of the moor, but melted into blue squares and ovals over the western stubble-fields, and glinted above Farewell Hanger into a pool of gold. Crossing two stiles, I came to a foot-bridge; beneath it the full Rother gurgled with song. The earth squelched under foot; a thrush whistled in a dripping copse of holly and oak.

In the still, dreaming heart of the Hampshire winter, the year turned, and would be made new. So wild and deep a mystery as this stirred the naked woods, whispered in the cold brook, whistled flutily from the holly copse. Immemorial Christmas, the year's turn, the sun's birth, the earth's cold saturnalia, whereat soft-footed elves patter and chuckle and gobble and trip, shaking silver drops from the holly, sucking their teeth as they squelch in the mud of the small deep lanes and cow-trodden fields. There is small friendliness in the year's end: it is secret, cold, a prehistoric act played each twelvemonth by the drowsy primeval gods who have scarcely yet, after these few thousands of brief years, observed the intrusion of the fussy little creature strutting on two legs through their ancient habitations.

There was a sighing, soft and cold, as if the year turned over in his sleep.

Or as if the sky slid earthwards in a sheet of rain, which in fact at that moment occurred.

Not going to parties

It is apparent which door the party is behind, for all down the street pours and swells its jocund rumour, as of Bacchus and his merry crew. It guides me to it, as the sweet church bells guide worshippers to prayer. Hark, hark, and yet again!

> This way the noise was, if mine ear be true,
> My best guide now; me thought it was the sound
> Of Riot, and ill manag'd Merriment,
> Such as the jocond Flute, or gamesom Pipe
> Stirs up among the loose unletter'd Hinds,
> When for their teeming Flocks, and granges full
> In wanton dance they praise the bounteous Pan,
> And thank the gods amiss. I should be loath
> To meet the rudenesse and swill'd insolence
> Of such late Wassailers; yet O where els
> Shall I inform my unacquainted feet?

Besides, I am all smugged up, all adorned for the party, all ready for the rout.

Yet, how hot it will be in there, up that flight of stairs to where they wassail in swilled insolence! How loudly shall I have to shout, to hear myself above all the ill-managed merriment! None will hear what I shout: I shall hear what no other shouts; all will be jocund revelry, with perhaps now and then an olive, a cheese straw, a glass of sherry or tomato juice, or a little sausage on a little stick. That is all very well when one is in the mood, and an excellent manner of employing an evening. But am I not also very well where I am, sitting in my car?

> Hence vain deluding joyes,
> The brood of folly without father bred,

How little you bested,
Or fill the fixed mind with all your toyes!

I turn my back on you; I trundle down small dim streets to the embankment, and along the dark, lit river, the night air, so delightful, so unwholesome, fanning my face and blowing through my hair, the wedge of a yellow moon, like a slice of cheese, rippling in black water among a myriad city lights. Tomato juice, strong drink, sausages, friendly faces, shouting, wassailing, and wit, I have rejected for lethargy, solitude, encharioted ease. I glide furtively home through streets and parks and embed in my own easy chair, as if I had never planned another evening.

But I shall never know what I have missed. What enchanting encounters, what faces new or long unseen, or all too often met; what jests, quips, cranks, quiddities, tales! They are occurring even now, in those high, lit rooms from which I turned. I am very well where I am; I prefer to be where I am; but who was it who said, 'God himself cannot give us back a lost party'?

Parties

Let me die (as Melantha would say), but this will be a good party. See how many people are flocking in at the door, gay butterflies, bright birds all silkily emplumed, or glossily black and white, with tails like tails of ravens hanging down behind. How fast they flock,

As thick and numberless
As the gay motes that people the sun beams!

What a noise already they make! Already they are gay, benign, inebriate, they drink and eat like to a harpy – Oh, Lord, walk this way – I see a couple, I'll give you their history. In that corner, close to the hock cup, poets stand grouped; tolerable poets, better poets, definitely poor poets, poeticules, poetitos, poetasters. (Poets have coined more derogatory names for other poets than any other professional men have done, is it not so? That is because they feel very strongly about poetry and about other poets.) They speak of poetry as they drink hock cup and eat olives. Spender, Barker, Day Lewis, Auden, Pudney, Isherwood, they mention these, they argue about the latest works of each; poetomachia rages. Near them is a Roman Catholic group; these do not go in for poetry but wit; they drink deep and sing gay songs. Then there are novelists; I always think novelists rather noisy, do not you? Let us move out of earshot. There stand three publishers, telling jovial stories of the frolic Greeks. Or is it about some books they hope to publish? I cannot catch the words; all speak, none hearkens. On the sofa near me two women murmur mysteriously one to another; one looks informed, and as if she knew the secrets of every one in the room; she seems the wisest aunt telling the saddest tale. I am not near enough to hear it.

What will happen at this party? Anything may happen. A man has just come in who stands charmingly on his head at parties. Perhaps he will stand on his head tonight. I hope that he will stand on his head. That is what people should do at parties of pleasure; it gives parties of pleasure the right note. At least, so I think, though to Cleisthenes the despot of Sikyon it seemed in the highest degree unseemly that his daughter's suitor should dance on a table on his head at a banquet. This only shows how times have changed since the days of Cleisthenes; if I had a daughter, I would present her immediately to a suitor who did that, and gladly would she go to him.

Other parties of pleasure which have been held come into my mind. Agathon's party, into which Aristodemus gate-crashed, on the specious suggestion of Socrates that 'to the feasts of the good the good unbidden go', and at which they praised love and Alcibiades complained of Socrates. That was a good party; I have heard that there are such parties now, but they do not come my way. Then I think of Trimalchio's party, where they began with dormice rolled in honey and poppy-seed, sausages, damsons, pomegranate seeds, and peahens' eggs containing each a fat becafico in spiced yolk of egg, and went on with a great dish of the signs of the Zodiac, and then really began to eat, every now and then washing their hands in wine. That was a vulgar party, a gluttonous, ill-bred Roman party; I should not like to be at that party. I would rather be at an English rout, assembly, or conversazione, nibbling dainty rout-cakes and sipping spiced wine, while the card tables are set out and the tea is brought in. Or at a party at the Royal Society's, where experiments in gravity and levity occur, bowls of goldfish are weighed before and after the goldfish are removed from them, fruits are frozen stiff, Æolian harps make music, and pyrophones their fiery moan. This is not a party such as that. Still, anything, or nearly anything, might happen at it.

There is a levity, a light and glittering quality, among the guests, as of revel routs on tiptoe for a feast. We quaff champagne, we gulp ices, we sit down with pencils and paper, we shall write a poem line by line. Some people leave the room, to return and perform for us; it is all most diverting. We eat again, we drink again; some are drunk, some sober. We all speak very loudly, but the time is past when I can hear much of what we say. It does not matter. It is a good party. Let me die but it is a good party.

So the brief night goes in babble and revel and wine. It is bed-time, but we are still here. To go home would be so odd. They would say that one was not enjoying the party, to be leaving it so soon. One must stay, though the black bat night has flown, though no silence falls with the waking bird, no hush with the setting moon.

It is a good party, an admirable party: but can it be that parties of pleasure go on just the fraction of a second too long?

Play-going

I am, on the whole, entertained by these agreeable cheats. At their best, they divert and please beyond measure; at their worst (which often occurs), they embarrass and fatigue. But to sit and watch the curtain rise on the mummers who will strut and mime for us for two hours of an evening to make us sport is an excitement never stale. They will perhaps display to us some lively tragedy: caught in a very torrent, tempest and whirlwind of passion, they will saw the air with their hands and tear a passion to tatters, to very rags. Hamlet would have had them whipped for this; but for my part, I like to see them at it; I consider that this is partly what they are put on that raised dais to do. They are in a fiction, in a dream of passion, and so, indeed, am I. Like Sir Thomas Browne, 'I can weep most seriously at a play, and receive with true passion the counterfeit grief of those known and professed impostures'. 'Tis true, they do often imitate humanity most abominably; but humanity we can see anywhere; it imitates itself; I would scarce cross the street to watch it. Yet here, set on this platform strutting above a row of lights, I will watch it for two hours (not, I think, for longer). On a stage meal I hang entranced, though I would not lift my eyes from my newspaper to see the same meal off-stage. I will delight in a stage dog, a stage baby, a stage quarrel, though all three are ever with us in the world without, and I think nothing of any of them. I will think with admiration. How well he said that! How wittily she took it! when I hear words well and wittily spoken all about me, and scarcely pause to mark them.

But sometimes the words are good words, well and wittily, or gravely and beautifully, written, and then how my pleasure is doubled; no, trebled, for there is the pleasure of the words, the pleasure of the speaking, and the pleasure of the fitness of the two conjoined. Should I ever hear, as I never yet have heard, the right Oberon sitting on a promontory to hear a mermaid on a dolphin's back, the right Titania deploring the confusing of the seasons, the right Prospero rounding our little life with a sleep, the right Macbeth in the to-morrow and to-morrow lines, the right Cleopatra in 'The crown o' the earth doth melt ... And there is nothing left remarkable beneath the visiting moon', and in the asp speech (which I have heard said to break the heart, but not on the stage), the right Beatrice, Rosalind, and Millamant in look, voice, and wit all joined, the right Restoration sparks to body forth the Restoration comic spirit ... but so one might go on for ever: should I ever hear these (as I have, once or twice, heard the right Hamlet), to be at the play would be to peer at heaven; such pleasure is more than one dare hope to purchase for the price of a plush seat. Normally, one must be content, or malcontent, with lovely lines blurred or flattened or coarsened in the speaking, or with plain speeches well enough spoken, as they are, or so it sounds to me, in most modern plays that I see.

Well enough, anyhow, for a theatre full of people to sit absorbed, smiling, laughing, moved, throughout the spectacle they have bought. We are, I suppose, easily entertained, and it was never hard to split the ears of the groundlings; even Punch and Judy will do that in the streets. As I said, there is that in the raised platform, the set piece, the ordination of players, the purchase of seats, which confers on common speeches and actions some strange cachet of prestige.

Anyhow, for my part I am pleased with these guileless impostures, and would watch them more often had I but more time, did the seats cost less, and would the play but run straight on without those dreary intervals that now break its thread and waste our time. If play-acting should ever cease among the human race, which, after so many thousand years of mumming, would seem improbable, it will be the intervals which will kill it. There is not enough time in a crowded human life to waste hours of it doing nothing in a theatre, removed from all other occupations, and unprovided with the spectacle we gave up an evening to see. Music should fill these spaces, or a puppet show, or what not, if the play must pause.

Pretty creatures

They strut and trip around us, all shapes, all sizes, all colours, all species (for even a pretty little black curly-tailed pig is at times to be admired, and the infant rhinoceros has indubitable charms). We may enquire, with Montaigne, what this beauty is that so pleases, and whether it has existence outside the individual eye and taste; we know that it has not, and that this in no degree diminishes its power to ravish and entice. 'The pre-eminence in beauty, which Plato ascribeth unto the spherical figure, the Epicureans refer the same unto the pyramidal or squat.' ... All the better, since Plato and the Epicureans are thereby both pleased. I dote on that gazelle, that tall, light-stepping girl with her slant eyes, her smooth and high-held head, her broad and smiling mouth; you on that fluffy kitten, that small and dainty person, with eyes large and round, clustering curls, pink roses in her cheeks. As to that, I dote on her also, as on all pretty creatures, from the sailing golden eagle to the gilded fly, from the splendid muscled athlete to the chubby babe in bath.

We are excelled, as we know, by many living creatures, earthly, airy, and marine. Yet this awkward and lumbering human biped has also power to ravish, and that not only its fellow-humans, who may be prejudiced in its favour, but those very creatures who, we think, so manifestly excel it. Fishes, notoriously amorous of the human race, have leaped from the water to the land if their angler be fair of face, have crowded round lovely bathers in embarrassing shoals, have carried beautiful boys across oceans. Unicorns have always loved young virgins to the point of rashness; lions, tigers, and wolves have followed beautiful youths and maidens with no anthropophagous dreams, merely to dote on their faces and forms; birds have lost their heads altogether –

When he was by, the birds such pleasure took
That some would sing, some others in their bills
Would bring him mulberries, and ripe red cherries,
He fed them with his sight, they him with berries.

While, as to dragons, they have frequently doted to distraction, forgetting their own kind in their attachment to some handsome human creature.

If our dumb friends, then, can so admire our curious form, perhaps ejaculating when they see it the thanks-giving of the Hebrew, 'Blessed be the Lord, who has made his creatures in such strange diversity of shapes', how much more should we. And do. For, if there is one thing for which we have ever admired one another, it is for our beauty. Whatever strange chance arrangement of features and colour it may be that pleases any given race, tribe, period, or personal taste, however little it may please any other race, tribe, or person, still, there it is, triumphantly, absurdly, irrationally victorious, enchanting such beholders as are to it susceptible. Beauty, as the intoxicated but truthful Comus remarked, is nature's brag. This amazing, confounding, admirable, amiable Beauty, than which in all Nature's treasure there is nothing so majestical and sacred, nothing so divine, lovely, precious, 'tis nature's crown, gold and glory – see where it goes, tripping and pacing about the common streets, about shop floors, uttering through its curled vermilion lips genteel remarks concerning art silk cami-knickers and hose, swaggering in old flannels about ancient college courts, singing, bronzed and limber, behind mules on Apennine paths, running and tumbling with hoop and ball in Kensington Gardens, speaking rich Californian to us in darkened palaces, lounging about raised platforms above footlights. Beauty can do with us what it wills; more effectual on a jury, as Phryne showed, is a prisoner's handsome appearance than any eloquence of counsel: not only was Phryne, 'following' (as reporters would say) the exhibition of her person to the court, discharged without a stain on her character (or without further stains than it had previously borne), but 'those intemperate young men of Greece' erected to her eternal memory, with infinite cost, a golden image.

And here our best Athenians seem owls indeed (as someone remarks somewhere about something else): for who would desire a golden image of a beautiful lady? I should not look twice at Phryne in that hard and yellow metal. The very charm of beauty is its moving evanescence, its fleeting hue and swift-sliding shape, that turns this way and that like a leaf on the wind, like the running sea in shadow and sun. Beauty vanishes, beauty passes: living beauty fixed in metal, all chained up in alabaster, is a poor and chilly thing.

Lounge, trip, stride, and run around me, then, oh lovely creatures of all sizes, ages, hues and shapes. You are a garden of bright flowers, a forest of saplings, like the young sapling shoot on Delos of which Nausicaa minded Odysseus; you are a very bestiary of such lithe and bright-eyed creatures as one may encounter leaping and slinking about jungle paths, or about ferny parks at Whipsnade, or prisoned in the small bright capitals of monkish missals. Speak not, oh beauteous idiots; move all in muted beauty like the moon; delight my eyes, and assault not my ears with your harsh or pretty jungle cries. I have no illusions about you; I know your limitations, and all I beg of you is that you will remain within them, and so continue to please.

Reading

Here is one of the oddest of the odd inventions which man has sought out, this conveying to one another by marks scratched on paper thoughts privately conceived in the mind. It shows, as all the arts show, the infinite publicism of humankind, the sociability, the interdependence, which cannot endure to have a thought, to conceive a tale, a tune, a picture, an arrangement of words, or anything else, but all must forthwith be informed of it. And how avidly we run to be informed; we have already consumed many thousands of tales, poems, essays, and what not, but we are never satiate, we are greedy always for more. We begin the day by running our eyes over those multi-paged printed rags which furnish us with potted selections of events which have occurred during the last twenty-four hours. What excitement! Here are countries plunging into war, politicians making speeches, governments, aeroplanes, and motor-cars crashing right and left, murders, thefts, and revolutions, Britons flung into foreign gaols, Etonians bowled by other Etonians in 1887 (they have remembered it ever since, amid all the uproar and confusion of life), outbreaks of healthy-Aryan-national-sentiment in Germany, of sacred egoism in Italy, of foot-and-mouth disease in Berkshire. It has all occurred many times before, it will all occur many times again, but still I devour the pages with eager appetite, stimulated and mildly stunned. My newspaper makes me realise, in the improbable event of my ever forgetting it, on to what an exciting, what a tumultuous world, the sun and I matitutinally rise.

Having risen, I endeavour for a time to bound my reading by what I regard as my proper studies, that is, by the requirements of such labours as I am at the moment committed to. These requirements, generously interpreted, may take me almost anywhere. They may take me, for example, to my dictionary; and, having heaved one of the somewhat ponderous volumes of this mighty work from its shelf (this is one of the main ways in which I keep in good athletic training) I continue to read in it at random, since it would be waste to heave it back at once. I need not expatiate on the inexhaustible pleasure to be extracted from the perusal of this dictionary, from the tasting of this various feast of language, etymology, and elegant extracts from all the periods of English literature. In this enticing pastime a whole morning may fleet itself idly away.

Or, on some slight pretext, the other works that beckon from my shelves like sirens from enchanted seas may win me to them, and, soon oblivious of the reason for my plunge, I am swimming in those deep voluminous seas, among poetry, masques, plays, history, lives, diaries, letters, zoology, navigations and explorations. These, last, above the rest, have the siren's power to drug and to detain. For they are, I suppose, what the psychologists call, in their uncouth tongue, wish-fulfilment, or dream-sublimation. They take you travelling over the globe, and with no further trouble than the lazy flick of a page. Why, as Samuel Purchas introducing his collection of travellers' tales, so plausibly asked, travel, when you can get all the benefits of doing so and suffer none of its damages, by reading of the travels of others? Why should gentlemen adventure themselves to see the fashions of other countries, where their souls and bodies find temptations to a twofold whoredom, and bring home a few smattering terms, flattering garbs, apish cringes, foppish fancies, foolish guises and disguises, the vanities of neighbour nations (I name not Naples) without furthering their knowledge of God, the world or themselves? For his part, for the benefit both of those who cannot travel far and those who cannot travel virtuously, he offers 'a world of travellers to their domestic entertainment'.

In brief, he recommends to us his travelogue, in which 'both elephants may swim in deep voluminous seas, and such as want either lust or leisure may single out what author or voyage shall best fit to his profit or his pleasure'. He would have us arm-chair travellers, and well he knew how to play on our indolence.

Here, then, we sit, as he suggests, at home and in peace under the shadow of our own vine and fig, and from the shore behold with safety and delight the dangerous navigations and expeditions of explorers, viewing their war-like fights in the watery plain as from a fortified tower, enjoying the sweet contemplation of their laborious actions. Most commodiously we peregrinate with Marco Polo over Persia, Thibet, Turkistan, and to the court of Khublai Khan; with Spanish Conquistadores and English pirate merchants to Mexico, the Indies, and the New World; with Portugal friars about Abyssinia; with the Hollanders to the Java seas; with King Solomon's navy to Ophir; with Captain William Hawkins, hindered all the way by proud injurious Portugals and wily Jesuits, to the court of the Great Mogul; with Sir John Hawkins in the *Jesus* to take five hundred negroes on the New Guinea coast and make vent of them to Spaniards in the Indies; with the good ship *Dog* to the Mexique Bay; with Captain Knox to the wild Highlands of Ceylon; with Thomas Gage, the disgruntled Jesuit, over Guatemala; with John Chilton over all New Spain, among Indians who dared not eat him for fear he might have the pox; with Anthony Knivet plundering chests of silver from the cells of Portugal friars in Brazil, eating the bark of cinnamon-trees at Port Famine, encountering cannibals, a crocodile, and a great dead whale lying on the shore like a ship grown with moss.

We may visit the island of Ferro and see that tree which rains continually; or chase after those flitting isles near Teneriffe which, when men approach them, they vanish; or behold the islands off Scotland swimming after the manner of the ancient Cyclades and flitting up and down in the water, the sport of tempests; on these same islands you may see (and still without moving a step nearer the Scotch express) trees from whose fruit falling into running water ducks and geese do grow. 'Whoever took possession of the huge oceans, made procession round about the vast earth? Whoever discovered new constellations, saluted the frozen poles, subjected the burning zones?' Whoever may have done so, I am as good as they, and far more at ease, sitting in my arm-chair and following them about the world with my eyes, doped and lulled with their enchanting lies. Without putting out a hand but to turn a page, I break off a sugar cane and suck it, drop into my mouth pears dripping honey, pluck store of oysters from the boughs of trees (but these have a flash taste), gather barnacle geese from the barnacle-trees, smell the sweetness of great lemon woods, watch Sierra Leonians slithering up high palm-trees to fill gourds with palmito wine, eat wood fruits called beninganions and beguills, as big as apples and tasting like strawberries, taste cooked friar, but reject it as unwholesome, visit the Castle at Agra, where in a fair court every noon the Rajah sees elephants, lions and buffles fight, and so on to Lahore, the way set on both sides with mulberry-trees; watch a Christian ape at the court of King Jahanjar pick out the name of Christ from those of twelve prophets shuffled in a bag, tearing up the eleven others with distaste; sail up the river Quame for gold, elephants' teeth, ambergris, and slaves; find turtles' eggs with Roger Barlow in the Indies, unicorns' horns with Sir John Hawkins in Florida; watch from the Florida beach the sea-fowl chase the flying fish; sail among these huge icy mountains which make such a dashing and crashing one against another in green Arctic seas; voyage, in brief, all oceans, peregrinate all lands, taste all foods, meet all people, enjoy all pleasures.

Meet all people. Yes; my humble dwelling-room becomes a salon, where I receive, without even troubling to rise or bow, an extraordinary miscellaneous crowd or rabble of persons, chattering in all tongues on all topics, in verse, in stately prose, in strolling, colloquial late-Stuart slang, in round and booming Johnsonian, in demure and ladylike Austenian, in sly and delicate Proustian, in gay modern English and French. Many are pompous, foolish, absurd, many have wit, many have ideas, many have neither. Some are wicked above the ordinary, some of a virtue only found among the angels and among earthly citizens of bygone centuries; of these my flat is not worthy, they shine oddly in it. Among them move people 'so beastly that they put themself to no manner of labour, but study only how to take their neighbours for to eat them'. Theological controversialists too I entertain; I hear the schoolmen thunder against one another on subtle points of doctrine, Jesuits and Jansenists furiously raging together, Puritan and Anglican at it hammer and tongs, non-Jurors smitten by the See of Bangor, the higher mathematics by that of Cloyne. Yet I do not greatly encourage these religious thunderings; I welcome more often blander and gayer guests, finding them apter for a salon. I prefer the urbane smile, the elegant jest, the fit phrase, the lovely line, the strange adventure, the subtle thought, or the sounding period of the historian.

At times, too, I like my salon to become a zoo, a bestiary, a setting for the infinitely strange habits of animals, of unicorns, elephants, dragons, manticoras, remoras, sea-serpents, dolphins, turtles, sparrow-camels, panthers, cockatrices, chameleons, and others of their curious kind.

Another and still more indolent salon I hold in my bed at night, in the hour before sleep. The guests here are of a different kind, less disturbing and exciting, for it does not do to be disturbed and excited before sleep. Poetry will not do at this hour, nor prose of a past and more splendid age. It is an hour reserved for the narrative fiction or biography of the present moment. As I drift in this agreeable ship towards sleep, I marvel drowsily at its good craftsmanship. How charmingly A writes, I think; how ingenious is B, how C's quick wit makes me smile, how D holds the attention nailed fast, so that if one slips a word one loses a sense. How sharp an irony sparkles from E's pages, how amiable a jester is F, how sound a workman G. How well they, for the most part, write. (Those who do not, do not detain me for more than a few pages.) Surely, I sleepily reflect, the standard of writing has climbed up and up through the past two decades. When I was young, we did not, I am sure, write as well as we nearly all write now. The standard has risen. There are, I believe, floods of tosh; fortunately, unless one is a publisher or a reviewer, one need not see it. But there is enough that interests, pleases or entertains to fill the ante-somnial hour night by night with company good enough for the occasion, which is all that one should demand of current literature.

So much for the home salon. One attends, also, the salons of others. There are within my reach two great places of entertainment. One is in a pleasant square; here one roams at will about gridded galleries, reading what one chooses, removing books by armfuls and leaving them scattered on tables to find their own ways back, or taking them away, either after being entered in ledgers if one is a person of probity, or concealed in despatch-cases if one is a thief; for this library is a notable hunting-ground for thieves; frail human nature has signally failed under the strain of seeing so many books at once, and the biblioklept, one of the lowest of God's creatures, may be prowling next you along those quiet corridors, his stealthy hand plucking the desired fruit from the bough and stowing it furtively away.

This is less possible in the other great London resort of readers, where they know better than to trust us. Here we are fed liberally, afforded every kindness, but we are marked men and women, we cannot easily steal away with pockets full of volumes. Unless, indeed, we chanced to be newcomers, gave false names, and were careful not to return. Something in this sort might, I suppose, be managed. But for most of us the strait and narrow way of rectitude is indicated.

We can, however, lick our fingers to turn the pages. I have been told that some readers even lick the pages direct with the tongue, but this habit is, I believe, confined to those who have been allowed special access to books not generally accessible, and denotes some peculiar pleasure.

For my part, I find it enough to sit drowsily in a great circular room, my wants supplied (in God's good time) by attendant elves, a great bank climbing volume by volume about me, shutting me off from the inky little student writing a research thesis on my right, and from the patriarch from the far deserts of Arabia on my left, leaving me dreamily alone, transcribing from crabbed texts in a crabbed hand, languishing agreeably in that hot-house clime, all the books in the world (or as near as makes no matter to me) within the call of a written order.

What is the extraordinary pleasure that we derive from this pastime? Why do we forget everything for it, feel by it transported, enlarged, enslaved, freed, impassioned, enlivened, soothed, drugged, delighted, distressed, entertained, sharpened in wits, ennobled in soul, winged in imagination, gratified in humour, stirred to pity, rage, love, rapture, enthusiasm, creation, zeal for learning, infinite zest, and curiosity for life? I do not know, nor anyone.

And, in the end, it wears down our eyes, never intended for this strange and crabbed use, so that we have to read through discs of magnifying glass. As to our health – 'the man whom about midnight, when others take their rest, thou seest come out of his study meagre-looking … squalid, and spauling, dost thou think that plodding on his books he doth seek how he shall become an honester man …? There is no such matter.'

No, indeed. Still, he has enjoyed his reading.

Shopping abroad

How strange it is, this passion that assaults the breast when the foot treads foreign earth; this lust to acquire, to carry away, to convey home in suitcases wretched pelting trifles which in our native land we should be the first (or so we hope) to disdain! With how fond pleasure have I purchased bronze models (green with *antichità*) of the Temple of Vesta in the shape of an inkpot, and of the extant fragments of the various structures that were reared, regardless of expense, to honour the triumphing monarchs and gods of Imperial Rome. With what delight have I bought in Taormina tiny painted mule-carts; in Palermo sections of a similar but larger cart, that would be of use, so one hoped, for a bed-head, for a wardrobe door, for a screen; in Naples coral charms against the evil eye and mother-of-pearl spoons; in Pisa the leaning tower in marble; in Athens the Erictheum in alabaster; (the seventh Lord Elgin, stirred by this passion on a grander scale, bore away, as we know, the Parthenon frieze); in Mexico painted pots, and walnut shells containing, preserved behind glass, tiny Mexicans; in New Mexico rugs and silver brooches made by Hopes; in Monterey huge abalone shells; in Florida twigs of worthless branch coral; in Spain fans illustrated with bull-fights; in Canada moccasins with fringes, and little canoes with Indians; in Quimper crockery; and I have known those who did worse than this in Brittany, and returned laden with giant oak dressers, cupboards and beds.

What is this foolish, this unconsidered mercery, this itch for having, this covetous desire for alien trifles, that mads the brain in foreign climes, emptying purse and bursting suitcases? What is it but that xenophilous lust that sent our great pirate traders a-merchandising to far coasts, plundering them for goods at which they would not have looked had they lain at their doors? Once across the seas, the bartering instinct wakes; we march into shops and markets, inquiring the prices of objects whose sole claim on our desires is their transmarinity; being informed, we exclaim 'Troppo, troppo', 'Trop cher', 'Demasiado', or 'Zu viel'; we make as if to walk out, but we are detained, met half way, the seller climbs down, we up, the bargain is clinched; we emerge happy, clasping in covetous hands this new and charming fragment of Abroad, which is to beautify, cheer and decorate our island life.

So Raleigh doubtless felt, a-homing from Guiana and Virginia with gold dust, tobacco, and potatoes in his hands; so Captain Smith, returning from Turkey with coffee beans; so Drake, sailing away from San Domingo, his fleet cargoed with the loot of that sacked city; so Warren Hastings retiring from Oude laden with the pearls of its Begums; so all British travellers preparing to re-cross to their island with pockets full of the bric-à-brac of foreign parts.

They will lie about our homes, bright and brittle intimations of past joy. This little coconut: when I caress its withered head, all the palm-fringed silver sands of the Florida Keys shimmer again before me. This gay and tiny cart, collecting dust on the chimney-piece, carries me along the hot white road from Palermo to Monreale. These walnut-dwelling Mexicans, with their bundles and their tall straw hats, take me to a lemon-grown plaza, warm and wan in pale dust beneath an orange moon, where mandolins eternally play and tiny *burros* trot patiently, bearing Mexican gentlemen larger than themselves. In this abalone shell sings the Pacific surf, beating on Fishermen's Pier and against the piles of Pop Ernest's Restaurant, where Spanish sailors lounge. To caress this bronze gondola is to see green water lapping against the rust-red brick walls of Renaissance palaces, to hear staccato cries, 'Sta-i', 'Premé!' while to touch this Vestal ink-pot is to stir all the dust of Imperial Rome.

The snag? Yes, you have guessed it, you who have also shopped abroad. Suitcases filled already to repletion, how should they distend themselves to absorb these alien o bjects? They will not; it cannot be done. More suitcases must be purchased; cheap, exotic suitcases; more, and more, and more …

Showing off

What is that you say you have done? Walked across Jamaica on your hands? That is nothing at all. Besides, it is probably not true. I once rode a dolphin across the Messina straits. And swam from Corsica to Sardinia. I ate seventy plums at one go, stones and all. I lived six days in a tree. I won a prize on the ocean for chalking a pig's head. I won a prize at school for the quarter mile. And for the high jump. I wrote out 'The Ride from Ghent to Aix' backwards. What did you say? You have a certificate of *what*? Signed by the Pope … And three children … Well, that was just a mistake, wasn't it; you should have told him … You gave ringworm to two archbishops? I really do not see that that is much to boast of. You converted Cherokee Indians when you were six? That is better. And had a tract written about you, called 'How Little — came to Jesus'. That is better still. But I have had my conversion prayed for by a Lama. No, not in Thibet; we met in Syracuse. Yes, I know Sicily well. I understand Sicilian more or less. And modern Greek. Yes, I know Greece. I didn't go there with one of those mass cruises; I went separately: I always think one sees it better that way. I know Greek literature pretty thoroughly. And Greek history, of course. I have done some verse translations of the Anthology that they tell me are not so bad. So bad as what? As most people's, of course. However that may be, I felt thoroughly at home in Greece. How long was I there? Well, I don't quite remember; certainly over a week. I had to get on to Constantinople after that. And then to Russia. I saw something of Stalin in Moscow; he wanted me to write something about my impressions, but the fact was I hadn't any, because I knew no Russian to speak of. You need to know a language really colloquially before you can begin to understand the people, I always say. The way I know Catalan, Mallorquin, and even Basque. Oh, yes, I know quite a lot of Basque words.

Well, where was I? Yes, after Moscow I visited Germany. I saw Goering and Goebbels; the Fuhrer would not see me; he had heard I was coming, and ordered Goering and Goebbels to send for me for an interview; they tried to trap me in conversation into saying something they could have arrested me for, but I wouldn't. Though I let them see my views all right. How they loathed me! They knew I was a writer of more influence in England than ... well, than most writers, I suppose I might say ... anyhow, they were scared to death. However, there was nothing they could get me on. I got safely over into France, and had a gay week in Paris; I know so many people there, I'm never at a loss. I had another proposal, too. Then I visited the place in Normandy my ancestors came from in 1066; they tell me one of the angels in the roof has my face, and that it must have been done from one of our family, in the thirteenth century. I must say, I always *feel* Norman, a kind of arrogant feeling, as if the English were under my heel. Not that ancestors matter: one makes one's own way. What do you say? Your ancestors were Saxon thegns? Well, some of mine were British druids. I always feel at home at Stonehenge. And I learnt to talk Welsh and Breton as easily as possible. And, of course, I could learn Erse and Gaelic too, if I cared to. But they don't seem very much use to-day, do they?

Well, I must go; I am going on to Buckingham Palace. No, quite a small party, I believe; no, the Garden Party is quite another thing; everyone is asked there. This one is for Ruth Draper; she is going to give a command performance, to a few special people. I don't know why *I* should be asked ... oh, you are going, too? How strange ...

Well, now they know what I am; now they, left behind in the house, are talking of me, saying it is not often one meets anyone at once so intelligent, cultured, travelled, handsome, modest, witty, and gay. I strut down the street, I get into my car, start the engine, trundle along Piccadilly. How well I drive! Traffic to right of me, traffic to left of me, volleys and thunders; I wriggle unscathed through the middle of it. I am thinking still of the lunch party I have left. I am trying to make sense of something someone seemed to be murmuring to someone else as the door shut behind me.

What was she saying? It sounded like 'Ho, ho! I am the Toad ...' But that does not seem to make sense, so it must have been something else ...

Solitude

What is this sensuous pleasure, this tide of starry peace, that flows around me like a Milky Way, making a heavenly music in mine ears? What is this space, this liberty, this balmy ease, that floods about me like a blue and buoyant sea, at once sustaining, stimulating and soothing? How rich, how sharply hued, how pregnant with meaning, does the universe appear, where but an hour since it was a wild and wandering globe lost in chaos and the chattering of voices. I am alone. I can look, listen, feel, apprehend, without muffling presences to bound imagination's flight, to maintain those human contacts which remind us always that we are gregarious creatures, running together in flocks. Good company is delightful bondage; to be alone is to be free. I may do what I choose, within the limits of capacity and means. So long as I keep myself unspotted from the world, there is none to stay or molest me or prevent me in my doings. I can, if I will, stand on my head, and none to comment, question, smile, or stare. The mountain nymph, sweet Liberty, trips hand in hand with me to the court of the reeling goddess with the zoneless waist and wandering eyes, there to tread that lordly pleasure house that none can share. Drony solitude; Dr Johnson's ill-meant adjective hums lovely in my ears, bringing to them the idle boom of bees among honeyed blooms, the sweetness of that happy garden state while Man there walked without a mate.

> But 'twas beyond a Mortal's share
> To wander solitary there ...

and has, alas, been increasedly beyond a mortal's share ever since, what with teeming humanity and minishing gardens.

Nevertheless, the two Paradises in one are still at times accessible. Aloneness can still be attained, by those who have the will to it. A perpetual and enforced state, it might cloy and irk; an occasional adventure, it might be wasted, unpractised, difficult; a frequent yet not immoderate indulgence, its drony beauty binds and snares, enspells and yet sets free; we come to it as prisoners for a space enlarged, as thirsty men to a tavern.

> If thou canst get but thither,
> There grows the flower of Peace,
> The Rose that cannot wither,
> Thy fortress, and thy ease.

Attired with stars we sit, or we can fly, or we can run, and joy shall overtake us as a flood.

But Dr Johnson said one day, 'Solitude is dangerous to reason, without being favourable to virtue. Remember' (continued he) 'that the solitary mortal is certainly luxurious, probably superstitious, and possibly mad'.

Well, there is no state without its drawbacks.

Sunday

All Sundays are not blue and hot and gay. In these latitudes few Sundays are blue and hot, though there is about Sunday a leisured gaiety that sets it, even when it is grey and cold, to what Milton called a dominical jig. Sunday strolls, sings, peals bells, dances, eats, drinks, sleeps, talks, in a care-free, slippered ease; it is different from Monday and the rest; it smiles like a holiday, it simpers like the spring; it is, as George Herbert observed, a day of mirth. Dr Johnson held that there should be relaxation, but no levity, that one may walk, but not throw stones at birds. In fact, there is both relaxation and levity; there is also love, for the parks, lanes, street corners, cinemas, and country places are thick enturbed with turtling couples who make the Cupid. Religion, too, much obtains; in churches there is singing, chanting, preaching, praying, and celebration of mysteries, in all the tongues in the world alive and dead, besides great ringing of bells. There is a hum of life, of pleasure, of leisure, of piety, of tranquillity.

For my part, when I say 'Sunday', I see a span of hours both blue and hot, a vault of sky without clouds, a floor of sea without waves and of white sand without shade. All Sundays, even in that place, were not blue and hot, but that is how I see them. No lessons; a day of pleasure, of bathing, wading, canoeing, reading, writing, taking out the goat, racing the rabbits, climbing trees and rocks, hearing the chanting of processions winding by. Gay stalls in the town, bells clanging, nets coming in, rounders on the shore in the evening, sitting in the ivy on the top of the *orto* wall. Time for everything; no lessons: that was, and always is, the point, the thing that sets Sunday apart. Even a grey Sunday, a wet Sunday, a cold English winter Sunday, when we can but stay indoors and read and eat and talk, is still a day of pleasure, since from our journal labours we do rest.

And yet, what assaults, what besiegements of misplaced pious intention, has the day of the sun, probably at all periods, endured! It would seem that there cannot be a day of pleasure and repose set up by man but some other men must seek to entrammel it in tedious bonds. We say, on one day in seven it is good to rest and make holiday and make our congee to the gods, laying aside diurnal toils. We say, put the spade and axe away, for we will do no work to-day. Then arise law-givers, priests, prophets, leaders, police, who enforce this gay intention, hedge it about with rigorous rule. Rightly, no doubt, since the heart of man is covetous and cruel, and there will beyond doubt enter into it the project of causing slaves and menials to perform those profitable labours for him from which himself he rests. Thus does his own native wickedness create tedious rules and fetters for sinful man. Then, since the lust to make rules, to embond and enshackle others, grows apace in the hearts of law-givers, they took this cheerful day, this septimanal jewel in the week's belt of toil, and set it about with prickles and with bars, minded to keep not only toil but mirth at bay. To this unavailing task Christendom early applied itself. Constantine forbade pleasurable spectacles in the circus, and all public celebrations and sports, except only that of the torture and execution of criminals. Charlemagne, that tremendous Sabbatarian, followed by emperors, kings, popes, and priests, sternly continued the losing battle against Sunday pleasures. The history of Sunday in all lands is the history of Pleasure, that indomitable goddess, assaulted, bound and fettered, even down to this day, but valorously slipping, now a shackle, now an imprisoning bar, negligently ignoring bondage and dancing and playing on the green, denounced by church and state, thundered at by minions of the law, kept at bay by parents (who shut up little Samuel

Johnson and made him read the *Whole Duty of Man* of a Sunday), menaced by papal decretals, by Genevan gowns, by Town Councils, by every tyrant in office, and yet breaking free, and yet enlarged, and yet on dominical pleasure bent, so that Sunday has ever been a glad day despite them all.

> For by th' Almighty this great Holy-day
> Was *not* ordain'd to dance, to mask and play,
> To slug in sloth, and languish in delights ...

Thus preceptors of all creeds and all lands have spoken down the ages. And Humanity has answered, not with defiance, but with that serene, intractable negligence that in the end defeats all law. Saying little about it, the majority have slugged in sloth and languished in delights each Sunday, thus recompensing themselves for the hard tedium of the week's travail.

And here it comes again, the sun's day, the Lord's day, merry and free and holy and bland. Hey! what comes here along, with bell-chiming and ringing? 'Tis Sunday a-coming... Hey! there again, how the bells they shake it! Come, come, ladies, come ladies out ...

Yes, that is all very well: but how am I to walk out, when my shoes that I forgot to fetch yesterday are still at the cobbler's, and the cobbler has shut his shop? And how shall I be happy staying in, when the book I meant to read is still in the library, and the library presents a shuttered face? Further, my wireless accumulator has run out, and I shall not hear Kreisler to-night, for those who keep accumulators have shut them behind locked doors and gone holidaying. I am frustrate, cribbed, and baulked, to make an English holiday.

Taking umbrage

Very good, then, very well; by all means attend to everyone else in the shop before me, though I was waiting here before any of them. There is such a thing as fair turns, as serving people in the order in which they come, but you do not seem to bother about that here. That old lady, that young man, both were after me, but you go up to each in turn, you say, 'What may I do for you?' and they, being deficient in sense of honour and fair play, both hasten to tell you, instead of saying, 'It is not yet my turn. You must serve that woman over there first'. Very good; I will make no movement to call attention to myself; I will stand here waiting, while you attend to these interlopers, and then to others who have pushed in even since they did. I suppose that in time someone will think of inquiring of me my pleasure, instead of hastening by with half questioning glances which I refuse to meet. I will not, even by a look, convey that I demand to be served; I coldly stand and wait: I have taken umbrage. I am wrapped in silence, an umbrageous mantle; I am shadowed about and umbraged with my pride; I have taken pet. I have joined the great company of the umbraged of all time. How they hover and shadow umbrageously around! Monarchs and subjects, priests, physicians, lovers, authors, actors, heroes, prophets, and gods, all cloaked in dudgeon, uttering high, cold words of proud offence, or else, wordless, wreaking deeds of vengeful ire. Kings, queens, emperors, outraged beyond mercy, exclaiming, 'Who will rid me of this traitor?' 'Little man, little man ...' 'Fling him to the fishes!' Offended gods and goddesses jealous of their honour and their rights; Apollo flaying upstart rival musical performers, Achelous the river god transforming into islands the naiads who omitted him from a party, Latona and her archer twins potting at the insolently excessive progeny of Niobe, Diana enstagging Actæon for his ill-judged bagniospection, Zeus and Hera each so unflaggingly alert for slights, so ingeniously efficient in avenging them, Jehovah, so easily provoked to wrath, so apt to turn his face from his Israelites, so quick to send them plagues. The umbrage of deities has been, very naturally, fruitful and well gratified, above that of others. But by no means contemptible has been that of authors, of actors, of prima donnas, and leading men; of John Milton, Alexander Pope, Lady Mary Montague, Dean Swift, Lord Byron, Samuel Coleridge, Andrew Marvell, Ben Jonson, and, for that matter, practically all who have lived by the pen. With what gusto have these beaten their pens into swords, envenomed them, and plunged them into the quivering breasts of rivals, calumniators, mockers, and reviewers. How their turbulent and impassioned phrases beat about me, darkening the air like eagles' wings! Could I but utter some of them, how those who pass me by in neglect would start and pale and fly to do my bidding. Then there are too the huge grievances of Parents, more particularly against daughters; the Capulets, Lear, Egeus, Squire Western, and the rest, all loud with Vexation, disappointment, and threats. 'Full of vexation come I, with complaints' … that has been the burden of parental life down the ages. A thousand umbrages wing and buzz about me like exultant wasps. Doctors, hearing that rivals have been called in, and refusing in their turn to come when implored. 'Certainly not: I hear that you have Dr Blank now …' Slighted lovers, slighting back, avenging neglect with cold pride. And, hovering and looming, a huge and purple cloud, the tremendous umbrage of Churchmen down the ages. A thunderous cloud, out of which come forth mighty claps and darting fires that play about the heads of heretics and disputants, striking upstart dogmatists to annihilation, sending empassioned eristics and direful fulminations over sea and land. The terrific voices of offended clergymen quiver and vibrate in the air about me. How they would strike these oblivious so-called salesmen to nothingness, could the salesmen but hear what I hear!

So, compassed about with so great a cloud of witnesses, luxuriantly umbraged, I stand and wait for the moment when one of these minions will turn to me at last with 'What may I do for you?' I shall not immediately tell them what they may do for me; I shall tell them first what they have already done to me; how they have kept me waiting long past my turn, kept me for ten full minutes out of my busy life; how this is the last visit I shall pay them; how, the next time that I require a new fountain pen, I shall seek it elsewhere; how no flourishing commerce can be built up on a foundation of injustice, on a system of breaking the law of Fair Turns; how I did, indeed, half an hour ago, wish to purchase a pen, but, during the hour that has elapsed since then, I have lost the desire, I no longer require a pen, or anything but a couch on which to repose after my two hours waiting; how, when my friends ask me where they shall buy pens, I shall reply, 'Anywhere but at Messrs Penley & Inkman's, for there they do not attend to you, but keep you waiting from three to six, and then they shut and you have to go away unserved'; how …

'What can I show you, madam?'

'Oh, is it you at last? Fountain pens, please. I have been waiting …'

'Certainly, madam. What make of pen do you require?'

They will never know, it seems, of my umbrage.

Talking about a new car

Yes, the time has come. The two low gears make a noise like the large cats at the Zoo at lunch-time, and even top is like the large cats purring *after* lunch, or like an aeroplane zooming just overhead. I must have a car which makes noises like small cats purring in their sleep, or, at worst, like an aeroplane a thousand feet up. Besides, the thing takes so long to pick up speed. And it groans. And drinks petrol like a fish. And it can't get up Primrose Hill on second now. And ... but what I mean to say is, it's eight years old, and has had its day, and I am looking about for another. Still, did you say? Yes, I always look about for another.

Do you like the Garnet ten-four? The Grasshopper, you know. It is roomy, accelerates from standing like an arrow from the bow, and climbs like a cat. Only sixty; but one seldom really wants to do more than that, I find. And thirty-five to the gallon, they say; I dare say actually thirty. The only question is, how well it holds the road. I must say, I incline to the Grasshopper. A green one, should you say? Or a red? Or beige? Of course black or navy is less *noticeable*. What I mean is, supposing a policeman saw a lot of cars all speeding, he might pick out the brightest coloured for an example. And a bright colour shows up more in the night, if it is left in the street without lights, or over time in a park. Black or navy melts into the night. But then beige melts into the day better, I suppose. And green into the parks, supposing one were doing rather over twenty there. Not red, I think; that does not seem to melt into anything. Into an accident, you say? Pray do not let us talk like that; I do not have accidents.

See, here is a Rapide 1933 – cost £350, and offered for eighty. Yet it is exactly like new, the advertisement says. Super-clean, absolutely indistinguishable from new. Mileage nominal. Then why, I wonder ... Oh, I see, it says why – owner giving up driving. I suppose he has had his licence suspended. Perhaps he is in prison. I wonder what the accident was, and how much the Rapide was damaged. They put them together again so strangely sometimes. Some friends of mine bought a car which had been in collision, and its back axle had been put in again upside down. I might go and look at the Rapide's inside. Outside, it sounds charming – splendid condition, red leather upholstery, long wheel base, everything de luxe, silent engine, super appearance. What a delightful car. One wonders why the owner so seldom used it, in two years – why, I mean, he only did a nominal number of miles. No, he does not say how many; the number is nominal, like other numbers, but he seems to have forgotten its name.

Then here is a Daimler which cost approximately £1,285 in 1932. Approximately. One would think one would remember spending such a sum as that. I suppose he put it out of his mind at once, not caring to dwell on it, and now has mislaid both the bill and his pass-book. Perhaps actually it did not cost quite so much. Anyhow it is in super condition, like the Rapide, and he will take £275, though there is absolutely no depreciation. A fluid fly-wheel, too; and fitted with smart owner-driver ... dear me, how odd. Well, anyhow one cannot buy a Daimler, of course, though one likes to toy with the idea.

Let us turn to the Austins and Morrises. The year really does not seem to matter, since they are all indistinguishable from brand new in every way. I wonder how many miles and years it does take to make a car distinguishable from brand new. How different they are from people! Here is an Austin Seven De Luxe Sun Saloon, 1931, for £10. Now I call that cheap. Oh, I see, it says 'down'. There would be a little more payment to follow ... Well, never mind, I do not want an Austin Seven, it is quite too small. What about the 1933 Morris Ten? I always say, you know where you are with a Morris. But wait, here is a Moonbeam 1928, deposit £3. Luxury riding, for small outlay. Looks like 1933 …

Well, really, it is all almost too confusing. Do you think perhaps I had better go on with the old car for the present? After all, when I have bought a new one, I shall not be able to talk about all the others so well, shall I? As it is, I seem to possess them all, which is delightful.

The only drawback is that I get given so many cards with the names of car salesmen on them, and these gentlemen are all so kind in taking me out for runs and writing to me that I hate the thought of disappointing any of them. Yet on the whole I think I had better disappoint them all, and go on as I am. After all, you know where you are with your old car.

Telling travellers' tales

Yes, I had a marvellous time. I went first to ... But I will get my picture postcards; I can explain it all better with them. No, indeed, no bother at all; no, really, I should like to – that is, if you would care to see them – or even if you would not. See, here they are. Yes, they *are* a great many; yes, everywhere I went I got some; they make a complete picture diary of the trip. Look, this is the Acropolis ... but that is too soon, they are in the wrong order; Marseille comes first; see, here is Marseille; I have six of Marseille. That one is the Rue Cannebière; and there we have the Château d'If. That is the old port, and ... dear me, this is Progreso, Yucatan, and must have got into the wrong set, for that was quite another trip. Yes, I must show you my Mexican postcards too; no, really, no trouble at all, I like it; but we'll do the Greek trip first. There is Marseille harbour, which we saw, of course, as we steamed away. Our next stop was Genoa; that one is the west porch of the Duomo; here is a close-up of one of the lions. This is the south aisle, and ... Oh, must you really? I'm so sorry. It is quite early still, and we've only got to Genoa. There is all Greece to come; we had the most marvellous adventures there. I must tell you all about it next time. Well, if you really must go ... It has been delightful to see you. I like to tell you about Abroad, for I know you understand. I remember all those postcards you showed me of Malta last year ... or was it Portugal? ... Yes; well, now it's my turn, is it not?

My turn. Yes, and I intend to take it. I hold them with my skinny hand, 'There was a ship', quoth I. The dinner guests they beat their breasts, yet cannot choose but hear. They listen like a three years' child; the mariner has his will. And that is really all the mariner can expect, in view of the strong travel-tale-resistance that flourishes in most modern human beings. It occurs to few travellers, as it occurred to Æneas, to be actually requested to describe their trip. Dido, with charming feminine and queenly courtesy, said to her just-arrived guest after supper, 'Now relate to us your wanderings from their first beginnings'; whereupon they all settled down to it, every tongue was still, every ear attentive, and Æneas, reposing upon his couch, began the tale of his long ramble, enabled by his hostess's courtesy to preface it by saying that it was the last subject he desired to dwell on, it being so sad and himself so sleepy, but that, since she longed to hear of it, he would oblige her. He was allowed to proceed uninterrupted with a travelogue which must have taken quite three hours. Odysseus took similar advantage of the kindly invitation of King Alcinous, on his visit to Scheria. Few of us meet with such good fortune; in fact, but for our picture postcards, we should find ourselves hard put to it to get any way at all without interruption, without the travels of other people breaking roughly in. The Wedding Guest was, one imagines, very young, and had not yet travelled himself, or one cannot but think that he would have put up a more efficient travel-tale-resistance than he did. Most returned travellers seek in vain their Desdemona, who shall seriously incline to hear of antres vast and deserts idle, and of the cannibals that each other eat, the Anthropophagi, and men whose heads do grow beneath their shoulders. These last peculiar people have usually had but a poor reception; practically all travellers have told of them, but the diffidence with which both the ancients, and such bold enlarging Elizabethans as Sir Walter Raleigh, put them forward (he wished he had brought one home with him, to put the matter out of doubt) seems to indicate that those reporting them were, except by the credulent Desdemona, found on the far side of the line which divides liars from mere bores. For one has to be on one's guard; one must not try one's audience too far. An air of elegant reticence is often advisable; a touch of Herodotean scepticism; and Raleigh's lofty, 'And if to speak of them were not tedious and vulgar ...' will sound the right note of sophisticated deprecation of our own adventures, and is a good preliminary to speaking of them just the same.

But it seems to have been always recognised that relating one's rambles viva voce is a somewhat chancy business; the wisest aunt telling the saddest tale is not always listened to; hence travellers have usually committed their trips to paper, knowing that the printed word breaks resistance down where the human voice does but strengthen it. Thus, it has always been the custom for returned travellers to write travel books, whether in the form of fictional narrative, or of true; and it is said that this form of literature is the greatest in bulk of any in the world. So, if you can prevail on none to give ear to your saga, or eye to your postcards and your photographs, take a pen and write your heart out, as did the lusty voyagers of all time. Join that great romantic company of enlarging travellers who have held it more commendable to publish unto the world what they have seen and done abroad than to permit it to fester perilously in their bosoms. Tell the world how the ice-bergs crashed around your bark, how fishes flew for you and whales spouted, how you spied a ruined city in a jungle and a phœnix in a date-tree, a gila monster up a barrel cactus, a chaparral cock fighting a rattlesnake in the mesquite, a golden eagle carrying a lamb, anthropophagi making a meal of a missionary; a unicorn with his head on a virgin's knee; and any other of the strange relations of authors that you think good. Do not fear to expand: you are in admirable company; the best company, many hold, in the world. It is a fine bold thing you have done, this going abroad, and you deserve that people shall hear about it. Telling them, you will relive your happy journeyings … Ah, me, how Delos, dropped from heaven, swung moorless on a violet sea …

Let me show you my postcards; indeed no, it is no trouble at all …

Turtles in Hyde Park

They lie close-locked, arms entwined, face on face, oblivious, loving, and dumb, strewn like chrysalises about the littered, burnt-up August sward. No speech passes; they bill, but do not coo; it is better so. John Donne has described their state.

> And whilst our souls negotiate there,
> We like sepulchral statues lay:
> All day the same our postures were,
> And we said nothing, all the day.

Another poet, a century later, mentions a young woman less wise than these:

> Sabina has a thousand charms
> To captivate my heart;
> Her lovely eyes are Cupid's arms,
> And every look a dart:
> But when the beauteous idiot speaks,
> She cures me of my pain;
> Her tongue the servile fetters breaks
> And frees her slave again.

> Had Nature to Sabina lent
> Beauty with reason crowned …

But Nature is seldom thus lavish, and Sabina and her swain are happier dumb. So dumb they lie, turtling it in the turtle-haunted parks, thick as autumnal leaves that strow the brooks in Vallombrosa, while the night dews gather on the grass, and the Park exhales the warm stale breath of the long summer's day, and policemen, simply and plainly clad, pace among their flock, their firm expressions saying, 'Thus far and no farther', and the keepers blow their whistles for time up. To bed, to bed, kind turtles now!

Delightful it is to see Cupid thus busy, to see lovers thus emparadised in this park of pleasure. But how we stumble over them as we walk! Impossible to help it, since there are so many billing pairs, so little space between each pair and the next. Not all our stumbling can break that subliminal peace in which they lie intranced; but, through the pillowing clouds of love on which they rest, does some faint jar from the lower world ever so faintly shake them, as one passer-by after another trips over them, kicking their entwined forms? Love gives courage; love gives oblivion; they do not appear to notice. It is we who trip and fall.

Yes, sweet turtles, to bed! It is really time you removed yourselves out of our way.

Walking

What is there in this so primitive, so outmoded motion of legs and body that gives so fine a lusty pleasure to some of those who practise it? One leg before the other, feet planted swiftly on the ground in turn, lifted, planted again, carrying the whole person, slowly, indeed, (as traffic travels to-day) but surely, (until intelligence revolts and the motion ceases) along: wherein lies the charm of this animal pastime? I suppose in the fact that we are, in fact, animals, and the mere exercise of the body pleases. 'The race of wild pedestrian animals,' says Timæus, 'came from those who had no philosophy in any of their thoughts, and never considered at all about the nature of the heavens, because they had ceased to use the courses of the head, and followed the guidance of those parts of the soul which surround the breast.' Very true; and so we stride along, walking vegetables, one with the earth we traverse, empty of thought, lazily gluttonous of eye and ear and nose, scrambling up hill, pushing through holt and hanger, emerging on to thorn-grown, wind-swept, close-cropped down, below which spreads a far, hazy glitter of sea, plunging down the hill's steep shoulder into green bottoms where cressy brooks wind, following ancient footpaths where they run on ancient maps, paths sometimes long lost and forgotten, leading over broken stiles and blocked hedge-gaps, across foot-bridges long vanished, over fields long ploughed, through copses and thickets which have run riot and made impenetrable with their jungly growth what was once the way through the woods. The path broadens; it becomes for a space a deep dark lane, alder- and hazel-hidden, sunk in mud. It is called on the map, for half a mile, Cockshut Lane. It comes to Standfast Barn, plunges through a gap into Cuckoo

Copse, becomes again a footpath, tilts up across two steep fields towards the beech-hangered ridge of Farewell Hill. And so on and along, and it will lead you round by the Oak-hangers to Cheesecombe Farm, and home by the moors.

What is there to it? You walk, you look, you hear, you smell; life arranges itself easily into a sensuous dream, a feast of sound, sight, scent, and always that light, swinging motion carrying you along, without effort, without thought. So doubtless, do the other animals feel, padding the earth, with their soft, quick feet, nose to ground, ears pricked, eyes bright. Yet they have an effect of following something; they seem ever on the chase, questing and nosing after some dream they have. Here I have the advantage of them; I follow nothing, beyond sometimes a path. I walk for walking's sake; do they also engage in this pastime, that some consider so odd? In America, I am told, it is not practised; if you walk, it is because you have no means to drive or ride.

Some walkers, such as Socrates, seem to walk only to talk, or to think about something, and even so they prefer to stroll about cities. Socrates enjoyed the green bank of Ilissus when he was taken there, since it offered a charming spot wherein to rest and bathe his feet while he was read to; but (said Phædrus to him), when you are in the country you are like a stranger being led about by a guide. I think you never venture even outside the gates. Very true, my good friend (said Socrates), and I hope you will excuse me when you hear the reason, which is that I am a lover of knowledge, and the men who dwell in the city are my teachers, and not the trees or the country. But (added he), you have found a spell with which to draw me into the country, as hungry cows are led by waving before them a bough or a fruit. For only hold up in like manner a book before me, and you may lead me all round Attica and over the wide world. And now, having arrived, I intend to lie down, and do you choose any posture in which you can read best. Begin.

A hopeless walker, you see; the kind of walker who would read a book as he walked, or argue about the absolute, or want to sit down and rest after a hundred yards; a walker only suited to pacing meditatively about cloister or peristyle, or strolling about the agora, hailing friends and hearing news. Walking for pleasure should not be an intelligent, discursive, gossiping or bookish pastime; it should be solitary and dumb, placid and vacant of mind, an unimpeded, undistracted error over earth's face, leg after leg, corporeal frame and urgent soul to timeless motion set.

So on we go and on, in delicious rhythm, until we tire. And the worst of that is that, when we tire, we are so many miles from home, and have to walk as many again to reach it, so that by the time we arrive there, we are fatigued indeed. A little forethought, you say, will prevent this? Very true; but walkers are not intelligent, and do not think ahead; they walk themselves weary, and develop all manner of ailments in the process. A good walk, you say, is worth them all? Again, very true.

Writing

Of all the animals, man appears to be the only one who enjoys this peculiar pleasure of writing. This is unfortunate, as it would be interesting to read the written works of the dog, the cat, the fox, the hog, the hippopotamus, and others, did they commit any. Besides, it would keep them quiet. Or would it not? Now that I come to think of it, I do not know that the human beings who write most are the quietest. Still, for the time being, the occupation of writing does prevent those engaged on it from making much noise, beyond that emitted by the typewriter or the pen. Parents find this, and all intelligent parents instruct their children early in the art, provide them with pencils and paper, and leave them to it. I myself was early thus instructed and, though I am told that for some time my only form of literary activity was to write in block capitals on every available space the boast 'I CAN WRITE', still, this I assiduously did. Step by step, I graduated to higher forms of the art; very early I collaborated in the fictional efforts of my elder sister, and a little later commenced poet. By the age of seven, I was a confirmed addict. Ever since, the pile of my written works has grown and grown; it has always been to me, if a rather shame-making, yet an insidious amusement.

Wherein lies its charm? Mainly, I believe, in arranging words in patterns, as if they were bricks, or flowers, or lumps of paint. That is, to me. Heaven never, I think, destined me for a story-teller, and stories are the form of literary activity which give me the least pleasure. I am one of the world's least efficient novelists; I cannot invent good stories, or care what becomes of the people of whom I write. I have heard novelists complain that their characters run away with their books and do what they like with them. This must be somewhat disconcerting, like driving an omnibus whose steering-wheel, accelerator, and brake are liable to be seized by the passengers. My passengers know their places, and that they are there to afford me the art and pleasure of driving. Are there not, for that matter, already enough people in the world, without these beings intruded from my imagination? Shall they puff themselves up because they are allowed on paper? I have heard of novelists who say that, while they are creating a novel, the people in it are ever with them, accompanying them on walks, for all I know on drives (though this must be distracting in traffic), to the bath, to bed itself. This must be a terrible experience; rather than allow the people in my novels to worry me like that, I should give up writing novels altogether. No; my people are retiring, elusive, and apt not to come even when I require them. I do not blame them. They no doubt wish that they were the slaves of a more ardent novelist, who would permit them to live with her. To be regarded as of less importance than the etymology and development of the meanest word in the dictionary, must be galling.

And so we come to words, those precious gems of queer shapes and gay colours, sharp angles and soft contours, shades of meaning laid one over the other down history, so that for those far back one must delve among the lost and lovely litter that strews the centuries. Such delving has rewards as rich, as stirring to the word-haunted fancy, as the delving into the deeps of human motive and emotion has to the novelist of psychology, or the weaving of intricate plot and counterplot to the story-teller, or the laying down of subtle clues to the detective problemist. Words, living and ghostly, the quick and the dead, crowd and jostle the otherwise too empty corridors of my mind, to the exclusion, doubtless, of much else that should be there. How charmingly they flit before me, heavy laden with their honey like bees, yet light on the wing; slipping shadowy out from dusty corners, hiding once more, eluding my reach, pirouetting in the air above me, now too light, too quick, to be caught in my net, now floating down, like feathers, like snowflakes, to my hands. They arrange themselves in the most elegant odd patterns; they sound the strangest sweet euphonious notes; they flute and sing and taber, and disappear, like apparitions, with a curious perfume and a most melodious twang. Or they abide my question; they offer their pedigrees for my inspection; I trace back their ancestry, noting their diverse uses, modes, offspring, kin, transformations, transplantations, somersaults, spellings, dignities, degradations, lines, and phrases which have enambered them for ever, phrases and lines which they have themselves immortally enkindled. To move among this bright, strange, often fabulous herd of beings, to summon them at my will, to fasten them on to paper like flies, that they may decorate it, this is the pleasure of writing. England, the pirate, has ransacked the countries of Europe for her speech: Greece, Rome, France, Germany, Scandinavia, have poured in tribute to her treasury, which shines and jingles with the most confused rich coinage in the world. To play with these mixed coins, to arrange them in juxtaposition, to entertain oneself with curious tropes, with meiosis, litotes, hyperbole, pleonasms, pedanticisms, to measure the words fitly to the thought, to be by turns bombastic, magniloquent, terse, flamboyant, minishing, to use Latinisms, Gallicisms, Hellenisms, Saxonisms, every ism in turn, to scatter our native riches like a spendthrift tossing gold – this is the pleasure of writing. It is this, rather than concern with relating of human beings, which can hold me thralled through a night, until, in the long street outside my high windows, the pale morning creeps, and the scavengers arrive with little carts to remove the last day's dust. It is dalliance with this pleasure that I promise myself when I think of work; it is, alas, dalliance with it that too often abets me in my day-long and easily accomplished business of keeping work at arm's length. For to hunt language, to swim lazily in those enchanted seas, peering at 'whatsoever time, or the heedless hand of blind chance, hath drawn from of old to this present in her huge drag-net, whether fish or seaweed, shells or shrubs, unpicked, unchosen', may well fill a day with such pleasure that to put pen to paper in the way of business, of getting on with some task in hand, seems too rude an interruption. Rather let me set down lines of verse, phrases of prose, experiments in rhythm and sound, images and pleasing devices, as they come into my mind, without relation to any larger work to be accomplished. Let me be an amateur of verse and prose, dealing in fragments only.

But here is a trouble and a hindrance, that has ever impeded and hampered the dilettante in his enjoyments: one believes that one has to live, and to live one must try to earn. And who will buy these fragments, unstrung, unset, without context or co-ordinated form? Who will buy the fish or seaweed, shells or shrubs, caught in my drag-net, scattered loosely like the twigs of white coral and the oyster shells with which Italian fisher lads pursue the foreigner, crying *Frutto del mare*? No one (heaven forgive readers and heaven help writers) desires such loose jetsam. They desire books. And, oh, God of literature and of achieved tasks, how incompetent do I feel adequately to produce these!

Notes on the Text

BY KATE MACDONALD, with assistance from Emer O'Hanlon, Maria Vassilopoulos and Sharon Craig.

Cowper, *The Task*: a poem in six books written in blank verse by William Cowper, published in 1785. It was the result of a challenge to Cowper by a new friend, Lady Austen, who, when asked for a subject for the new poem she had requested, said 'Oh, you can write upon anything. Write on this sofa.' The first book is called 'The Sofa', which would surely have appealed to Macaulay. In the poem Pleasure is the antithesis to Domestic Happiness.

Chapman, *The Blind Beggar of Alexandria*: an Elizabethan stage comedy first performed in 1596, heavily reliant on disguises and changes of identity.

FRATRIBUS SORORIBUSQUE: Latin, brothers and sisters. Macaulay was the second child in a family of two boys and five girls, although one sister died as a young child.

Foreword

as I recently did: Macaulay's previous book was her anthology of extracts and quotations *The Minor Pleasures of Life* (1934).

Had I but world enough and time: from Andrew Marvell's 'To His Coy Mistress' (1681), which aligns Macaulay's enjoyment of reading about pleasure with the lover's pleasure in 'reading' his mistress's body.

Clive: Major-General Robert Clive, 'Clive of India', in a speech to the Select Committee on the East India Committee, remarked that after the East India Company's military victory at Plassey, Bengal, in 1757, 'an opulent city lay at my mercy, its richest bankers bid against each other for my smiles; I walked through vaults which were thrown open to me alone, piled on either hand with gold and jewels! Mr Chairman, at this moment I stand astonished at my own moderation!' (1772).

Abroad

Thomas Coryat: English courtier, clown and travel writer of the early seventeenth century. His memoirs were published as *Coryat's Crudities* (1611).

Thomas Cook: the first populariser of modern tourism and package holidays.

boat train: the train service from London to Channel ports was scheduled to make connections with Atlantic liners or boats to France, with ticketing through to most Continental and North American destinations.

Grand Tour: the ritualised extended journey to continental Europe made by young gentlemen of means in the eighteenth and nineteenth centuries, which lasted several months and was intended to 'finish' the young man in the ways of the world, and return him polished and ready to take his place in society.

cered: to wrap in wax or waxed cloth, referring to Ulysses stopping his ears with wax to avoid being driven mad by the Sirens' song.

packet: the passenger boat crossing the English Channel.

setting of beans: planting beans, that is, quietly cultivating their garden at home.

St Grison: Macaulay seems to have invented this saint. The canton of Grisons in Switzerland lies as far from the sea as it is possible to be in Europe.

sepulture: burial, or the place where the body is placed after death.

a fig for the waves: I give or care nothing for the waves.

Par ici pour la douane: French, Here for the customs officer.

chalk them: after the contents of travellers' baggage had been passed by the customs officers, the cases were chalked.

Allons, allons, facteur: French, literally 'go on, postman!' Macaulay is making a joke at the expense of the narrative voice, who, like many British travellers abroad, has muddled their vocabulary, here using the word for 'postman' (facteur), in place of 'conducteur' or 'porteur' for porter.

deuxième classe, s'il vous plait: French, second-class [carriage], please.

Mettez mes bagages: French, put my luggage.

Je suis bien entourée, n'est-ce-pas: French, I'm surrounded nicely, aren't I?

Vite, vite, facteur: French, quickly, quickly, postman (conductor).

Je me plaindrai au consul anglaise: French, I will complain to the English consul.

Allons, allons, mes braves compagnons: French, Onward, my brave companions.

Αθήναςε! Ολυμπίαςε!: the older form of Greek for στην Αθήνα! (To Athens!) and το Ολυμπία! (To Olympia!).

Αθήναι είσι καλαί: Greek, Athens is beautiful; Macaulay's translation of 'Athens are beautiful' is a joke pluralising Athens as if it were an English noun.

who do not comprehend their own ancient tongue when we speak it to them: a Macaulay joke at the expense of foreigners who assume that the ancient Greek they learned at school is the same as modern Greek.

Vale of Tempe: a gorge in northern Greece south of Mount Olympus, between Thessaly and Macedonia.

Pompeii: a town of the Roman Empire that was smothered in ash by the eruption of Vesuvius in 79CE, and which became a tourist destination from the early nineteenth century.

Rome, Florence, Siena, Umbria, Venice, the lakes: important Italian tourist sites.

Ligurian sea shore: the coastline west of Genoa towards the French border, where Macaulay lived for many years of her childhood. Until the 1930s it was extremely popular with British visitors and residents.

Buon giorno, signorina, sta bene oggi? Benissimo, grazie, signore; mi bagnerò nel mare, dopo di prendere il caffé: Italian, Good morning madam, how are you today? Very well, thank you sir; I will bathe in the sea after having coffee.

bianchetti: whitebait, young sardines and anchovies caught early in the year.

curling papers: the traditional way of curling hair was to roll and pin damp hair in strips of paper to dry.

futbal: Spanish, football.

comida con vino incluso: Spanish, a meal with wine included.

'You Sardinian, you Bavarian': Macaulay quotes extensively here from Walt Whitman's poem 'Salut au Monde', published in his *Leaves of Grass* (1855).

Apra la sua valigia!: Italian, Open your suitcase!

Sin duda quejaré al consul ingles: Spanish, I will certainly complain to the English consul.

Album

mondaine: French, of the world, in society.

Du Maurier children: the artist and author George du Maurier was famous for his drawings in *Punch* in the later nineteenth century, featuring instantly recognisable children wearing sailor suits, with heavy fringes and suspicious expressions.

fashionable school in Dorset: Macaulay may be inventing a school derived from a mixture of Bedales (founded 1893, in Hampshire), Summerhill (founded 1921, in Suffolk), or Dartington Hall School (founded 1926, in Devon), all of which place importance on the student's choice of how and what to study from a varied curriculum.

Tractarian: a mid-nineteenth century movement within the Anglican Church which wished to assert the primacy of Catholic doctrine in the church.

Eastward Position: when the priest saying Mass stands on the west side of the altar and faces east, a practice introduced into the Roman church in the eighth century. It became a contentious subject.

one of those who rode back: that is, he survived the Charge of the Light Brigade during the Battle of Balaclava in 1855, in which 118 men died.

chatelaine: a hanging pocket for the lady of the house to keep the keys for the sugar and the tea, and other valuable household stores.

habit: a woman's dress made for riding side-saddle which had bloomers or trousers underneath for modesty.

bend: the bustle was a small cage worn under the skirt at the back, over which the skirt was draped to create a new profile for women in which their bust and bottom protruded in opposite directions, creating the 'swan bend', supposedly like a swan's neck.

Newnham: women's college of Cambridge University, founded in 1871.

There was some story: this is a private joke, because Macaulay had been having an affair with a married man since around 1920, and almost nobody would know about it until after her death in 1956.

Arm-chair

I love it: from 'The Old Arm-Chair', a poem by Eliza Cook, first published in 1838.

Pay-Way system: paying for an item in instalments.

in chronic use: in use all the time.

twiring: an archaic term, meaning either to look intently at something, or to merely glance at it.

sedilian: a word that Macaulay seems to have invented, from Latin sedile, a chair; also from sedilia, one of the three chairs in the sanctuary used by the celebrant and other ministers during High Mass.

***tranquillo animo*:** Italian, with a calm mind.

the innocent toils which you cultivate: from diarist John Evelyn's *Kalendarium Hortense*, or, *The Gardner's Almanac*, dedicated to poet Abraham Cowley in 1666.

***cacher sa vie*:** French, literally, to hide his life; here, to preserve or conserve good living.

Steele: Sir Richard Steele, seventeenth-century Irish writer and co-founder of *The Spectator*. This and later quotations in this essay are from his diatribe on spleen published in the *Guardian* on 1 August 1713.

Queen's Hall: Macaulay describes listening to a concert broadcast from Queen's Hall, London.

long enough: Macaulay was a notably tall woman.

Astronomy

The sand is cool: Macaulay recalls here an event from her childhood in Italy.

lackeyed: attended by servants, or lackeys, which are its satellites.

proprio come il Signor Iddio, che sa tutto, tutto: Italian, just like the Lord God, who knows everything, everything.

siderial: sidereal, relating to or connected with the stars.

I will believe of the stars all you would have me: from Bernard le Bovier de Fontenelle's *Conversations on the Plurality of Worlds* (1686), in which a philosopher and a marquise walk in gardens by night, discussing the stars.

The Story of the Heavens: an immensely popular work of introductory planetary science for the general reader, by Sir Robert Stawell Ball, an Irish astronomer, published in 1886.

Hesperus: from Ben Jonson's 'Ode to Cynthia', 1599.

Mutianus: sixteenth-century German humanist.

Bakery in the Night

ichthyophagi: derived from Greek, persons who eat principally fish.

manna: the food that was provided from heaven for the Israelites in the wilderness, see Exodus 16.31.

ambrosia: from Classical myth, the food of the gods.

Lucullus: first-century Roman general and consul, famous for his luxurious feasts.

Bathing

1 Off the Florida Keys

enisle: to create islands in.

cœlenterate: a type of coral that is related to the jellyfish in having a bag-like body, stinging tentacles and a single mouth.

Rise, rise, and heave thy rosie head: from 'Sabrina Fair' in John Milton's masque *Comus* (1634).

2 Off the Ligurian Coast

putti: winged cherubs used decoratively in Renaissance paintings and sculpture.

bagnanti: Italian, bathers.

3 In the Cam

may-bushes: white blossoms of hawthorn which blooms in May.

the gold and white chalices: water-lilies.

chestnuts light their candles: the flowers of horse-chestnut trees look like cream and pink candles.

but suddenly there sprung: from 'Ringdale and the Granta' in Michael Drayton's *Polyolbion* (1622).

cantiferous: an invented word, their dominant quality is their singing.

Bed

1 Getting Into It

Thou shalt lie in a bed: from Act Scene 2 of John Webster's play *The White Devil* (1612).

And to your more bewitching: from Robert Herrick's poem 'A Nuptiall-Song' (1648, in his *Hesperides*).

a good deed in a naughty world: from Act 5 scene I in Shakespeare's *The Merchant of Venice* (1596).

somnifacient: conducive to sleep.

oneiric: deriving from dreams.

unentomologous: an invented word, meaning to be without insects.

transaudient: admitting all sound.

somniloquent: someone able to sleep easily.

eoan: of or relating to the dawn.

2 Not getting out of it

Go to the ant, thou sluggard: from Proverbs 6.6.

exsuscitation: the action of rousing or stirring up.

entomological: of or pertaining to insects.

gentlier lie than tired eyelids upon tired eyes: from Tennyson's 'Song of the Lotos-Eaters' (1832).

somniatory: pertaining to dreams or dreaming.

matutinal: occurring in or during the morning.

formicarian: of or relating to ants.

Thou shalt have thy Caudles: The first verse in the second part of a seventeenth-century English ballad, 'A Country new Jigge betweene Simon and Susan, to be sung in merry / pastime by Bachelors and Maydes', from the collection made by Samuel Pepys, now held at Magdalene College, University of Cambridge (EBBA 20129).

Æneas: see Acts 9.32–33.

tenebrizing: passing one's time in darkness.

journal: used in this sense to mean a daily event.

philoclinic: another invented word, meaning the love of the bedside.

Believing

Slow *Boötes* underneath him sees: from Joshua Sylvester's 1608 translation of *Du Bartas his divine weekes and works*, on the transformation of barnacles into barnacle geese.

Athanasian Trinity: the creed which states that God, Christ and the Holy Spirit are equal, a point of importance for Anglicans.

French angels: in the first weeks of the First World War, after the Battle of Mons in southern Belgium, a legend emerged that angels helped the British Army from defeat by the invading German forces. Arthur Machen's story, 'The Phantom Bowmen', published on 29 September 1914, elaborated the myth with bowmen from Agincourt, and the story propagated the legend due to the enthusiastic adoption of the story as fact by many readers, despite his denials.

Ulster angels: one of Macaulay's more obscure references, this may be connected to the 1689 Siege of Derry.

Thomist angels: Thomas Aquinas helped to popularise the scholarly debate of how many angels could dance on the head of a pin.

sirloins: a joke on the 'sir' in the name of this steak, which derives from French, *surlogne*.

Diogenes: this Classical Greek philosopher slept in a large pottery jar in the Athens marketplace, making a virtue of his self-imposed poverty.

St Simon Stylites: this fourth-century Syrian ascetic lived on a small platform on a pillar near Aleppo for 37 years.

gull: both verb and noun, to be and to fool a foolish believer.

teratologize: to collect stories about marvels or fantastic beasts.

aniles: of or like feeble old women. See also 148.

tenebrios: those who prowl at night.

lucence: radiance.

And there is nothing left remarkable: from Shakespeare's *Antony and Cleopatra*, Act 4, scene 15 (1607).

'misse-stories, hisse-stories' to 'forbidden fruit': from Samuel Purchas' *Hakluytus Posthumus or, Purchas his Pilgrimes* (1625), a collection of travellers' tales including material from papers left by Richard Hakluyt after his death.

Bird in the box

Herodotus: famed Classical historian who prefaced many of the more extravagant anecdotes in his Histories with this disclaimer.

he breathes ... on earth: a quotation from Izaak Walton's *The Compleat Angler* (1653), although Walton considered that the nightingale was female, rather than male.

Book auctions

emulous: closely resembling.

flirt: a darting wave or indication.

agonists: those who compete to win.

agonarch: the presiding overseer of the events.

beclumpsed: to make numb.

My nerves are all chain'd up in Alablaster: from John Milton's masque *Comus* (1634).

guinea: one pound one shilling, ie twenty-one shillings.

Two pounds: forty shillings, quite a jump up from the thirty shillings the auctioneer had last been bid.

Booksellers' catalogues

Vergil (Polydore): sixteenth-century Italian author of the *Anglica Historia*, an influential early history of England.

In the Black Letter: a heavy black typeface already old in the mid-seventeenth century.

woodcuts: early form of printed illustration, in which the design is carved into wood plates, and then inked.

Decapla in Psalmos: a multilingual commentary on the Psalms by John Viccars (1639).

Insectorum sive minimorum animalium theatrum: The *Theatre of Insects* (1634) was the first book about insects published in Britain, edited and collated by Thomas Moffet (also Moufet and Muffet), a physician and natural philosopher.

The Silkewormes, and their flies: two volumes in verse about silkworms, also by Thomas Moffet (1599).

French physician: Moffet was English.

Bishop of Chester: John Wilkins was Bishop of Chester from 1668 until his death in 1672. He was a polymath and one of the founders of the Royal Society, the first organised association of British scientists.

stood up for the Church: taken from 'The Life of the Author' prefacing Wilkins' collected works *The Mathematical and Philosophical Works Of the Right Reverend John Wilkins, Late Lord Bishop of Chester* (1708), which includes *The Discovery of a New World in the Moon*, his speculations on the Earth's relationship to the planets and the moon, and *Mathematicall Magick*.

John Maplet's *Greene Forest*: an alphabetical list of animals (natural and fantastical), plants, stones, metals, and natural phenomena, compiled when Maplet was studying at Cambridge, published in 1567.

***Sacred Theory of the Earth*:** Thomas Burnet's speculative cosmogony, in which he explains the earth as a sphere containing the water later deployed in Noah's Flood (1681–90).

Yonge: Charlotte M Yonge's most famous work was her Romantic novel *The Heir of Redclyffe* (1853).

protophilism, protomania: neither word exists, but Macaulay was presumably trying for a word to mean a passion for firstness.

Ezra Pound … *The Way of an Eagle*: this appears to be an anti-Modernist joke, placing first editions of High Modernist authors Pound and Lawrence at the same price as the hugely popular and very much not highbrow Jerome K Jerome (probably *Three Men in A Boat*) and massively successful romance novelist Ethel M Dell's *The Way of an Eagle*.

Bulls

Bashan: from Psalm 22, meaning a lawgiver and spiritual authority rather than a lively animal.

Did he that made the lamb make him?: paraphrasing from William Blake's 'The Tyger' (1794).

That lordly Bull of mine: from Robert Southey's 'Brough Bells' (nineteenth century).

Candlemas

Candlemas: 2 February, the day in the Christian calendar on which the church candles are blessed.

parroco: Italian, parish priest.

***bonne bouche*:** French, delicious mouthful.

Canoeing

bark: archaic term for a boat.

Tethys: the Greek goddess of the sea.

out of compass: cannot be known or encompassed.

Cook, Columbus, Cabot, Magellan, Raleigh, Drake: celebrated Western European navigators and commanders of ships from the fifteenth to the eighteenth centuries, who 'discovered' lands and sea routes not previously known to white people.

Jack, Ralph and Peterkin: boy heroes of R M Ballantyne's novel *The Coral Island* (1857).

fraught with: archaic, to be freighted with, to carry a cargo.

chanties: obsolete spelling for 'shanties' a rollicking song of the sea and sailors.

main: shortened archaic term for the main sea, the open sea.

the peculiar joys of Italy: from the *Diary* of John Evelyn, 11 October 1644.

home from the sea: adaptation of 'Home is the sailor, home from sea' from Robert Louis Stevenson's 'Requiem' (1879).

angelus: a pattern of three sets of three strokes rung on a church or convent bell at morning, noon and sunset to indicate the time for the angelus devotions to be recited.

plain: obsolete term for making a grievous complaint.

Chasing fireflies

orto: Italian, a vegetable garden.

Dr Browne of Norwich: Sir Thomas Browne, polymath and also a medical doctor who practised in Norwich from 1637 to 1682.

lucent: shining, bright or luminous.

empatining: Macaulay has invented this word from patinate, to cover with another texture to alter the colour.

St John's Eve: 23 June, the day before the feast day of St John the Baptist.

Christmas morning

Venite, venite, il Signore v'aspetta, levatevi pronto, pronto, e fatte il dovere: Italian for Come, come, the Lord is waiting for you, get up ready, ready, and do your duty.

Full little thought they than: from John Milton's 'On the Morning of Christ's Nativity, Compos'd 1629'.

Church-going

1 Anglican

Audite hæc, omnes: from Psalm 49, by Thomas Walmsley.

richly dight: archaic, to be richly appointed.

quire: archaic, choir.

For he shall carry nothing away ... perish: also from Psalm 49.

rubrics: notes as to how a church service should be conducted, traditionally printed in red at the side of the devotional text.

the Magnificat: the text of Luke 1:46–55 sung as a hymn at an evening service of the Anglican Church.

the oppressions: from John Milton's *Considerations touching the likeliest means to remove hirelings out of the church, wherein is also discoursed of tithes, church-fees, church revenues, and whether any maintenance of ministers can be settled by law* (1659).

the Ceremonies of Liber Pater: from Sir John Suckling's *An Account of Religion by Reason* (1646).

lectisternia: another invented word, probably meaning that which was read aloud from a lectern to the public.

2 Roman Catholic

dark and dumb ceremonies: from the Anglican *Book of Common Prayer,* in the section 'Concerning Ceremonies, why some be abolished and some retained'.

dog-Latin: a debased or uneducated form of Latin.

censer: the miniature metal brazier in which incense is burned for church ceremonies, swung from a chain to spread its scent throughout the building.

stoups: carved basins in the walls or special bowls, containing holy water in which the congregation dip their fingers to cross themselves.

Per l'onore di Dio, e per l'igiene, si pregono di non sputare: Italian, For the honour of God and for hygiene, do not spit.

beads: their rosary beads, an aid to repeating prayers.

orisons: archaic term for prayers.

Ave Maria ... nostra morte: Italian, Hail Mary, full of grace, a penny, lady, for the love of God. Holy Mary, Mother of God, pray for us sinners, now and in the hour of our death. The woman automatically addresses a beggar's plea to Mrs Macaulay while she recites this popular Catholic prayer.

a black savage, an Australian aborigine: Macaulay is reaching for the figures most far removed from the baroque complexities of the Italian Catholic church she knew in her childhood, to suggest the universality in how gods are addressed.

hagiary: an invented collective noun for the models of saints in a church, combining 'aviary' and the prefix for saints.

peregrinating: in formal procession.

agoral: an invented word, suggesting the quality of an agora, the public space for people to gather in.

pomps and gauds: a splendid display with plenty of visual excitement and drama.

sputato: Italian, spat upon.

vestured: wearing the ceremonial clothes of their calling.

genuflect: to make the formal bow or obeisance before the altar, also making the sign of cross against the chest.

drogheria: the grocer's shop.

miniations: an invented word, from minatory, to utter a threat, so probably intended to mean threatenings.

cosmography: the mapping of the universe and the heavenly bodies.

Credo in unum … invisibilium: the Creed, I believe in one God, the Father, the Almighty, maker of heaven and of all things visible and invisible on earth, recited in Roman Catholic and Anglican churches at the end of the service.

3 Quaker

meeting for worship: Quakers in the British tradition have no programmed service but meet for worship in stillness, with occasional ministry from those present as led by the Spirit.

Pelagius: a fifth-century theologian who advocated free will, and was objected to for thus denying the need for divine intervention.

Charles Dickens: his novels quite often feature angelic children dying young and in purity or innocence.

When the Friends: when Quakers emerged from seventeenth-century nonconformist turmoil to separate from the Established Church of England, they were persecuted for their transgressive views about equality in the sight of the Lord, in all aspects of life.

in this very house: Macaulay occasionally attended Meeting at Jordans in Buckinghamshire, one of the oldest Quaker settlements and Meeting House.

conventicling: going to a meeting for illicit or clandestine worship in the seventeenth century.

4 Unitarian

Unitarian: a nonconformist church which rejects the Trinity of the Father, Son and Holy Spirit of the Christian church, and maintains that God was a single individual.

deal: pine wood, often used for cheap furniture.

Athanasian creed: the formal statement of faith in a Trinitarian God.

Triune Mystery: the essential belief that God consists of three equal parts or entities.

Ecclesia Anglicana: the Church of England.

the barren fig-tree: from Luke 13: 6–9.

Arians: a Christian sect that emerged in Egypt in the fourth century, holding that Jesus Christ was separate from and subordinate to God the Father.

Photinians: a fourth-century Christian bishop from present-day Serbia, whose followers believed that Jesus Christ was a man and not divine.

Macedonians: also known as the Pneumatomachi, this late fourth-century sect based near the Hellespont in present-day Turkey rejected the divinity of the Holy Ghost.

Sabellians: followers of a third-century priest who believed that the Father, Son and Holy Ghost were aspects of a single god, rather than three distinct persons.

Socinians: also anti-Trinitiarians, rejecting the existence of Christ before his birth, deriving from sixteenth-century Italy.

Ebionites: a vegetarian Jewish Christian sect from the very early years of Christianity who held that the righteousness of Jesus in his life made it possible for him to become God's prophet, rather than any innate divinity.

Dr Martineau: James Martineau was a Victorian religious philosopher who was influential in the evolution of Unitarianism.

Cinema

news reel: early cinema performances often included a reel of short film clips with overdubbed commentary on events from the past few weeks.

Mussolini: Benito Mussolini had been the Fascist Prime Minister of Italy since 1922.

bull of Bashan: from Psalm 22, in this sense meaning strong and fierce creatures.

Silly Symphony: one of what would be a long series of short musical animated films from Walt Disney.

apotheosising: raising to greater heights.

it is like women preaching: Macaulay is quoting Dr Johnson, who said when his biographer Boswell mentioned having attended a Quaker meeting where a woman preached, 'Sir, a woman's preaching is like a dog's walking on his hind legs. It is not done well; but you are surprised to find it done at all.'

Waterloo and Plassey: the Battle of Plassey was fought in Bengal in 1757, and did involve elephants. The Battle of Waterloo was fought in 1815, and did not.

too solid flesh: 'Oh that this too too solid flesh would melt', from *Hamlet*, 1:2.

square: square up to, to confront each other.

Mr Laughton: Charles Laughton had recently starred in *The Private Life of Henry VIII* and *The Barretts of Wimpole Street* (1934).

Harold Lloyd: a celebrated silent film comedian.

Mr Cantor: the actor, singer and comedian Eddie Cantor was famous for his trademark eye-rolling.

Jack Hulbert: a very popular British film star, a comedian and early alumnus of the Cambridge Footlights.

Miss Courtneidge: Cicely Courtneidge was an Australian actor and comedian of great distinction, who in the 1930s was a long-standing performer in film and on stage with her husband Jack Hulbert.

Ralph Lynn: British comic actor, famous for his 'silly ass' roles, starring in farces at the Aldwych Theatre.

Lynn Fontanne: great British actor who was famous for her work in 'high comedy' on the American stage, particularly with her husband Alfred Lunt and with Noel Coward.

bock: a strong German lager.

Clothes

eximious: excellent, distinguished.

gaudy: a great feast or entertainment, often connected to a college or university, used here as a scholarly filter for much sociability.

prank: flaunt, show off.

Eve, walking forth ... quainte Mandilion: from *Du Bartas his divine weekes and workes*, translated by Joshua Silvester (1608).

estrich: ostrich.

medly: medley, multi-coloured, patchwork.

Mandilion: a loose upper garment for men of fashion in the sixteenth century, with the side seams open, the garment turned around 90 degrees so that the sleeves can be displayed open over the chest, demonstrating the stylishness of negligence.

Dr Watts: the theologian and minister Isaac Watts was a prolific writer of Anglican hymns. 'Why should our garments' was published in 1715.

Croesus: a king of Lydia, present-day Anatolia, in the sixth century BC, renowned for his fabulous wealth.

Solon: an Athenian statesman from the sixth century BC who failed to reform the excesses and lawlessness of the city-state.

prick up: archaism for dressing elaborately.

emplume: to cover with feathers.

decking: to be decked out is to be ostentatiously dressed with the intent to impress.

Montaigne: Michel Eyqem de Montaigne was a sixteenth-century French philosopher, author of a monumental collection of *Essais*. The passage quoted is from John Florio's translation of 1603, of 'The Apology of Raymond Sebond'.

A multibus animalibus decore vincimur: Latin, We are overcome by many animals' beauty.

Simia quam similis, turpissima bestia, nobis: Latin, quoted in Cicero's *De Natura Deorum*, I, XXXV, How like us is the degraded ape!

Soon the grave: from William Cowper's poem 'On A Similar Occasion For The Year 1790' (1800).

Green as the bay tree: from William Cowper's poem 'Stanzas Printed At The Bottom Of The Yearly Bill Of Mortality Of The Town Of Northampton; Dec. 21, 1787' (1788).

Cows

cornigerous: producing or bearing horns.

Passchendaal: Passchendaele, a small village in West Flanders, in 1917 the site of the Third Battle of Ypres, at which between 400,000 and 600,000 men died.

the female of the species is far deadlier than the male: the refrain of Rudyard Kipling's eponymous poem from 1911.

Departure of visitors

Fair Quiet, have I found thee here: from Andrew Marvell's poem 'The Garden' (1681).

Disbelieving

Suetonius: historian of the early Imperial Roman period, and biographer of twelve Roman rulers and emperors.

Sir Thomas Browne: from chapter 23 of Browne's *Pseudodoxica Epidemica* (1646).

puerile hallucinations and anile delirations: from John Gaule's Πῦς-μαντία *The Mag-Astro-Mancer, or the Magicall-Astrologicall-Diviner posed and puzzled* (1652), chapter 14 'On the Absurdity of Errours'.

What are they that think there are Antipodes: from the fourth-century Christian philosopher Lactantius, in his *Institutiones Divinae*, chapter 24, 'Of the antipodes, the heavens and the stars', in Book 3, 'Of the False Wisdom of Philosophers'.

Doves in the chimney

turtle: turtledove.

soughing: to make a rushing or murmuring sound like the noise of wind in branches.

Steele: Sir Richard Steele, eighteenth-century Irish writer and playwright, and co-founder of *The Spectator*.

Mrs Cornelia Lizard: these lines are by Thomas Tickell in his article 'On pastoral poetry' in *The Guardian* of 6 April 1713, not by Sir Richard Steele, who loathed Tickell.

As a turtle-dove did I chatter, and as a dove did I mourn: from Isaiah 38, verse 14.

culver: a dove or a pigeon.

Basil: Basil of Caesarea, a fourth-century Greek bishop in modern-day Turkey, wrote in his collection of homilies the *Hexaemeron*, that the tortoise, rather than the turtle (though this may be an error in translation), 'gorged with the flesh of the viper, finds in the virtue of marjoram a specific against this venomous animal' (Homily 9 'The creation of terrestrial animals', verse 3).

passing chaste: exceedingly faithful in marriage.

ensample: archaic term for an illustrative instance.

chimney-cole: possibly a chimney-top, but this is only a guess guided by the OED.

jeune homme de Dijon: The subject of a French limerick: Il y avait un jeune homme de Dijon, / Qui n'avait que peu de religion. / Il dit, 'Quant à moi, / Je m'encule tous les trois – / Le Père, et le Fils, et le Pigeon. (There once was a young man of Dijon / Who had no time at all for religion. / He said: 'As for me, / I detest all the three, / The Father, the Son and the Pigeon.)

the Phœnix and the Turtle: a poem by Shakespeare about perfect love embodied by an allegorical phoenix and a turtle-dove. 'Beauty, truth, and rarity, / Grace in all simplicity,/ Here enclosed in cinders lie. / Death is now the phoenix' nest / And the turtle's loyal breast / To eternity doth rest.'

Driving a car

Mulciber: an alternate name for the Roman god Vulcan, who was not known for his speed. This description seems to be more suitable for Phoebus Apollo in the chariot of the sun.

Phaethon: the son of the sun-god Helios, who was unable to control the horses drawing his father's chariot, burnt up the world and was killed by a thunderbolt.

Nero: the Emperor Nero prided himself on his prowess as a charioteer in the arena.

fifteen: fifteen miles per hour.

Sceveling: Wilkins mentions the Sceveling chariot in his *Mathematicall Magick* (1708) as designed by Stephinus or Simon Stevin.

Peireskius: Nicolaus Claudius Fabri de Peiresc, seventeenth-century French astronomer whose works included establishing the measurements of longitude at different points in Europe and North Africa.

Grotius: the Dutch polymath Hugo Grotius wrote admiringly about his trip to see Stevin's sailing chariot in 1600 in his *Farraginis Liber.*

scud: to be blown lightly over the tips of the waves.

volatile spirit: petrol.

juggernaut: an English and pejorative mistransliteration of the name of the Hindu god Jagannath, whose icon is ceremoniously pulled from its temple precincts on a wheeled chariot. Now used to mean a vast and all-consuming wheeled terror of the roads.

translated: removed to after death.

Easter in the woods

enverdured: covered in green leaves.

Wheatham Hill: a hill in the South Downs between Surrey and Hampshire.

hangers: hillside plantations of deciduous trees.

galline: of or pertaining to poultry.

this is what I believe that I am hearing: it is an impressive list of common English woodland birds and their songs.

cuculan: an invented word, presumably intended to be the adjective of cuckoo.

solvitur cantando: Latin, solved by singing.

agrimony: a yellow spiked flower of woodlands.

Eating and drinking

gule: medieval term for the gullet, and for gluttony.

the confessor: John Gower's long poem in English, *Confessio Amantis* (1390), is the narrative of a lover called Amans.

ingorged: also engorge, to feed to excess. Macaulay is quoting from Book 9 of John Milton's *Paradise Lost* (1667), the source of the lines about Eve that follow.

Timæus: an eponymous dialogue by Plato from about 360BC, which discusses the nature of the universe and the creation of the 'world soul'.

kickshaws: small, elaborate and decorative things to eat.

Piers Plowman: *William's Vision of Piers Plowman* by William Langland (late fourteenth century).

shrift: to be shriven or to have his confession heard.

H W Fowler: the English lexicographer and authority on the English language.

recked: to care or think about, to esteem.

the Lady: a character in John Milton's masque *Comus* (1634) a young woman imprisoned in Comus's castle, where he tries to seduce her metaphorically with delicious food.

Antonio de Herrera: seventeenth-century Spanish historian and Chief Chronicler of Castile and the Americas.

comestive: another word invented by Macaulay, an adjective from comestible, or edible foodstuff.

Sylvester: from Joshua Sylvester's 1608 translation of *Du Bartas his divine weekes and works*.

ichor: the liquid flowing like blood in the veins of the Greek gods.

Heliogobalus: also Elagabalus, the third-century Roman emperor Antoninus, who seems to have broken more taboos than any other Roman emperor, and whose reign was noted by contemporary historians for its excess and decadence, undoubtedly in food as well.

Aldermen: English Aldermen traditionally held annual feasts for their guilds.

Nicholas Wood: called the Great Eater of Kent in a seventeenth-century promotional poem by John Taylor.

Elephants in Bloomsbury

bitter foe the dragon: one source among many on the enmity between dragons and elephants that Macaulay may have enjoyed reading is the thirteenth-century work by Bartholomeus Anglicus, an English Franciscan monk, *De proprietatibus rerum*, 'On the properties of things'.

mandragora tree: the British Library's thirteenth-century Bestiary in the Harleian Miscellany (MS 3244) contains this interesting theory about how elephants mate, which was a common belief in the medieval west.

I remember how: Macaulay appears to be drawing most of this lore from various medieval bestiaries and later collections of travellers and fabulous tales, but it would also be in character for her to have made some of these up. The source of the tale about elephants eating a chameleon is particularly obscure.

Yea (if the Grecians do not mis-recite): from Joshua Sylvester's 1608 translation of *Du Bartas his divine weekes and works*, in 'The Sixt Daie of the First Weeke'.

Fastest on earth

Morris: a popular and reasonably affordable make of car for the British middle classes.

scuffle: driving around Hyde Park Corner, even in the 1930s, was a competitive stretch of road.

Atalanta: in Greek myth she prided herself on her fleetness of foot, until she stopped to pick up the golden apples thrown in her path during a race.

travels post: stagecoaches of the eighteenth and nineteenth centuries travelled post by exchanging their tired horses for new teams at the staging posts, thus achieving the fastest possible speed for their journey.

Mercury: the Roman god of travellers, who had winged shoes.

turnpikemen: when public roads began to be maintained by different parishes, the turnpike or toll-house would mark the next stage of the road when a new toll had to be paid by the carriage driver for use of the road. Those who let the turnpike keepers know of their approach with a blast on a horn would have the barriers thrown open ready for them, and they would drop the fee into a bag held ready.

St James's Square: this is in the opposite direction from the Marble Arch-Baker Street route: Macaulay must be lost. St James's Square is also a sedate area in the heart of London's clubland, where racing around corners is not desirable.

Finishing a book

embosked: another word invented by Macaulay, evidently from bosky, the adjective for a thicket or bushy clump.

lotus eaters: in the *Odyssey*, Odysseus visits the land of the lotus eaters who do nothing all day, which in the end turns out to be an unsatisfactory way of living.

I have done, you get no more of me: from Michael Drayton's sonnet *Idea 61. Since there's no help, come let us kiss and part* (1594).

Fire engines

pyromach: Macaulay invented this word from the Greek pyromachy, the use of fire in combat.

lachrymose: to make the tears flow, to suggest a sad emotion.

brass-helmed: firemen of the 1930s wore imposing metal helmets.

pyrolatry: an adoration of fire, from which Macaulay invents the adjective pyrolatrous, fire-worshipping.

panolethrous: another invention by Macaulay, possibly meaning all-destroying, from ὀλετὴρ (oleter) a destroyer.

Flattery

contemners: those critical of her.

write a thesis: three German-speaking students did write theses on Macaulay's work: Margarete Kluge in 1928, Margot Brüssow in 1934, and Irmgard Wahl in 1936.

Come è bellina, simpatica, graziosa!: Italian, How pretty, how nice and pretty!

'Think'st thou,' asked Silvia: from Act IV, scene 2 of Shakespeare's *The Two Gentlemen of Verona* (1589).

flattery pleases very generally: from James Boswell, *The Life of Samuel Johnson* (1824).

He will commend: from 'A Flatterer' in John Earle's *Microcosmographie* (1628).

Flower shop in the night

erred denizens: transgressing inhabitants, ie Adam and Eve.

pines: pineapples

medlar: an uncommon fruit, unusual in being available into the winter, so for it to be in season with lilies, pears and hydrangeas suggests that either the fruit or the flowers are fake. Or that this is a flight of Macaulay's imagination.

Flying

Klemm: could be any of several two-seater Klemm touring and sport planes manufactured in the 1920s and 1930s.

taxy: a variant of 'taxi', used in the 1930s for a plane travelling slowly on the ground.

climbing th'aerial height with eager haste: echoing lines in Book VIII of the *Aeneid*.

enormous bliss: from Book V of Milton's *Paradise Lost* (1667).

Down thither prone in flight: also from Book V of *Paradise Lost* (1667).

volant automata: part of the title of Chapter VI of Wilkins' *Mathematicall Magick*, volant meaning flying.

Elmerus ... Antipodes: taken almost verbatim from Chapter VII of *Mathematicall Magick*, 'Concerning the art of flying'.

winnow: from Book V of *Paradise Lost* (1667).

Following the fashion

She was a grand girl ... hell with your noise: this section is an extension of Macaulay's story 'Week-End At The Hoppers', to be published in Leonard Russell's *Parody Party* (1936), in which she parodies the style of Ernest Hemingway.

'To the Barricades': this appears to be a parody of the style of T S Eliot.

εἰς τὸ πῦρ εκ τοῦ κὰπνου: Greek, Into the fire from the smoke.

Dites donc, monsieur, si qu'on irait se coucher, n'est-ce pas?:
French, So, sir, are we going to go to bed or what?

Festinare nocet, tempore quæque suo qui facit, ille sapit:
a Latin adaptation of a quotation in the style of Ovid; it is bad to hurry;
the wise person is the one who does everything in its proper time.

Allons, allons, faites donner la garde!: French, Come on, come on,
take him in charge!

Fraternal

a background of hot Indian plains: Macaulay's brother Aulay served
in India in the Royal Engineers, and was murdered in 1909.

prairies roll, skis and sledges glide: Macaulay's brother Will farmed
in Canada from 1908 to 1914.

Miss Edgeworth's Frank: Maria Edgeworth wrote two collections of
moral tales about a small boy called Frank in the nineteenth century.

Getting rid

scavengers: before modern recycling and wartime salvage drives,
unwanted materials were collected from households by the rag
and bone men, or scavengers (scaffy, an abbreviation from this,
is still a dialect term for dustmen), who would take all household
rubbish and sort it for resale to specialist customers.

Neglected heaps we in by-corners lay: from the translation
by Sir William Soame and John Dryden, *The Art of Poetry* (1680),
of Nicolas Boileau-Despréaux's *l'Art poétique* (1674).

stolephage: another word invented by Macaulay, possibly meaning
stole-eater.

encharted: possibly a reference to rags being made into a sturdy
paper for printing maps and seafarers' charts.

Hatching eggs

Unnumber'd comforts to my soul: from the hymn 'When all Thy mercies o my God' (1882).

Heresies

ergotising: a verbal form of the Latin 'ergo', suggesting an authoritative conclusion, see also 246.

frapling: an obsolete word for disputing or blustering in argument.

Origen: one of the most influential of the early Church Fathers, active in the second and third century CE, who seems to have made a career of proposing heretical theories.

Eustathian: a follower of Eustathius of Antioch, from the fourth century CE, who objected to Origen's teachings.

Sir Thomas Browne: the seventeenth-century English author, most famous for his *Religio Medici* (1643).

Anabaptists: this Protestant sect became notorious in 1534–35 for its radical rule of Munster and the subsequent siege by opposing authorities, during which polygamy was forcibly but briefly instituted in the town by the male leader of the sect.

Mormons: the Mormon church advocated polygamy until the twentieth century when US law made it illegal.

Adamite: a short-lived Christian sect active in North Africa in the second, third and fourth centuries, who attended their church services naked.

Jeremy Taylor: with Obadiah Walker one of the two supposed authors of *Several Letters between Two Ladies Wherein the Lawfulness and Unlawfulness of Artificial Beauty in Point of Conscience are Nicely Debated* (1701), in which one writes to the other of 'rustick or *Adamitick* impudence, to confine Nature to itself, and to strip our Bodies of all

Additaments of fair Vestments or other Ornaments of humane Art and Invention'.

Manichee: one of the many beliefs of Manichaeism, founded in Persia in the third century CE, was that natural phenomena were linked to the soul's condition.

Pelagian: Pelagianism, originating in Britain in the fifth century CE, held that humans were not afflicted with original sin.

Arianism, Socinianism, Photiniansim: sects which held that Jesus was subordinate to God, which directly contradicted Athanasian teachings.

Fraticelli: the Spiritual Franciscans objected to the wealth of the Catholic Church and relied on begging to sustain their travelling mission.

Dulcinists: supporters of the Dulcinian heresy wanted a return to holy poverty and egalitarianism.

Waldensians: a twelfth-century sect who demanded a return to the ways of the Apostles by owning no possessions. Their objection to Catholic dogma seems to be a secondary concern.

Agonyclites: the seventh-century Agonocites prayed standing, rather than kneeling.

Collyridian: an alleged fourth-century Christian sect who purportedly worshipped the Virgin Mary rather than Jesus, but primary evidence for its existence is lacking.

Messalian: another possibly fictitious Christian sect, condemned in the fourth century, who were led by a man called Peter who claimed that he would rise from his grave as a wolf.

Quartodeciman: not so much a sect as an early Christian practice of observing the Passover on the 14th day of the month instead of moving with the times and celebrating Easter on the Sunday following the vernal equinox.

Montanist: a late second-century Christian movement which preferred its worship supported with prophetic revelations.

Donatist: a schismatic sect from sixth-century modern Tunisia, which expected complete purity and infallibility from its clergy.

Christianophagous: a word invented by Macaulay meaning eaters of Christians, ie lions in the Roman arena.

odium theologicum: Latin, theological hatred, engendered by the disputes between sects of very narrow divisions.

Hot bath

vespertine: of or occurring in the evening.

gellid: gelid, ranging from extremely cold to distinctly chilly.

ennebuled: a Macaulay invention, to be surrounded by a cloudy mass.

choking pores and lungs: before the Clean Air Act of 1956 London was routinely smothered in a choking yellow fog in the winter, when coal and wood fires filled the atmosphere with heavy particles. In 1933 Macaulay had written the introduction to a new edition of John Evelyn's *Fumifugium, or, The Inconvenience of the Aer and Smoake of London Dissipated*.

verdurously: with an abundance of greenness.

And on old Hiems' thin and icy crown: from Titania's speech in Act II, Scene 1 of Shakespeare's *A Midsummer Night's Dream* (1595), in which she mourns the breakdown of natural things.

Alcinous: ruler of a wide dominion, and the father of Nausicaa, whom Odysseus visits and tells the stories of his wanderings in the *Odyssey*.

floating gardens of Montezuma: the Aztec civilisation created artificial islands for cultivation.

The fringed bank with myrtle crowned, and universal Pan: from Book IV of Milton's *Paradise Lost* (1667), from the description of Eden.

Commodus: the emperor may well have been a keen bath-taker, but is more famous for killing a bathhouse attendant, and for being strangled himself in his bath.

alone and palely loitering ... sing: the first stanza of 'La Belle Dame sans Merci' by John Keats (1819).

Ignorance

3 Of gossip

Daphnis and Chloe: the protagonists of the eponymous novel, by the second-century CE Greek author Longus, here used to typify all romantic couples of whom we have heard but know nothing about.

Phyllis and Corydon: conventional names for characters in English Arcadian pastoral poetry from the sixteenth and seventeenth centuries. Macaulay's narrative voice is being mischievous in mixing her genres, but also indicating that she doesn't care enough about these characters.

5 Of one's pass-book

being made up: depositing money in your account at your bank used to involve taking one's pass-book to the branch with the money. The bank clerk would enter the amount you had deposited in the book, and post it back. Interest would be calculated and added annually in the same way. Thus you would rely on your pass-book to know how much money you had in the bank.

take no thought for the morrow: from Matthew 6.34.

National Benzole: a brand of petrol sold in the UK from 1919 to the 1960s.

quarter days: the traditional days when, among other events, rents were paid and the teaching term began. They were: Lady Day (25 March), Midsummer Day (24 June), Michaelmas (29 September) and Christmas (25 December).

indigence: of being in need, usually of an income or other support for daily living.

R D: bank abbreviation for 'refer to drawer' meaning 'send this back to the account holder as there is not enough money in their account'.

Yet ah! why should I know my fate: from Thomas Gray's poem 'On a Distant Prospect of Eton College' (1742).

Improving the dictionary

Dictionary: Macaulay means the Oxford English Dictionary. Supplementary volumes of new words and revised definitions began to be printed from 1933.

Murray, Bradley, Craigie, and Onions: James Murray was the principal editor of the OED, Henry Bradley was the second editor of the OED from 1888 to 1923, and William Craigie and C T Onions were co-editors of the 1933 Supplement.

Had I but world enough and time: Macaulay adapts the first line of Andrew Marvell's 'To His Coy Mistress' (1681), which discourses on all the joys that could be possible.

Listening in

Listening in: listening to BBC radio programmes, which at this period were all on one channel, broadcast at set times of the day and evening.

calling shapes ... virtuous mind: Macaulay paraphrases from John Milton's masque *Comus* (1634).

*def*ects, figyures, ideels, currencee: Macaulay had joined the BBC Advisory Committee on Spoken English in 1934, and was much concerned with the way the pronunciation of English words was changing due to regional and generational influences.

The turning vault of heaven formèd was: from Sir John Davies' 'Orchestra, or, A Poem of Dancing' (1596).

the heavenly tune, which none can hear: from John Milton's masque *Arcades* (1634).

Pythagoras: Greek philosopher from the fifth century BC, who posited the idea of *musica universalis*, by which the heavenly bodies moved in orbits understood through mathematical equations, and thus created the music of the celestial spheres.

So dear to Heav'n is Saintly chastity: a quotation from John Milton's masque *Comus* (1634).

Er: a man whose story is recounted in Plato's *Republic*, in which he died and was revived two days later to describe the afterlife.

That sit upon the nine enfolded Sphears: a further quotation from Milton's *Arcades* (1634).

Erinnyes: the Greek Erinyes or Furies pursued those who had committed crimes against natural law and justice.

Orestes: killed his mother Clytemnestra to avenge his father Agamemnon, whom she and her lover had murdered. Variations upon his story are told in the plays by Sophocles and Euripides.

Phineus: a king of Greek myth encountered by the Argonauts, whose punishment for revealing the future through his long sight was to be blinded and have his food continually stolen by flying harpies.

Procne: in a particularly bloody Greek myth she and her sister are brutalised by her husband Tereus, and then turned into birds by the gods.

chelidonian: from Greek, of or pertaining to a swallow.

Oberon: he recounts this adventure to Puck in Act 2 scene 1 of *A Midsummer Night's Dream* (1595).

xylites: this is a puzzle, since it is a scientific term rather than musical; perhaps Macaulay meant the xylophone?

ashes: the annual series of cricket matches between England and Australia.

wicket: three posts standing upright behind each of the two batsmen in cricket, which need to be knocked down by the bowler's ball.

innings: the section of a cricket match in which a player or a team are batting.

Italian-Abyssinian crisis: this political-military aggression lasted from 1935 to 1937, so was current while Macaulay was writing.

Logomachy

Logomachy: argument or contention about the meaning of words.

dominical: of or pertaining to a Sunday.

Whipsnade: the celebrated Bedfordshire zoo and safari park, north of London.

putting a gloss: adding meaning.

etymological: of the derivation and history of words.

litotes: the figure of speech to achieve understatement by using double negatives, or suggesting an affirmative by negating its opposite, eg 'A citizen of no mean city'.

meiosis: a figure of speech in which something is presented as smaller than it really is, for ironic or other effect, eg 'The bomb blast was a little noisy'.

ilk: commonly used in Scottish genealogical or heraldic contexts, meaning a person is of the same family as another.

anthropophagi: an archaic term for a cannibal.

ergotising: a verbal form of the Latin 'ergo', suggesting an authoritative conclusion, see also 239.

poetomachy, bibliomachy, angelomachy, theologomachy, gastromachy, erotomachy: arguments that, respectively, debate the nature of poetry, books, angels, theology, food and passionate love.

Meals out

1 On the roof

Nansen: Fridtjof Nansen was one of the West's most famous explorers.

2 On the pavement

Hey, mozo! Otro aguardiente! Y mas azucar: Spanish, Waiter, another brandy! And more sugar.

New Year's Eve

saturnalia: a Roman festival of several days held around the winter solstice.

Not going to parties

Bacchus: the Roman god of wine.

This way the noise was: a speech by the Lady from John Milton's masque *Comus* (1634).

rout: a term used widely in the eighteenth century for an evening party with dancing.

wassail: a medieval practice of singing at Christmas and Twelfth Night, the wassailers often being rewarded with drink.

Hence vain deluding joys: the first stanza of John Milton's *Il Penseroso* (1645).

embankment: the north bank of the Thames in central London.

Parties

Melantha: a pushing court lady from Act V of John Dryden's *Marriage à la Mode* (1673), who wishes to impress the Princess by (over)using fashionable phrases, of which 'let me die' is one.

As thick and numberless: from John Milton's *Il Penseroso* (1645).

poeticules, poetitos, poetasters: respectively, an insignificant poet, an inferior poet, a mere versifier.

Spender, Barker, Day Lewis, Auden, Pudney, Isherwood: respectively, Stephen, George, Cecil, WH, John and Christopher, all prominent twentieth-century writers.

Cleisthenes: Cleisthenes of Sicyon (sixth century BCE) is known from Herodotus to have been a despotic tyrant who made far-reaching decisions based on his whims rather than principles.

Agathon: a Greek tragedian from the fifth century BCE whose party was gatecrashed by Alcibiades, Socrates and Aristodemus, as narrated in Plato's *Symposium*.

Trimalchio: an enriched former slave from Petronius' *Satyricon* from the first century CE, who held ostentatious and lavish dinner parties.

becafico: Italian, a fattened song-bird eaten in the autumn.

Æolian harp: a stringed instrument placed in an open window to be played by the wind.

pyrophone: a nineteenth-century musical instrument designed to produce sound by the action of fire or explosions.

though the black bat night ... setting moon: paraphrasing lines from *Maud* by Alfred Tennyson (1855).

Play-going

I can weep: from Sir Thoms Browne's *Religio Medici* (1643).

Beatrice, Rosalind, and Millamant: assertive female characters in Shakespeare's *Much Ado about Nothing* and *As You Like It* (both 1600), and in William Congreve's *The Way of the World* (1700).

groundlings: those who stand in front of the stage, in the cheapest places.

Pretty creatures

When he was by, the birds such pleasure took: stanza 184 of Shakespeare's *Venus and Adonis* (1593).

art silk: artificial silk, considerably cheaper than the real thing.

Phryne: a fourth-century Greek courtesan who was tried for impiety.

small bright capitals: illuminated letters in medieval manuscripts often have delightful small creatures frisking around the capital letters.

Reading

matitutinally: Macaulay's own derivation from matutinal, of the morning.

this mighty work: by 1933 the Oxford English Dictionary consisted of ten volumes and one supplementary volume.

Captain William Hawkins: one of the earliest English traders with India for the English East India Company, whose ship *Hector* anchored at Surat in 1608. He rivalled Portuguese merchants and Jesuit missionary interests in that region.

Sir John Hawkins: William Hawkins' uncle, a prominent naval commander in Queen Elizabeth's service and one of the first Englishmen to profit from slaves taken from West Africa and sold in Spanish-controlled Central and South America.

Captain Knox: Robert Knox was a seventeenth-century sea captain in the British East India Company, who was shipwrecked and then imprisoned in Sri Lanka for nineteen years. His account, *An Historical Relation of the Island Ceylon*, was published in 1681.

Thomas Gage: a seventeenth-century missionary who chose to join the Dominican order rather than the Jesuits, whom he despised. He lived in central America for ten years.

John Chilton: Macaulay is probably referring to the author of *Voyage to the West Indies and New Spain made by John Chilton in the year 1560, containing an account of their people, manners, cities, mines, riches, forests, &c., and a list of the Provinces and Governments in New Spain.*

Anthony Knivet: an English privateer who was captured by the Portuguese in Brazil in the early 1590s, was enslaved on a sugar plantation, escaped and lived with a Brazilian tribe for a year. He sold his account of his adventures to Hakluyt who sold them to Samuel Purchas, where they reached print.

beninganions: a fruit described in the Abbé Prévost's *Histoire générale des voyages* (1746), as about the same size as a citron, or large lemon.

Roger Barlow: an English merchant and traveller who petitioned Henry VIII with a proposal to open up a new English trade route to the East Indies with a background volume describing his travels, *Brief Somme of Geographia* (1541).

See of Bangor: an Anglican diocese in the Church of Wales, pitted here against the schismatic non-Jurors who refused to take the Oath of Allegiance to the Protestant monarchs William and Mary after the abdication of the Catholic James VII and II.

Cloyne: George Berkeley, Bishop of Cloyne, was also a philosopher who published a critique of the theory of calculus in 1734.

the ante-somnial hour: the hour before sleeping.

One is in a pleasant square: this is the London Library in St James's Square, off Piccadilly in central London, which lends its books out to its subscribing members.

the other great London resort of readers: this is the old British Library Reading Room in the British Museum in Bloomsbury, where one could consult the books, but not borrow them.

the man whom … no such matter: from Montaigne's Essays.

Shopping abroad

antichità: Italian, antiquity.

Hopes: from the Hopi tribe.

xenophilous: loving strange things.

Transmarinity: their quality of having come from across the seas.

'Troppo, troppo', 'Trop cher', 'Demasiado', or 'Zu viel': 'too much', in Italian, French, Spanish and German.

Captain Smith: better known now for founding Jamestown in Virginia and bringing Pocahontas to England, in his youth John Smith had fought against the Turks and marched to Constantinople.

Drake: in the Battle of San Domingo (1586) Sir Francis Drake led a successful expedition to attack and loot the well-established Spanish fortified city on Hispaniola.

Hastings: Macaulay's great-uncle, the historian Thomas Babington Macaulay, described Warren Hastings's wife at court, with 'the galaxy of jewels, torn from Begums, which adorned her head-dress' in the *Edinburgh Review* in October 1841, an image which the younger Macaulay no doubt retained. Hastings received the treasure from the son and grandson of the Begums, the Nawab of Oudh, in lieu of his debts to the East India Company.

bric-à-brac: modern readers will notice that what Macaulay calls bric-à-brac is in the instances she gives more correctly termed loot.

Palermo to Monreale: a short distance from the Sicilian city to the cathedral outside its boundaries.

Pop Ernest: this abalone restaurant on Fisherman's Wharf at Monterey, California, was popular in the 1930s.

Showing off

Corsica to Sardinia: a distance of just over nine miles.

'The Ride from Ghent to Aix': 'How They Brought The Good News From Ghent To Aix' by Robert Browning, a popular poem for recitation, is 60 lines long.

Ruth Draper: American actress who specialised in monologues and monodramas, performing with only a few props to great acclaim in the interwar years. She apparently did give a private performance for George V and Queen Mary in the 1920s.

Traffic to right of me: a parody of Tennyson's poem 'The Charge of The Light Brigade' (1854).

I am the Toad: a reference to the character in *The Wind in the Willows* (1908) by Kenneth Grahame, who is notable for his rash boasting.

Solitude

the reeling goddess: from Book III of William Cowper's poem *The Task* (1785), as a personification of Pleasure.

drony solitude: from Hester Thrale's *Anecdotes of the Late Samuel Johnson* (1786).

But 'twas beyond a Mortal's share ... two Paradises: from Andrew Marvell's 'The Garden' (1681).

minishing: archaic version of diminishing.

If thou canst get but thither: from the seventeenth-century poem 'Peace' by Henry Vaughan, better known now as the anthem 'My soul, there is a country', set to music in 1916 by Sir Hubert Parry.

Attired with stars ... joy shall overtake us as a flood: lines from the poetic address 'On Time' by John Milton (1645).

Solitude is dangerous to reason: from Hester Thrale's *Anecdotes of the Late Samuel Johnson* (1786).

Sunday

enturbed: a Macaulay invention, from the eighteenth-century term turb, meaning a crowd or gathering.

turtling: as in turtledoves, cooing and courting noisily.

orto: Italian, the vegetable garden.

congee: French, congé, to formally take one's leave.

septimanal: weekly.

Sabbatarian: one who keeps the Sabbath, not permitting work to be done on a Sunday.

For by th' Almighty this great Holy-day: from 'The Seventh Daye of the First Weeke', in Joshua Sylvester's translation of *Du Bartas his divine weekes and works* (1608).

wireless accumulator: a lead-acid battery for home radio use that had to be recharged frequently at a local shop or garage.

Kreisler: Fritz Kreisler, acclaimed Austrian-American violinist.

Taking umbrage

umbrage: offence, displeasure, deriving from its earlier meaning of a shade or a shadow.

dudgeon: indignation or offence.

Who will rid me of this traitor: the words held to have been said in rage by Henry II of his recalcitrant Archbishop of Canterbury Thomas à Becket. The Latin record uses 'traitor' rather than the more common paraphrase 'turbulent priest'.

Little man, little man: part of a cross retort reportedly spoken by Elizabeth I to Robert Cecil when he urged her, shortly before she died, to go to bed.

Fling him to the fishes: possibly referring to Achilles' taunt to the dead Lykaon whom he had killed and flung into a stream.

Apollo: Apollo objected to the flautist Marsyas' audacity in challenging him to a musical contest, and when Apollo won, he flayed him.

Achelous: the story is in Ovid's *Metamorphoses*.

Latona: mother of Apollo and Artemis, who punished Niobe for boasting of her superiority in having fourteen children: all were killed by the twins.

enstagging: a Macaulay invention. Actaeon was turned into a stag and hunted to death, for having spied on Artemis in her bath.

bagniospection: the surprisingly common and often fatal practice across many mythologies of men spying on women bathing.

calumniators: those who spread calumny and insult.

Capulets, Lear, Egeus, Squire Western: from, respectively, *Romeo and Juliet* (1595), *King Lear* (1605), *A Midsummer Night's Dream* (1595), and Henry Fielding's *The History of Tom Jones, A Foundling* (1749).

Full of vexation come I: Egeus's complaint to Demetrius about his daughter Hermia.

Talking about a new car

Garnet ten-four: possibly an invented marque to avoid litigation.

I do not have accidents: she did.

Rapide 1933: possibly the 1933 Lagonda M45 Rapide touring car, apparently one of the fastest British sports cars of its day.

Daimler: an elegant and luxurious long-engined sport saloon.

Austins and Morrises: the nearest thing to a cheap car in the 1930s, reliable and affordable.

Austin Seven De Luxe Sun Saloon: a very popular compact economy family car.

Morris Ten: a medium-sized family car first on the market in 1932.

Telling travellers' tales

There was a ship: from Coleridge's *The Rime of the Ancient Mariner* (1798), in which a sailor grips a guest hurrying to a wedding and will not let him go until he has listened to his tale.

Æneas: he arrived at Carthage as a refugee from Troy, and was entertained by Dido.

antres vast … shoulders: from Act 1 scene 3 of Shakespeare's *Othello* (1603). Antres is a Shakespearian invention, thought to mean caverns.

Sir Walter Raleigh: leader of early Elizabethan expeditions to the New World, bringing some of the first reports of its people and plants back to England.

credulent: credulous, inclined too much to believe.

Herodotean: the first known historian, Herodotus, from the fifth century BC, distanced himself from tales in his *Histories* which were likely to be disbelieved with prefatory remarks about their unlikeliness.

viva voce: Latin, in speech, orally.

Turtles in Hyde Park

sward: grass.

And whilst our souls negotiate there: from John Donne's 'The Ecstacie' (1633).

Sabina has a thousand charms: a lyric by the Carolinean organist John Blow, probably 1700.

turtling it: as in, behaving like turtle-doves.

autumnal leaves: from Book II of John Milton's *Paradise Lost* (1667), a simile for uncounted numbers of devils.

Walking

Timaeus: a dialogue by Plato, named after the eponymous narrator, which discourses on the physical nature of the world and its creatures.

the way through the woods: the title of a poem by Rudyard Kipling from 1899, repeating the ideas and images in the previous passage.

Ilissus: the river flowing outside the walls of ancient Athens, where Socrates liked to walk and teach.

Writing

did they commit any: if they had written any.

taber: tabor, a small drum used to accompany medieval musicians on the pipe or trumpet.

enambered: more properly used to mean to scent with amber, but here Macaulay uses it to mean preservation as if in amber.

whatsoever time, or the heedless hand of blind chance: from John Milton's essay 'Of Prelatical Episcopacy' (1641).

amateur: an enthusiast for, a hobbyist of, a specialist in.

Frutto del mare: Italian, fruits of the sea, seafood.

What Not

A Prophetic Comedy

by Rose Macaulay

Rose Macaulay
What Not
A Prophetic Comedy

What Not is Rose Macaulay's speculative novel of post-First World War eugenics and newspaper manipulation that influenced Aldous Huxley's *Brave New World*.

Published in 1918, *What Not* was hastily withdrawn due to a number of potentially libellous pages, and was reissued in 1919, but had lost its momentum. Republished in 2019 with the suppressed pages reinstated for the first time, *What Not* is a lost classic of feminist protest at social engineering, and rage at media manipulation.

Kitty Grammont and Nicholas Chester are in love. Kitty is certified as an A for breeding purposes, but politically ambitious Chester has been uncertificated, and may not marry. Kitty wields power as a senior civil servant in the Ministry of Brains, which makes these classifications, but she does not have the freedom to marry who she wants. They ignore the restrictions, and carry on a discreet affair. But it isn't discreet enough for the media: the popular press, determined to smash the brutal regime of the Ministry of Brains, has found out about Kitty and Chester, and scents an opportunity for a scandalous exposure.

Aldous Huxley was a frequent guest at Macaulay's flat while she was writing *What Not*. Fourteen years later, his *Brave New World* borrowed many of Macaulay's ideas for Huxley's own prophetic vision.

The introduction is by Sarah Lonsdale, senior lecturer in journalism at City University London.

'Her writing is stirring, funny, uniquely imaginative. This book should not be forgotten again' — *The Guardian*

'*What Not* is a forgotten gem in a prolific career' — *The Times*

Rose Macaulay

Potterism

A Tragi-Farcical Tract

A novel in which truth battles slander.

Potterism

A Tragi-Farcical Tract

by Rose Macaulay

Rose Macaulay's 1920 satire on British journalism and the newspaper industry is about the Potter newspaper empire, and the ways in which journalists struggled to balance the truth and what would sell, during the First World War and into the 1920s. When Jane and Johnny Potter are at Oxford they learn to despise their father's popular newspapers, though they still end up working for the family business. But Jane is greedy, and wants more than society will let her have.

Mrs Potter is a well-known romantic novelist, whose cheap novelettes appear in the shop-girls' magazines. She has become unable to distinguish fact from fiction, and her success gives her an unhealthy estimation of her own influence. Arthur Gideon resists the fake news and gushing sentiment peddled by the Potter press, but an unexpected tragedy binds him even closer to their influence.

The Introduction is by Sarah Lonsdale, senior lecturer in journalism at City University London.

Non-Combatants and Others

Writings Against War, 1916–1945

by Rose Macaulay

Rose Macaulay
Non-Combatants
and Others
Writings Against War, 1916-1945

Rose Macaulay was a columnist, reviewer and pioneering critic of BBC radio in its early days. Here all her anti-war writing is collected together in one fascinating and thought-provoking volume.

- *Non-Combatants and Others* (1916) was the first anti-war novel to be published in the UK during the First World War.
- Her witty, furious and despairing journalism for *The Spectator*, *Time and Tide* and *The Listener* from 1936 to 1945 details the rise of fascism and the civilian response to war.
- 'Miss Anstruther's Letters', a short story of the Blitz, relates the devastating loss of a home, and of all a dead lover's letters.

The Introduction is by Jessica Gildersleeve of the University of Southern Queensland. The cover illustration, 'Peace Angel', is by the Norwegian caricaturist Olaf Gulbransson, published in the German satirical magazine *Simplicissimus* in 1917.

'Reading the whole in sequence is to witness a deliberately cultivated indifference towards war harden – many would say strengthen – into pacifist resolve.' —*Brixton Review of Books*

Dreaming of Rose

by Sarah LeFanu

In 2003 the former Women's Press editor and literary critic Sarah LeFanu published her acclaimed biography of Rose Macaulay with Virago Press.

She was also keeping a detailed journal of her research trips and her processes as a biographer, arguing with herself over what to include, what to pursue, and what to leave behind. Her immersion in her research led to Rose intruding in her dreams, and fantastical imaginings of what Rose would say or do, at each fork in the road. In 2013, LeFanu published *Dreaming of Rose*, a remarkable record of the art of biography, and the search for another woman's life. This new edition from Handheld Press is revised and updated.

Dreaming of Rose is a woman's memoir of teaching, researching and writing while dealing with what life throws at you. LeFanu's work on Rose was squeezed in between writing for the BBC and teaching creative writing and English literature in Bristol and Wales. She managed research trips to Varazze in Italy to look for Rose's childhood, and to Trabzon in Turkey to find traces of *The Towers of Trebizond*, lucky intuitive ventures that found treasures in unexpected places.

For life writers, for lovers of biography, for admirers of Rose Macaulay.